SIX CENTURIES OF THE
PROVINCIAL BOOK TRADE IN BRITAIN

Six Centuries
of the
Provincial Book Trade
in Britain

EDITED BY
PETER ISAAC

ST PAUL'S BIBLIOGRAPHIES

The papers published in this volume were presented
at the Eighth Seminar on the British Book Trade,
Durham, July 1990, the silver jubilee of the History
of the Book Trade in the North.

Cover illustration: Copper engraving after Edward
Burney, engraved by S Springsguth. Illustration from
an unknown title (London, *c*.1840).

© 1990 The Contributors

First Published 1990 by
St Paul's Bibliographies
West End House
1 Step Terrace
Winchester
Hampshire SO22 5BW
England

British Library Cataloguing in Publication Data
Six centuries of the provincial book trade in Britain.
   1. Great Britain. Book trades, history
   I. Isaac, Peter
   380.1450020941

ISBN 0 906795 96 6

Typeset on Ventura by Peter Isaac
Cover designed by John Mitchell
Printed in England on long-life paper by
Henry Ling Ltd, Dorchester

Contents

Contents (continued)

Contributors

CHARLES BENSON is Keeper of Early Printed Books in Trinity College, Dublin. He is at present working on a dictionary of the book trade in Dublin 1801–50.

Dr JEREMY BLACK graduated from Queen's College, Cambridge, with a starred first. After research at Oxford he was appointed Lecturer in the Department of History at Durham University in 1980 (Senior Lecturer 1990). He is a Fellow of the Royal Historical Society, and has published many books and papers.

JOHN C DAY has been Senior Lecturer in Bibliography, Local Studies and Archives since 1968 in the Department of Information and Library Management at Newcastle upon Tyne Polytechnic. His publications and interests range from library history and literacy in the Northeast to industrial archaeology and preservation and conservation of nineteenth-century materials. Regional contributor to Revised STC, Wing and LA Rare Books Directory.

Dr A I DOYLE is Hon Reader in Bibliography, University of Durham since 1982. He was Keeper of Rare Books in the Durham University Library 1958–82. He was Lyell Reader in Bibliography, Oxford, 1967. He is a Vice-President of the Bibliographical and Surtees Societies, and is a member of the Comité International de Paléographie Latine and of the Council of the Early English Text Society.

Dr BRIAN HILLYARD has been an Assistant Keeper in the Department of Printed Books, National Library of Scotland, since 1977. He has edited the Library Association Rare Books Group Newsletter (1983–9), and is editor of the *Transactions* of the Edinburgh Bibliographical Society (1984–).

VINCENT KINANE works in the Department of Early Printed Books in Trinity College Library, Dublin. Besides being co-editor of the Graisberry account books, he is writing a history of the Dublin University Press.

WESLEY McCANN is Librarian of Stranmillis College, Belfast. He was formerly on the staff of the libraries of Durham University and of Queen's University, Belfast. He is at present at work on a biographical dictionary of the Belfast book trade to 1860.

ADAM McNAUGHTAN is a Glasgow schoolteacher who has been involved in the Scottish folksong revival since the 1950s. His research into Glasgow songs led him to ephemeral printed sources, particularly song-sheets and garlands published in Glasgow.

IAN MAXTED was formerly Assistant Keeper at the Guildhall Library, London. For thirteen years he has been Local Studies Librarian at Exeter. His series of Exeter Working Papers in British Book Trade History has made a variety of source material available in the form of indexes and concordances.

PAUL MORGAN worked in Birmingham University Library 1946–60, and in the Bodleian 1961–83, where he is now a consultant. He is interested in Warwickshire history and book trade, and has written numerous articles on bibliography, binding history and topography. He was Editor of the Dugdale Society to 1982, and Vice-President of the Bibliographical Society until 1990. He was president of the Oxford Bibliographical Society 1980–4. He was a Fellow of St Cross 1978–83.

DAVID PEARSON works at the British Library, but was previously at Durham, where he helped to recatalogue Cosin's Library. His research centres on bookbindings and the history of private and institutional libraries. His publications include *Durham Bookbinders and Booksellers 1660–1760* (1986) and *Provenance Indexes for Early Printed Books and Manuscripts* (1987).

MICHAEL PERKIN was formerly Curator of Special Collections, Liverpool University Library, and sometime Secretary, Liverpool Bibliographical Society and editor of *The Book Trade in Liverpool to 1850: a Directory* (1981 & 1987). He is now working part-time at Reading University in the Library and in the Department of Typography, in Winchester Cathedral Library, and on freelance bibliographical and editorial work for a publisher.

Dr F W RATCLIFFE is University Librarian, Cambridge, and Fellow of Corpus Christi College. After research in German literature and language at Manchester and in Germany, he worked in four University libraries. He played a major part in merging the John Rylands Library with that of the University of Manchester. His main professional interests are in collection building, conservation and the recruitment of academic library staff. He has published widely in various areas of librarianship and bibliography.

Miss EILUNED REES, a native of Carmarthenshire, worked as an Assistant Keeper in the Departments of Printed Books of the British Museum and of the National Library of Wales. She was appointed to her present post of Conservation Coordinator at the latter institution in 1984.

Dr PETER WALLIS graduated at Cambridge in mathematics as a Wrangler, and was subsequently MA and PhD in English. He moved from headmastering to the School of Education of the University of Newcastle upon Tyne, becoming Reader. His research has been unified in the Project for Historical Biobibliography, of which he has been Director since its inception in 1975. The Project has an integrated approach to the advancement of knowledge, particularly in the fields of education, book publishing, science, mathematics and medicine, concentrating on the eighteenth century.

W MALCOLM WATSON was a practising librarian in public libraries 1949–59. He taught analytical, historical and descriptive bibliography 1959–88, and was Head, Department of Librarianship and Information Studies, Newcastle Polytechnic at the time of his retirement, December 1988. He has spent ten years as specialist adviser in librarianship and information studies to the Council for National Academic Awards. Founder-member of Newcastle Imprint Club and of History of the Book Trade in the North Group.

Foreword

This collection of papers associated with the 1990 Seminar on the History of the Book Trade illustrates well the growing strength of studies in the provincial book trade in the United Kingdom and Ireland. It demonstrates also the enthusiasm with which a growing number of individuals with a wide variety of backgrounds are currently pursuing worthwhile research into the history of printing, publishing and bookselling in provincial towns.

Dr Ratcliffe in his paper 'The contribution of book-trade studies to scholarship' refers to Allnut's paper given to the Library Association's Annual Meeting in 1878 listing 276 printers in provincial towns in England and Wales 'with the hope of stimulating librarians...to collect and preserve the local literature of their respective districts' and comments that Allnut's plea 'has been answered, if not fully, certainly enthusiastically'. Ratcliffe rightly argues that there is much work yet to be done on the interpretation and analysis of listings and other records of printing, publishing and bookselling before the comprehensive economic, social and cultural history of the provincial book trade can be written. He suggests that the study of the provincial book trade suffers from 'being the province of specialists in other subjects who happen to take an interest in the subject...it has no hard core of professionals dedicated to the subject'.

That this is substantially true in no way detracts from the value of the work now being done by a growing body of librarians, historians, bibliographers and schoolteachers, as well as publishers, printers, scientists and engineers; indeed the enthusiasts come from all walks of life and perhaps the only point they have in common is that they share the same passionate, dedicated interest in local printing and its history. At a time when much research and scholarship has become so specialised and is so dependent upon many years of professional training, and upon resources which are beyond those of the private individual, it is particularly gratifying to find an area of study which still provides great scope for the enthusiast and 'amateur' to do invaluable work – to list, to date, to map out from the surviving evidence the course of local printing and publishing and its influence in the British Isles. The provincial book trade provides a rewarding area for study which demands the highest standards of scholarly discipline from those who engage in it; there is much untapped source material to be worked through in local libraries, in the county record offices, in public and private archives, and, indeed, in some provincial towns, in the bookseller's or printer's basement. The chance find of a local broadsheet from the 18th century which has never been previously listed, or use of an ornament or device on a piece of local printing which could only have come from the sale of a printer's type in another county can be the start of a rich adventure in assembling detailed evidence from often quite unpromising clues which can contribute significantly in the history of printing and publishing.

The work of groups such as the History of the Book Trade in the North in bringing together individuals working often in private and often in isolation is of enormous importance to the well-being of the study of the provincial book trade. John Day and Malcolm Watson's paper in this volume tells of the substantial achievements of this group over the twenty-five years since it was formed: C J Hunt's work *The Book Trade in Northumberland & Durham to 1960*, P J Wallis's Project for Historical Biobibliography, the Subscription List Project, the formation of the British Book Trade Index, and the large and varied collection of published Working Papers. The History of the Book Trade in the North has indeed established an enviable reputation for both the quantity and the quality of its work, under the watchful eye of its Chairman, Professor Peter Isaac. It is a splendid model for the development of similar local groups, drawing its membership as it does from the Universities of Newcastle and Durham, the Polytechnic School of Librarianship, and from the public libraries etc. I hope the Centre for the Book which we are planning in the British Library will itself act as a national focus for the development of studies in the history of the book and of the provincial book trade. I look forward to the creation of strong links between the Centre for the Book and groups such as the History of the Book Trade in the North which will further encourage and develop research and the dissemination of information which will add to the proper understanding of the rich heritage of our national printed archive. I am sure the History of the Book Trade in the North Group will have much to contribute to such work in its next twenty-five years.

J Michael Smethurst
Director General
British Library Humanities & Social Sciences
July 1990

The Contribution of Book-trade Studies to Scholarship

F W RATCLIFFE

Most publications dealing with the provincial book trade in its widest sense cite Allnutt's 'Notes on printers and printing in the provincial towns of England and Wales'[1] and Plomer's *Dictionary of Printers and Booksellers in England, Scotland and Ireland*.[2] There are very good reasons for this. They are the planks on which so much of the study of the provincial book trade in Britain has been built. Of much greater interest, however, both from the point of view of a 'good read' and as a contribution to mainstream scholarship is Miss Plant's now classic study of the English book trade.[3] Allnutt and Plomer provide facts, lots of them, and very important they are too; Miss Plant gives them meaning and makes them live. Much of the published literature on the provincial book trade, perhaps inevitably, extends Allnutt and Plomer. Extending Miss Plant's study is a very different matter and, perhaps understandably, examples of this are relatively few. The accidental omission of 'provincial' from the title of this paper in the published programme gives me an excuse to dwell on the wider implications of the book trade and the significance of provincial studies.

Everyone interested in the book trade must be aware of the massive contributions of such as Eisenstein, Febvre, Martin, Hirsch among many others to the history of the book. Their works contain much that has to be relevant to the book trade in this country, but they are more concerned with the growth and spread of printing and the trade in Europe than in Britain and that for some three centuries, was of a quite different order from that in this country. It is important to remind ourselves of what the implications of this were both for the book trade in Britain, in particular in the provinces, and for education in general. It explains in part why provincial book-trade studies in Britain, as we know them, have no real counterpart in Continental Europe.

In Miss Plant's words 'in 1586 all provincial printing was abruptly ended by a decree of the Star Chamber'.[4] Henceforth printers were to operate 'onelye in the cittie of London, or the suburbs thereof (except one presse in the universitie of Cambridge, and one other presse in the universitie of Oxforde, and no more)'.[4] It should be recognised that these drastic new regulations hardly eliminated a thriving provincial press or, indeed, a thriving industry in London. The paucity of English printing in the fifteenth century, its very late start, was for all practical purposes simply endorsed by the output of printing prior to the decree of the

1

Star Chamber. A comparison, for example, with Germany at this time suggests that the decree was hardly necessary at all. Just how great the disparity is seems often to be overlooked by those concerned with the book trade in this country.

A few statistics about Luther's published works illustrate clearly this disparity. No fewer than 226 named printers and 95 unidentified presses produced one or more of Luther's works during his lifetime, a total of 321 in all. It was estimated by A G Dickens[5] that 'between 1517 and 1520 Luther's thirty publications probably sold over 300,000 copies'. By the time of his death in 1546, excluding his collected works and the many printings of his Bible, some 3 702 printings of his various works by different printers had appeared. His *Septembertestament* of 1522 was already being reprinted by Adam Petri in Basel in the month when the revised so-called *Dezembertestament* appeared. In regard to his Bible, Hans Lufft's press alone issued forty-four editions between 1534 and 1572 in an estimated total of 100 000 copies. The famous 95 theses, originally in Latin, were available in German translation throughout Germany within a fortnight of their appearance. By contrast, according to Miss Plant 'only thirty-six men are known to have printed in London between 1500 and 1550, and all of these except twelve belong entirely to the period following 1530'.[6]

Luther's prodigious output points to an already highly organised trade. Evidence for this is to be found in 88 pages of the account book of the second Peter Drache, printer in Speyer, which were discovered in the binding of a volume in the Staatliche Bibliothek Dillingen in 1957. The 88 pages cover the period 1475 to 1503. During this time Drache's recorded output was 185 titles, including many substantial works, but the number of titles handled, including those of many other printers, is 550. He is described by Geldner[7] as a European 'Grossbuchhändler' – book wholesale dealer. He distributed books far and wide, usually in the sheet in barrels. He can be seen doing business on a significant scale in Augsburg, Landshut an der Isar, Prague, Brünn, Leipzig, Halberstadt, Stendal, Cologne, Strassburg and Basel. He had representatives or associates in each of these cities. He was a printer, book dealer, bookseller and bookbinder. His output and trade dealings by English eighteenth-century standards were huge. Like his father and his son he belonged to the Guild of Master Weavers.

Given this kind of organised trade, it is little surprise that the Reformation literature on the Continent was so prolific. It provides clear evidence of widespread literacy. Among Drache's proof-readers were schoolmasters and university students. In Luther's *An die Raddhern aller Stedte deutsches Lands,*[8] of 1524, he is pleading for the expansion of education in a way that was not heard in Britain until the nineteenth century. Printing he described as 'God's highest, most extreme act of grace',[9] but by 1541 in his Preface to his Bible he complains that his work has been so much reprinted that he cannot recognise it. The contrast with the printing trade in England could hardly have been more striking. In some ways we may regard the spread of provincial printing post-1700 in this country as an attempt to catch up with the European past.

The general censorship Bulls issued in 1487, 1501 and 1515 must have been quite irrelevant in Britain. The Church, having first welcomed printing on the assumption that it would have control of it and benefit by it – for example, in the printing of indulgences for wars against the Turks – was soon alarmed by its rapid spread and secularisation in Europe. In this country, the press can never really have constituted any such threat to the Church and it was a simple matter after the Reformation to introduce the 1586 decree restricting its practice. The reasons for the decree can only have been narrowly political and commercial. Printing was hardly a burgeoning trade even in the context of the small population. Despite Shakespeare and all those other literary greats, despite a Civil War, it was to be 250 years before this country was seized of printing in the way it had long been in Europe. This retarded development, even then restricted by all those other forces which Feather[10] described so well, determined largely the publishing practices in Britain today.

The Star-Chamber decree ensured a North/South divide in communications and trade that was still intact in some respects into the nineteenth century and in a broader sense is one of those factors lying behind the North/South divide so frequently referred to today. There were, it is true, clandestine presses during the century in which the Star-Chamber decree was in force but they hardly point to significant demand. The Act of 1662 sanctioning printing in York saw no great upsurge in output. Even when the Licensing Act of 1662 was not renewed in 1695 there was no rush to start printing in the provinces. When Feather writes that 'from the late sixteenth century onwards there is copious evidence for the existence of a provincial book trade',[11] he is nevertheless referring to very modest activity. The fact that in 1644 John Awdley of Hull had 832 books in stock[12] hardly points in itself to a dynamic book trade in the provinces, especially in view of the trade on the Continent. The extant inventories of two booksellers in York of the sixteenth and early seventeenth centuries tend to confirm that the reverse might be easier to accept. Boswell's comment on Johnson's father, Michael, a bookseller in Lichfield, that such shops 'in the provincial towns of England were very rare, so that there was not one even in Birmingham, in which town old Mr Johnson used to open a shop every market-day'[13] seems to confirm this. Johnson's own comment in *The Idler* in 1758 that 'almost every large town has its weekly historian, who regularly circulates his periodical intelligence'[14] indicates that a century later not all large towns yet had their local newspaper.

Plomer[15] noted and many have repeated that by 1725 all important towns had
their own printers. Put somewhat less positively it could be said that some thirty
years were to elapse after 1695 before most important towns had their own
printers. Feather and others have suggested that the London-based copyright
controls, the regulation of the trade by London, inhibited development in the
provinces and there is much substance in this. The conclusion seems, however,
inescapable that the still modest output generally in the early eighteenth century
met the needs of a comparatively small population with limited educational
opportunities and a high degree of illiteracy. It is questionable whether the
picture would have been very different without the Star-Chamber decree, the
Licensing Acts or the cartel-like control of the Stationers' Company and the
London trade. The gradual spread of printing in the eighteenth century does not
encourage belief that it would have been otherwise. If anything, it reflects the far
from enthusiastic growth of the trade in the sixteenth century. Only during the
Civil War, 1639-40, do we learn from the Stationers' Register that output briefly
increased but that could not remotely be compared with the publication levels
promoted by the Reformation in Europe or, more specifically, the output in
Germany during the Peasants' Revolt.

Allnutt complained 'that the history of our provincial presses...should hitherto
have been almost entirely neglected by local historians'.[16] He writes

> It is surely not too much to expect of the historian that he should devote a tithe
> of his researches and one chapter of his book to the history of that noble art by
> means of which he is enabled to communicate the result of his labours to the
> literary public and to hand it down to posterity.

His paper concludes with a list of 276 printers found in provincial towns by the
end of the century. The list was compiled in his words [16]

> with the hope of stimulating librarians of town libraries to follow the example
> already set by Birmingham and other centres, to collect and preserve the local
> literature of their respective districts, and especially to secure while yet
> obtainable any books, pamphlets, ballads or broadsheets, having the slightest
> pretence to be called early specimens of local presses not only of their own
> cities or towns, but of other places in their several neighbourhoods.

It is now 112 years since Allnutt's paper was published. In the years between
his plea has been answered, if not fully, certainly enthusiastically. Librarians,
collectors, bibliographers have collected imprints and statistics and preserved
much which could well have been lost for posterity. In making his plea, Allnutt
did not enlarge on why this should be done and many lists remain just that, lists.
Plomer's *Dictionary* provides one kind of answer. In the continuation of 1932, his
co-editors described Plomer as 'interested in the history of printing and publishing for its own sake, and only very slightly...for the sake of the authors'.[17] This
interpretation certainly emerges from his Dictionary and from the many later

listings by other compilers. In Feather's preface to his admirable *Provincial Booktrade in Eighteenth-Century England*, he writes 'We have lists of names, trades, places and dates, but no attempt...to flesh out these bare bones of knowledge'. 'Despite all this effort...surprisingly little is known of the provincial book trade as an economic entity'.[18] This is reminiscent of Morgan's paper in Birmingham of 1958: he writes[19]

> Whether the study of the printing history of a particular locality is worth doing except from a purely antiquarian view is most doubtful; one has to rake over such a mass of intrinsically worthless material, only of interest to the local historian. There is no doubt, however, that much remains to be done in investigating the economic aspect, especially in the 18th century and later.

He goes on to suggest investigations of provincial firms' accounts, the kinds of machines used, the origins of the type, the source of employees and the like.

Miss Plant's book was 'designed as a contribution to the economic history of Great Britain...a strangely neglected chapter'.[20] She notes that bibliographers, students of literature, historians of political movements, of censorship and of freedom of the Press, had all given their attention to the history of the printed book, and, she writes[20]

> Yet the history of the economic development of the English book trade itself, the structural form which it gradually evolved, the problems of supply and demand which it encountered and overcame, the techniques which it adopted and discarded, the social and economic relationships which arose between masters and men, have not hitherto been described and appraised.

That Miss Plant achieved her objectives is not in doubt: she threw little light, however, on the history of the economic development of the book trade in the provinces. In the meantime, much of the material referred to by Morgan has been raked over in many different parts of the country.

It still remains to attempt for the book trade in the provinces what Miss Plant did so splendidly for it at a national, essentially London, level. Feather made an excellent contribution to the understanding of it in the 18th century but he would be the first to admit that much there remains to be done. He was 'primarily concerned to solve a single problem: how those living outside London obtained their books'. In achieving this 'the structure and organisation of the book trade; its growth and development; the demand for books in the provinces; and the economics of provincial bookselling and printing'[21] were considered in some depth. His remarks stand now very much as pointers to what still needs to be done. Much more still remains to be extracted from Record Offices. Then there is the massive still-growing evidence being provided by the Eighteenth Century Short Title Catalogue (ESTC). In a certain sense the 'list' to end all lists, this should also cast a searching light into the remotest areas of book production in the Eighteenth Century. It is certain to reveal detail of a kind and on a scale never previously available whilst offering insights and interpretations of the trade of which the ESTC Newsletter, *Factotum*, has already given a tantalising taste.

Feather is concerned with the eighteenth century. It is in the nineteenth century when the provincial cities and towns begin truly to shape the nation. It will be a long time before the STC for that century is complete. The main source of direct information until then is likely to remain the directories and lists which much 'raking over' has produced.   These can only be described as 'labours of love'. Feather referred to the stories of the pioneer printers of the 18th century as 'almost tediously uniform'.[22] There is certainly tedious uniformity in the directories and lists which have appeared.

Evidence of this uniformity comes clearly from the studies of provincial newspapers in the eighteenth and nineteenth centuries which reveal much in common in their historical development.   NEWSPLAN[23] endorses this convincingly and since newsagents played such an important role in the distribution and development of the book trade, it may be that the story has already been largely told. It is also important to acknowledge the limitations such studies reveal: local newspapers are of great interest to the public they serve, but are little more than objects of idle curiosity to others. Their significance, in a collective sense, beyond their locality has yet to be established.

Nevertheless, it should also be recognised that since the 1840s the provincial book trade is more than a mere corollary to London's book trade.   The largest publishing houses today are in Cambridge and Oxford, and if that seems to perpetuate 1586, it was not intended to work out that way. Moreover, following the Industrial Revolution, Cambridge and Oxford are, paradoxically, more provincial than they were. As wealth and influence grew in the Provinces, so did the provincial book trade so that today presses like that of Manchester University represent real forces in the publishing world.

Feather anticipated his 'fleshing out of bare bones' by a checklist of secondary sources in 1981. It lists publications on *The English Provincial Book Trade before 1850*[24] on a county by county, town by town, basis with a short section referring to the whole country. It records for the most part lists of the kind pioneered by Allnutt and Plomer, publications about individual presses, printers and booksellers, and accounts of local newspapers. There is little to be found in the list by way of interpretation of the materials, whether from the economic, literary or social historical point of view. Seen objectively, many such lists seem of limited value. For example, the checklist of bankrupts in the British book trades, 1731–1806, by Maxted[25] is only of interest if placed in the context of bankruptcies in general in that period. Marginally more printers are seen to have 'gone under' in London than in the provinces, but that is what would be expected given the concentration in the London area. It interests me personally to learn that in my home town of Leek, Francis Hilliard, bookseller, and Mary Maddock, bookseller, went bankrupt in 1795 and 1797 respectively but only because the names are familiar to me, as is the town itself. Doubtless it would interest other people in my home town but for much the same reasons. The list still awaits conclusions to be drawn. Many of the lists assume that they speak for themselves. In the foreword to Hunt's *The Book Trade in Northumberland and Durham to 1860*, Moran writes that 'it presents a picture of the spread of learning in the North-East during a period of expansion',[26] and the directory conveys much in the body of the text that is highly informative about those engaged in the book trade and their local standing. In the introduction a modest contribution to the economic history of the book trade is made, but primarily the work demonstrates the rich potential of such detailed listings. It is directly in the Plomer tradition. Miss Plant's work apart, it is not until Feather's monograph of 1985 that the real value of such lists begins to be realised.

The listing of types of publication, such as chapbooks, or analyses of subscription lists à la Wallis,[27] are by and large more capable of speaking for themselves. In the case of chapbooks it is questionable whether they provide much really new evidence: they fill out for the most part what is already known. Chapbook production has long been seen as an indication that the population of the lower orders in the nineteenth century was more literate than in the eighteenth century, but that confirms conclusions already drawn from much evidence of a different kind. Perhaps more important is the information provided about printers in a given area, which even if they were largely jobbing printers, meeting local printing needs rather than embarking on book production, is a valuable pointer to the economic development of the place. The Northeast, in particular Newcastle upon Tyne, exemplifies this particularly well. It would be interesting to see from Gazeteers and census returns just how important this occupation was in such a major port. By contrast the study of the subscription lists have revealed much that is new and important for provincial book-trade studies. Wallis's Project for Historical Biobibliography (PHIBB) cannot, however, be claimed purely as a provincial study since the publications have very clear national implications. They embrace the trade as a whole and offer additional evidence for interpreting its economic development.

At the other end of the spectrum of provincial book-trade studies is the essay or monograph on an individual printer working in one of the regions. Isaac[28] on Davison is a good example of what such studies can achieve. It is full of facts about life in Alnwick which not only add genuinely to the vision of the book trade, but also bring it alive in the context of a small community in the early nineteenth century. The very appearance of Davison's Book of Common Prayer and his Universal Holy Bible was in itself, as Isaac puts it, 'startling'. The fact that his splendid folio Bible was not a 'financial success' must be of equal interest. The account of Davison's relationship with John Catnach and his dealings with Thomas Bewick have an interest and relevance which goes far beyond the purely 'local'. Catnach's bankruptcies are set in context and have meaning. It becomes easy to appreciate Charles Hindley's remark that Davison was 'by far the most enterprising printer that had settled in the North of England'.[29] Hindley also tells us that Davison, pharmacist and printer, was no less distinguished for his 'chemistry' and 'medicine'. Isaac on Bulmer[30] is no less interesting, but this friend of Bewick and Robert Pollard, though an apprentice in Newcastle upon Tyne, distinguished himself in London. He cannot really be said to be representative of the provincial book trade. The growth and spread of printing in the Northeast, especially in Newcastle upon Tyne, raise questions of the connections between Newcastle and London, of the maritime links of two great ports on the East Coast.

Morgan's reference to the local historian recognises that the study of the provincial book trade is essentially an ingredient of local rather than mainstream history. The position of local history in the discipline of History has itself never been established and it is questionable whether it has ever secured a place in the curricula of any university in this country. It suffers first and obviously from the fact that it rarely determines national events and secondly from being the province of specialists in other fields who happen to take an interest in the subject. Unlike military history, which had apparently similar beginnings but is now secure in the teaching of History, it has no hard core of professionals dedicated to the subject. Miss Plant observed that 'the eighteenth century publisher was not always fully occupied by his profession. Book production from quite early days was often carried on in conjunction with some other trade, or with one of the learned professions'.[31] She notes that for some booksellers that part of their business was virtually a 'sideline'. Morgan comments that 'it is the exception rather than the rule to get a living by selling or printing books and nothing else'.[32] Study of the book trade seems also to be more of a 'sideline'. Perhaps significantly it is in the Extra-Mural Departments of English universities where supervised or organised research into this area is now most frequently to be seen. Previously, it was the province of many a dissertation for the fellowship of the Library Association.   Inasmuch as Extra-Mural Departments are parts of universities, this involvement, particularly where university-accredited certificates are awarded, must be seen as a step towards professionalising the subject in terms of university teaching and research.

The most that local history could hope for is to be recognised as an option, or Special Subject, in the way that Military History is now established in certain universities. Historical bibliography found a way into the curricula of English Departments essentially 'on the back' of textual criticism, in the way that palaeography and diplomatic, essential aids to historians, found their way into History Departments. The History of the Book, where it finds entry at all does so on the coat tails of historical bibliography. It is still very much a scholarly minority interest. The book trade clearly has some affinity with historical bibliography, the make-up of the book and hand printing, but how far that is established as a valid subject for scholarly enquiry it is difficult to say. Miss Plant's book demonstrated clearly the validity of the book trade in the context of economic history and it is there where its study is most likely to be found. In that context its role is likely to be supporting, one element among many. It is difficult to put the history of the book trade with all its fascination side by side with the content of one of its products such as J P Kay Shuttleworth's *The Moral and Physical Conditions of the Working Classes* of 1832 and expect it to claim equal attention.

The book trade is one of many vehicles which offer insights into the growth of the nation. The provincial book trade is an important part of it. It is a salutary fact that the index to Miss Plant's book refers to the provinces only seven times, yet each of its twenty one chapters could be applied to the provincial book trade. The first edition of her book appeared in 1939, the second in 1965. The time to extend her work to the provinces, amplifying and completing it, seems long overdue. Certainly the material is there and Feather has provided a taste of what could be achieved. Miss Plant's book made historians take note of the importance of the book trade in the way that the History of the Book has been brought before the eyes of scholars. Despite the 'History of the Book Trade in the North', other regional groups and annual seminars and conferences, their published works remain in the main apart, outside the required reading of scholars. It is a sobering thought that many of the articles published in *The Library*, the most respected of all bibliographical journals, will never come to the notice of many who need to read them. If the full potential of the study into the provincial book trade is to be brought before scholarship, the subject needs to be focused and brought into an integrated whole.

All this may seem to be negative if not uninformed. After all, my contribution, if one overlooks a now far distant bibliography of Scottish chapbooks in the University Library of Newcastle upon Tyne, is confined to perusing the hard-won findings of so many indefatigable scholars, not least of those involved in the 'History of the Book Trade in the North'. I read with pleasure Isaac on Bulmer or Davison, with admiration the Wallises and PHIBB, Robin Myers, John Feather,

C W Chilton and so many others. I have considered many lists. I would like to read a book on the provincial book trade which, to quote the *Economic Journal* reviewing Miss Plant 'every book-lover should read and from which every economist interested in industrial organisations can cull unending examples of the infinite adaptability of structure to circumstances'.

NOTES

1. W H Allnutt, *Notes on Printers and Printing in the Provincial Towns of England and Wales*: a paper read at the first annual meeting of the Library Association, etc., Oxford, 1878.

2. H R Plomer, *A Dictionary of the Printers and Booksellers who were at work in England, Scotland and Ireland from 1668 to 1725* (London, 1922).

3. Marjorie Plant, *The English Book Trade: an Economic History of the Making and Sale of Books*, second edition (London, 1965).

4. Plant, *English Book Trade*, p 81.

5. A G Dickens, *Reformation and Society in Sixteenth-century Europe* (London, 1966), p 51.

6. Plant, *English Book Trade*, p 83.

7. F Geldner, 'Das Rechnungsbuch des Speyrer Druckherrn, Verlegers und Gross-buchhändlers Peter Drach. (*Archiv für Geschichte des Buchwesens, Bd 5*) Frankfurt a M, (1964), pp 2–196.

8. M Luther, *An die Radherrn aller Stedte deutsches Lands: das sie Christliche schulen auffrichten und hallten sollen* (Wittemberg, 1524).

9. Two frequently quoted comments of Luther, see for example, M N Black, 'The printed Bible' in *The Cambridge History of the Bible*, p 432, etc.

10. J Feather, *The Provincial Book Trade in Eighteenth-Century England* (Cambridge, 1985).

11. Feather, *Provincial Book Trade*, p 1.

12. C W Chilton, 'The inventory of a provincial bookseller's stock of 1644', *The Library*, 6 ser, vol 1 (1979), pp 126–43.

13. Quoted from Plant, *English Book Trade*, p 85.

14. Quoted from Feather, *Provincial Book Trade*, p 27.

15. Plomer, *Dictionary...1668–1725*, p vii.

16. Allnutt, *Notes*, pp 1, 2 & 4.

17. H R Plomer, G H Bushnell and E R McC Dix, *A Dictionary of the Printers and Booksellers who were at Work in England, Scotland and Ireland from 1726 to 1775* (London, 1932), p vi.

18. Feather, *Provincial Book Trade*, p ix.

19. Paul Morgan, *English Provincial Printing*: a lecture delivered at the School of Librarianship, College of Commerce, Birmingham, 7 May 1958 (Birmingham, 1958), pp 17 & 18.

20. Plant, *English Book Trade*, p 7.

21. Feather, *Provincial Book Trade*, p x.

22. The same, p 16.

23. NEWSPLAN. A sub-committee of the Library and Information Services Council, representing all library authorities in the regions and promoting newspaper micro-filming programmes.

24. J Feather, *The English Provincial Book Trade before 1850*: a checklist of secondary sources (Oxford, 1981).

25. I Maxted, *The British Book Trades, 1731–1806*: a checklist of bankrupts (Exeter, 1985).

26. C J Hunt, *The Book Trade in Northumberland and Durham to 1860* (Newcastle upon Tyne, 1975), pp xi & xii.

27. P J Wallis: the investigations into subscription lists have been pioneered by P J Wallis resulting in various publications, eg *The North-east Book Trade to 1860: Imprints and Subscription Lists* (Newcastle upon Tyne, 1977). They represent a major contribution to book-trade studies.

28. P C G Isaac, *William Davison of Alnwick: pharmacist and printer, 1781–1858* (Oxford, 1968).

29. C Hindley, *History of the Catnach Press* (London, 1886), p 15. Quoted here from Isaac, *Davison*.

30. P C G Isaac, 'William Bulmer, 1757–1830: an introductory essay', *The Library*, 5 ser, vol 13 (1958), pp 37–50.

31. Plant, *English Book Trade*, pp 95 & 96.

32. Morgan, *Provincial Printing*, p 8.

The English Provincial Book Trade before Printing

A I DOYLE

People familiar with the era of printing sometimes speak as if the expression 'book trade' were virtually synonymous with the whole of book-production and distribution, even though today there are still significant non-commercial segments. For most of the middle ages the situation was very different and even by the fifteenth century it is doubtful if the majority of books were being made or changed hands for money. The term 'book trade' is more exactly employed to embrace three sorts of activity for remuneration: (1) the practice of various handicrafts towards making the physical objects; (2) the provision of texts and the coordination of the crafts to produce copies; (3) the selling of books, old or new, and of the requisite materials. None of these activities need be full-time occupations and one or more of them cannot give a living until the accessible market is large enough. That is clear from much of the provincial trade after printing, and it is all the truer in the middle ages.

The term 'provincial' is of course used in opposition to 'metropolitan', but it must be remembered that in the early middle ages London was not yet so dominant a centre commercially, while the political and cultural capital moved from Winchester to Westminster only after the Norman Conquest, and most medieval manuscript books do not state where they were made, who made them, or why. Moreover there is a paucity of explicit narrative or documentary evidence about book production or acquisition,especially in the earlier centuries, and in later ones for many places. From relatively few specific instances we have to venture hypotheses concerning the circumstances of origin of most manuscripts by comparative study of every detail of their form and content. For the question under discussion, what elements of trade there were in production and sale of books outside London before 1450 or 1476, we ought to think firstly of the supply of the materials, membrane, paper, inks, pigments and foils, threads, cords, boards, leathers, fabrics and metal fittinqs, secondly of the skills of design, writing, decorating, illustrating, binding, thirdly those of compiling or procuring what in the printed era we call copy, fourthly the availability of existing books, and last but not least who might have been willing to pay for books new or old.

I can say very little about the period before the Norman Conquest, except that books were probably for the most part made within monasteries and by monastic craftsmen or by other clerics in the service oI bishops, kings and noblemen or women.[1] That is not to say that vellum or parchment and leather may not have been prepared by lay servants, and some pigments and fabrics purchased from merchants, and there may have been some migratory artists who received fees besides bed and board. No doubt cash or its equivalent was sometimes given by the commissioner of a new book for any necessary outlay by its makers, and rewards in cash or kind, and future patronage, after the product. You may think this was a sort of trade, since it was obviously known where to go (such as Winchester and Canterbury in the 10th and 11th centuries) to get a book done, but the relationship was probably often one of reciprocal favours. Some books presumably passed for money from owner to owner, but I am not aware of anything like professional bookselling, unless you count the ransom of gold given by an ealdorman and his wife in the middle of the ninth century to the Norsemen for the Stockholm Codex Aureus of the Gospels which they had looted (since they specialised in such transactions).[2]

The situation for a century after the Norman Conquest was not very different except for the multiplication and expansion of monasteries, of their libraries and their book-production, the increased importation of foreign books and replacement of Old English in law and administration by Latin and French.[3] From the late 11th century major monasteries began to employ specialist scribes and artists, some of distant origins, most probably clerics, for longish periods, in addition to their own members, to enhance their collections – at St Albans from the time of the first Norman abbot until the early 13th century and at Abingdon in the early 12th century.[4] Throughout the middle ages a very considerable proportion of book-production was done by the hands of temporary or permanent employees of religious communities or lay households, who were often not engaged full-time on that but also on other duties. Thus it was a relationship of service rather than of trade. It is however from the middle and second half of the twelfth century, with the great development of the use of written records, that we begin to find more signs of the professionalisation of parts of the process of book-production.[5] It is not surprising that it is from about 1150 on that the term *pergamentarius*, later in French *parcheminier* and English 'parchmener', is found steadily, for what was the most messy, laborious and large-scale of the require-ments – not of course only for books but also and perhaps more for the rising tide of documents and, it is said, for windows. If an appellation like that is given to a man (or woman – there was one called Idonia in Lincoln in 1328) in the pipe rolls, assize, court, subsidy, account, or guild rolls, etc. it must be because it was recognised as their main distinctive occupation, down to the time, about the end of the 14th century, when occupational names begin to be merely hereditary, though even then not mostly so.[6] Parchmeners are found in many, probably most towns, throughout the country from the earliest records (which are mostly 13th or 14th century) and frequently more than one at a time in each place. They naturally occur along with butchers, skinners, tanners, whittawers and other workers with animal carcasses and pelts. Obviously their presence did not necessarily imply book-production, nor did the latter require parchment manufacture at hand, but proximity was no doubt cheaper if quantity mattered. For quality an ample supply of skins to be sorted, good methods of handling, and competitiveness in price were, I imagine, more likely in the bigger market-towns and cities.

The other early term is at the other extreme of skill: in Latin *illuminator*, French *alumpnour*, from 1135, and 'limner' in English. This noun and its verb seem to be used only of book or comparably delicate work; 'pictor', or 'peyntour', which are more frequent, and not infrequently applied to artists engaged on books, of course are not so restricted in use. If not already in the Anglo-Saxon era, then by the Norman, there were specialist migratory book-illustrators and decorators, some moving between countries, such as Master Hugo and the Alexis Master who worked for St Albans and Bury St Edmunds and the artists of the Winchester Bible, one of whom is also thought to have done murals in Spain.[7] The recurrence of recognisable artists' hands in illumination of manuscripts of diverse origin throughout the middle ages suggests that they often were peripatetic, if only within one country, though of course the books, and parts of them, were portable.[8] But a painter or limner in a local list implies settlement where there was regular work within reach. Painters are found as members of town guilds at Shrewsbury and Leicester in the early 13th century.[8]

Most clerics knew how to write, and up to the 15th century the majority of books were probably copied by them, whether for their own use, for friends, as part of their service to an institution or to someone who employed them for other purposes, or possibly for direct payment, full or part-time, just as with documents. Clerics in the lowest orders could marry, and the number of laymen (and to a much lesser extent women) who could write, gradually grew through the 13th, 14th and 15th centuries.[9] *Scriptor, escrivain* in French, 'scriveyn', 'scrivener' or 'writer' in English, does not tell us if he was a copyist of books or documents: if he could do one he could probably do the other, but what did most of these men (and sometimes women) do most of, in most places? Surely legal documents, as the word 'scrivener' came to imply in London by the end of the 14th century, when 'text-scriveyn' and 'text-writer' became current and was formalised in a separate trade guild, with the limners.[10] It is nonetheless significant that the vernacular words 'escriveyn' and 'scriveyn' are found from 1246 onwards, the same period as the first record of *exemplarius* (later *exemplator*), which meant copyist, pretty certainly of books, running up to the early fourteenth century in Oxford,[11] and one 'bokmaker' (perhaps alternatively a binder) in Yorkshire in 1293.[12] So from the middle of the 13th century advances in literacy were creating good enough markets in various places for people to specialise as scribes, and in at least some as copyists of books. Likewise, a *ligator librorum* is recorded in 1255, and 'bokbynder' in several places from 1286 on.[13]

Stationarius occurs at Oxford from 1262, which was the term used in the universities of Bologna and Paris from somewhat earlier for a licensed shop-keeper dealing in old and new books, responsible there also for running the pecia system of price-controlled loans for copying of quires of standard works, which was believed by Destrez and Pollard to have operated in Oxford too but has recently become a disputed question.[14] The stationers at Oxford and Cambridge (where the name occurs from 1276) did however operate the caution system, not known as such in the continental universities, valuing the books pawned by scholars for loans from chests endowed for the purpose (existing from 1240 at Oxford) and selling the pledges if they were not redeemed within a year and a day.[15] And up to their expulsion in 1290 the Jews of Oxford performed the same service, whether you regard it as part of the book trade or of banking.[16]

The term stationer is not recorded in London until 1311 and 1319 in York only elsewhere in England before the arrival of printing so far as I know, but there was a 'libraire', a bookseller, at Lincoln in 1360.[17] *Librarius*, the ancient term for a maker or seller of books was used sometimes synonymously with *stationarius*. But both in London and Oxford most of the positive evidence, from actual books or in lawsuits, relates to stationers dealing with secondhand books rather than new ones. Scarcely any of the scribes who are named in books or can be identified are independently documented as settled craftsmen, and extant illumination and binding is with a very few exceptions anonymous. What we can see of the changing associations in books of different scribes' and illuminators' hands, and what the documents indicate of the small size of trading establishments suggest that though a stationer, his family, apprentices or servants might practice one or more of the book-crafts, he commonly needed others, parchmeners, paper merchants or middlemen for materials, and scribes, limners, or binders for their skills, for some or all of any new books which were ordered from him or which he might speculate on finding purchasers for. As Graham Pollard put it, the trade in newly-made manuscript books was largely a bespoke one, up to and after the advent of printing.[18] Stationers must have laid out money on secondhand books for stock and so may have also invested in the production of new ones in anticipation of demand, but it has yet to be shown that they ever did so for more than single copies of a particular text at one time, though ready to repeat it if an exemplar were in stock or could be procured, yet usually with variations to suit the tastes or pockets of individual customers. Then as now, secondhand books were cheaper than new ones and steady sales were likely for only a limited range: bibles, church service-books and standard works of theology, canon and common law, grammar, history and some vernacular literature. Steady sales also required a sufficiently large accessible market of people who wanted books, would from time to time return some of them to the market and would be regularly replaced by new buyers: a situation obtaining only in a few centres resorted to by many clergy and wealthy laity, such as the university towns, London, York and one or two other cities.

In the 1930s Graham Pollard set out to collect evidence for the medieval book trade in the provinces as well as London. What he found, regrettably only published in part but now available in his papers in the Bodleian Library, was much more for Oxford than the metropolis until the end of the fourteenth century.[19] Although the earliest records from Oxford, of illuminators, a scribe and parchmeners are of the same period, the 1180s or 1190s, as the beginnings of the university, he concluded from the number of illuminators recorded in the early and mid-thirteenth century and the extant illuminated bibles and psalters which can be connected with Oxford yet with contemporary owners from well beyond its vicinity (as far indeed as Scotland), that the trade was not at first academic.[20] He traced nineteen illuminators, twelve bookbinders, eleven parchment-makers and nine *exemplarii* in Oxford before 1300, and most of them situated together, especially in Cat Street, between where All Souls College and the Radcliffe Camera now are.[21] The most celebrated is the limner William de Brailes, a married cleric, from before 1238 till after 1252, who signs his work in two books and pictures himself in one, and whose style is discernible in others.[22] The comparatively low number of specialist scribes recorded may be because of the luxury nature of the books being produced at that stage, and no doubt because of the large reservoir of potential copyists particularly of academic texts, as demand developed, among the members of the university, working occasionally for pay as well as for themselves and friends. It is significant that when books survive with scribal names they are not mostly identifiable as known *exemplarii* or *stationarii* but students, masters or presumed professional freelances.[23] The stationers, recorded only from the middle of the thirteenth century on, were licensed to control buying and selling of books for the protection of members of the university, and it was no doubt their complaints of competition that led to a university ordinance in 1374, against excessive numbers of other booksellers, not duly licensed, as a result of which books of great value were being taken to foreign parts (which might I suppose mean Cambridge as much as Paris), that in future none except a stationer or his deputy should sell a book worth more than half a mark (6s.8d.).[24] Whether or not this was effective (and it could not prevent private sales) it is notable that there was no attempt to regulate the making of books by copyists of any kind on commission, either for individuals or for stationers. This is confirmed by the fifteenth-century phenomenon of a number of professional scribes of foreign origin (chiefly from the Low Countries and Germany) working in Oxford, expressly for individuals in most cases, but perhaps also for stationers, presumably because there were not enough comparably competent natives available, for they were not evidently cheaper.[25] The one contract I know of is directly between the scribe and the commissioner of the book, with no intermediary.[26] It is interesting that an Englishman, John Lutton, who signs three surviving books, two of them copies of Higden's *Polychronicon*, one of which belonged to Hyde Abbey, Winchester, the other to Bath Priory, and a biblical commentary for Reading Abbey, using two different practised though not polished scripts, is recorded as a scribe and brewer in Oxford in 1410.[27] It was still a centre for supply of books to other places, especially monasteries (including Durham) which sent students there; and even in Oxford a combination of trades was prudent (and brewing was for long one of the commonest everywhere, on a domestic scale).

There are fewer records for Cambridge and manuscripts which may have originated there have not yet had the amount of attention they call for.[28] The university began with a migration from Oxford in 1209, a statute embracing scribes, illuminators and stationers may date from c 1264, confirmed in 1276, to which bookbinders were added by 1353, and the first of a series of loan-chests was established by 1300.[29] In the accounts of Ely Cathedral priory in 1301/2 and 1374/5 there are payments respectively for currying parchment in Cambridge and for having it made there by Robert Parchymnyneur from calf-skins bought for the purpose, and all the materials for ink and binding were bought, while wages were paid for weeks of work by named scribes in copying, and for illumination, repairing and binding, apparently much of it on the spot rather than in Cambridge.[30] Ely itself was too small a town to give a permanent living to professionals, except probably clerks acting as scribes, and Cambridge was its nearest source of help.

If we look for products of the Cambridge book trade we can find a number of early fifteenth-century manuscripts given to Peterhouse (one of the two colleges retaining much of the evidence calling for study) in which there are notes of the costs of parchment, writing, illumination and binding, with a total, which may well imply that all the work was arranged through a stationer, rather than separately between the craftsmen and the customer.[31] And wherever one finds (as one may in the products of other places) note of just the cost of illumination and binding, it may imply coordination of the two crafts by a stationer, to whom sometimes an independently written book was brought for finishing. A mere price on a book proves nothing, for it may be a valuation for pledging or borrowing, not evidence of sale, new or secondhand. While Cambridge was never as important a centre of the book trade as Oxford, the annual Stourbridge fair just outside Cambridge was a larger affair than that of St Giles at Oxford, as an international market.[32] We do not know how often, before printing made widespread wholesale and retail distribution imperative, books were offered at fairs, but as today dealers anxious to get books off their hands for cash or by exchange must have used them sometimes.

It was to be expected that York, as the second city of the kingdom in size, occasional seat of government and head of the northern ecclesiastical province, with its own liturgical use, many churches, clergy and religious communities, and a centre of other trades, would develop one for books, but it is not till the end of the thirteenth century, that there are records in the 1270s of parchmeners, in the 1280s and 1290s scriveners, a 'bokmaker', a bookbinder, and illuminators.[33] It was during the thirteenth century that the dominance of the two liturgical uses of Salisbury and York had developed, along with papal, provincial and diocesan legislation prescribing better education for the clergy and instruction for the laity, supported by the composition and copying of pastoral handbooks.[34] All parish and collegiate churches and chapels had to be equipped with a set of service-books of the prevailing use, they had to be kept up to date with additions and amendments subsequently authorised, and repaired in text and binding from constant wear and tear. This alone provided enough work for a York book trade, apart from other business which would naturally come in to where the craftsmen where known to congregate. There can be little doubt, though it cannot easily be proved, that the majority of service-books of York use were made there in the 14th and 15th centuries, although as good texts spread they could be copied in other places. There is a detailed contract of 1346 by Robert Brekeling, *scriptor*, to copy and illuminate a psalter with calendar, office of the dead, a hymnary and collectar, for a Minster priest, in return for a total of 18s.9d. and some clothing.[35] By 1377 the scriveners, text-writers, limners, tourners and noters were numerous and prosperous enough to form a guild together (whereas in London at this time the scriveners had formed a separate guild, which only happened by 1425 in York); the flourishers are also named later.[36] The tournours and flourishers, not so discriminated in other places, specialised on the non-illuminated decorative initials, and the noters on musical notation, both of which played a crucial role in service-books. Professor George Keiser has counted in the York Freemen's

Register between 1327 and 1473 thirty-eight parchment-makers, one stationer, thirty-five scriveners, thirteen limners and six bookbinders.[37] Professor John Friedman adds three tournours between 1377 and 1450.[38] The scriveners and limners shared in one of the Corpus Christi plays and the parchmeners and binders in another.

Eventually in 1476 (the year Caxton set up at Westminster, when foreign printed books were probably already arriving in York) the binders and stationers joined in a new company. As in London these divisions and amalgamations point to changes in the balance of business over the years. Besides the scribes who were freemen there were in York many clerics who could and did do occasional jobs of writing to augment their income, and even full-time. As a result of one case of a priest taking an apprentice for the purpose, as late as 1487, which he was allowed to continue, there was an attempt to regulate this competition by an ordinance (which I guess was a reaffirmation of custom) of the guild that [39]

> noo prest within this citie, suburbs and fraunchesse...having a competent sallary, that is to say, seven marks or above, exercise the craft of textwritters, lominers, noters, tournours and florisshers within the same for his singuler prouffit and lucour, nor take noone apprentice, hirdman, or other servant into his service, nor make noo bargans or covenants to that intent, undre the pain of forfaiture of 13s.4d. Provided alway that it shalbe lefull to any prest to write, lomine, note, tourne or florisshe any maner of books to his propre use or to distribute to any place in way of elmose.

Seven marks was £4.13s.4d. and £5 was a common level of stipend for a curate or chaplain. There is no mention of clerks in orders below the priesthood, who would have smaller incomes and whose customary right to practice is thus tacitly admitted.

Of the other major regional centres one would expect to have developed a book trade by the end of the 13th century, at Norwich the accounts of the Cathedral priory have, in the second surviving roll, 1272, 20s. *to redeem a copy of Peter Lombard's Sentences* from the Jews, and in subsequent years up to 1317 many payments for the buying and making of books for church and library, in stipends and board for scribes and illuminators, the purchase of ink, parchment, vellum (with two lots of currying for writing), and on binding, with the names of a number of the practitioners seemingly lay professionals, one living in for a year, but the others presumably local men.[40] County assize rolls name a parchmener, bookbinder and scrivener in 1286, city deeds a limner in 1287, a parchmener in 1295, and so on subsequently.[41] Though Norwich did not have its own liturgical use the diocese had a distinct calendar and some of the many service-books in which it occurs must have been made in the city, though others perhaps in Lynn or Bury. And some of the books illuminated in what has been called rather too definitely the East Anglian style of the 14th century are closely connected with Norwich.[42] With a larger number of parish churches even than York (46 against 40), a somewhat smaller population in the 14th century but possibly larger in the 15th, there was a comparable market on the spot, and a more populous and prosperous region.[43]

At Lincoln, again with the cathedral of a very large diocese, several religious houses and 46 parish churches, there was a scrivener in 1246, an illuminator about 1250, a woman parchmener in 1275 and a male bookbinder in 1319.[44] In 1359–60 when King Jean le Bon of France was a captive his servants bought two books, one from a 'libraire' and paper and parchment from three grocers in the city, besides commissioning a book from an English scribe.[45] Grocers were retailers of miscellaneous household supplies and at this date (and until 1494) all paper was imported, and there are extant English instances from early in the 14th century, in particular the archives of Lynn, which was probably a point of entry and of distribution to dealers in its hinterland.[46] As an example of later professional production in the city, there is a note by John Weston of Lincoln, *scriptor*, in a finely-written and illuminated volume of a Latin commentary on the Sunday gospels that the writing was finished on 10 May 1425, how much parchment it took and how much was left over, which suggests he was accounting to someone else; the illumination was still to be done and no costs are stated, so a price for the whole job had already been agreed, or had still to be worked out.[47] Pamela Robinson has remarked how this naming of his place of residence by a scribe was a way of advertising to attract future business. Another instance is a *scriptor* of Newark, not quite so good, for a volume of Latin theology in 1442.[48]

Another cathedral city, Winchester, by this time no longer of its ancient status but with a population of approaching 8000, had two parchmeners and a scrivener before 1300 and more or less the same through the next two centuries, with a bookbinder shortly before and a limner shortly after 1400, when the new college there of Wykeham's foundation was equipping itself.[49] Its accounts show several men described as *scriptor* or *clericus*, apparently of the neighbourhood, one of whom had a servant, and one from St Mary's Abbey (where he must have worked for the nuns) copying books between 1398–9 and 1423–4, besides one (whom we know also to have been a stationer and limner) of London in 1400–1.[50] And volumes of a large set of five actually copied at Lanthony Abbey near Gloucester in 1432–7 were illuminated (and also bound ?) in Winchester, where Sir Walter Oakeshott thought he saw the same limners' hands in other surviving books.[51]

Smaller cities and towns, for which besides the fact that the documentation may not be so good, did not necessarily have a continuity of recognised professional practitioners of all the book crafts. As in post-medieval times they may have tried their luck, come and gone. Lichfield, with which an important group of copies of English religious texts can be associated about 1400, had a parchmener and scrivener in 1379/80 (the former taxed more heavily), another scrivener in the 1390s and early 1400s but only a parchmener in its guild in 1411, but once more we must remember the clergy of the cathedral, who may have made it hard for even one full-time scrivener to earn a livelihood there.[52] It had a limner however in 1327 and 1397–8.[53]

Durham, with its large cathedral priory but no other religious house, has record of only one parchmener in the late thirteenth or early fourteenth century, at a time when there were more luxury trades in the town than later, but there must have been a constant need of parchment for administrative and legal documents of the palatine and diocesan courts as well as the monastery, and there were a number of clerks employed by each.[54] The priory accounts from the later thirteenth century onwards have payments for parchment, paper and writing for those purposes, and also book purchase, binding and repairs, chiefly for appropriated parish churches, but few specifying the payees: for instance 12d. to Ralph Luminour for illuminating a book for Merrington in 1330/1, who perhaps was the same as Ralph de Langton illuminator fined at Durham in 1304.[55] The priory employed a Breton scribe, Guillermus du Stiphel, to write books in the 1380s and subsequently, and perhaps a son, both in books and documents, and he may have worked for people outside the monastery too.[56] In 1450 Richard Danyell of Duresme, yeoman and bookbinder, when charged with blocking the gateway of St Mary-le-Bow in the North Bailey, said he was a servant of the prior and did so by his command; he perhaps had to be a jack of all trades since in 1451 he was paid for making two sets of church vestments for Finchale priory, the dependency not far from the city.[57] We know that Durham priory in the fourteenth and fifteenth centuries got many, probably most, of its new acquisitions of books from Oxford, where its monks went to Durham College, some writing and some buying what they wanted there and bringing it home later.[58] If local provision was thus reduced other buyers might have resorted to Newcastle upon Tyne. Despite a bookbinder in 1292 and 1296 and an illuminator in the latter year there is an unfortunate lack of later evidence.[59] The only book I know certainly made in Newcastle is a volume of religious texts in Latin and English both handsomely written and illuminated by John Lacy, a Dominican friar living as a recluse, between 1420 and 1434, as a gift for the use of successive priests serving St Nicholas's church, now the Cathedral, there.[60] If he had not expressly told us, we could have thought either writing or illumination paid work, and we would not have known where it was done, for the English spelling has only hints of northern dialect. Friars of course were migrants; in the south of England another

Dominican, John Siferwas, was a notable illuminator at the beginning of the fifteenth century, and in the first and second half of the fourteenth century Augustinian friars were responsible for illumination of the highest quality, particularly those working for the Bohun family. These are properly called professionals, but their relationship to their patrons was that of family servants, not of trade.[61]

More important than Newcastle and with better surviving records, Bristol is a city in the same rank as York and Norwich, and second in wealth to London, for which there ought to be more explicit evidence than I have yet found. By 1312–13 it had a number of parchmeners and curriers and three scriveners.[62] It had religious houses, many parish churches and as a port a prosperous and literate laity. From the late fourteenth and early fifteenth century there are some finely written and illuminated English books with west-country links which I am inclined to think may be commercial products there, but so far I cannot clinch it.[63] In 1436–7 fifty-nine quires of large vellum were bought in Bristol for a book being copied at Lanthony Abbey near Gloucester for Winchester College.[64] In 1458–9 and 1466–7 the wardens of St Ewen's parish church were able to spend a good deal on vellum and writing for service-books, presumably from local resources,[65] and in 1479 a merchant, Philip Ringeston, had an illuminated book of hours made (or completed) for him, but we do not know what sort of craftsmen did it.[66]

In contrast at Bury St Edmunds, a much smaller town, the monastery continued in the fifteenth century to employ non-monks for book work as it had in the twelfth, and it can also be shown that a number of illuminated copies of the English poems of the monastic poet John Lydgate, some with series of pictures, and other books, were probably made by several scribes and limners in the town over the years 1440 to 1470, both for the abbey and for other owners.[67] In the period 1354–1430 two parchmeners and two scriveners are recorded in the town; from 1441 to 1530 two parchmeners, but nine scriveners, two limners and, in 1520 (with printing), two stationers.[68]

There are other towns from which one could cite sporadic records of craftsmen[69] and some actual books, but it ought to be realised that there were clerks from at least the middle of the thirteenth century in every locality of a few villages, who could be called on to make books as well as documents and might do a good job if they could get the materials and knew the conventions of structure and presentation. Professor Carter Revard has discovered that the scribe of two famous anthologies of English and French verse, well-designed and written, though without illumination, and made probably for noble household entertainment and edification, also wrote many deeds for modest people in a small rural area of Herefordshire over the same period of the 1320s to 1340s.[70] He may have been a clerk with cure of souls and we should probably style his scribal role as rather part-time professional than commercial.

There are two other aspects of the book trade which ought to be considered. By the late fourteenth century there was at least in London and possibly in some other centres a wholesale trade in parchment and vellum, and certainly in paper, but it is very doubtful if there can be said to have been any wholesale trade in books before printing, since that obviously means the supply of identical or similar articles in quantity. There were only a few types of book which were produced in large numbers to fairly uniform patterns, and almost never quite identical: in the mid-thirteenth century Latin pocket bibles, mostly from France but some probably from Oxford, in the late fourteenth and early fifteenth century Wycliffite English New Testaments, more probably from London than Oxford, and in the mid-fifteenth century English Brut chronicles, some possibly from an unidentified provincial centre but most from London; but I know of no evidence of their being supplied simultaneously in quantity to booksellers in London or elsewhere, or successively, as may however have happened. Extant manuscripts do show that some scribes seem to have specialised repetitively on certain texts, particularly in fifteenth-century London, but there is a group of copies of the English translations of the allegorical Pilgrimages by Guillaume de Deguileville from the mid-fifteenth century which from the style of illumination and early ownership may have been made in the north midlands, perhaps Lincoln or Nottingham, probably for money (as repetition suggests though it scarcely proves).[71] And there is nothing to prove that this repetition preceded individual commissions.

Speculative commercial importation of books very likely took place for the academic and ecclesiastical public, in the thirteenth and fourteenth centuries, of works of canon and civil law, for most of those that survive (many now as binders' waste) with marks of English medieval ownership are in the rotunda script of Bologna, and many with Italian or French illumination, though some with English. Some of these were no doubt bought by English clerics studying or journeying abroad, but they were an obvious costly item for Italian merchants to bring into London, Southampton or Bristol. The question is whether they themselves sold them there or at the general markets or if Oxford or Cambridge or York stationers found it worth their while to deal with them. In the *Philobiblon*, dated 1345 at Auckland Palace shortly before his death, Richard de Bury claims to have got to know stationers and booksellers not only in England but also in France, Germany and Italy, to send or bring books he wanted regardless of expense, distance or the seas.[72] That however was at his initiative, probably before he became Bishop of Durham in 1333, when he was himself travelling abroad; it may however imply some degree of international commercial correspondence, as there was in other commodities and as rapidly appears after the introduction of printed books, in the provinces at Oxford, Cambridge and York as well as at London.[73]

Although I have referred to the existence of local records of bookbinders and occasional notes of the cost of binding, most of the surviving work from the eleventh to the fifteenth century has plain whittawed covers over wooden boards, forwarded and finished in styles which indicate the period but not the place of execution. There is a handful of late twelfth-century richly blind-tooled tanned leather covers which can be connected more or less firmly with Winchester, London and Durham, imitating contemporaneous French work, which may have been done by professionals rather than monks, while single specimens with a few tools are found at Durham and some other monasteries in the thirteenth, fourteenth and early fifteenth centuries, but it was not until the middle of the fifteenth century that a growth in blind-tooling begins, from the details of which separate binderies can be identified at Salisbury, Canterbury and Oxford, where Graham Pollard attempted to match them with the names and dates of documented binders.[74] It must be remembered that many medieval manuscripts spent much or all of their lives not between hard boards but in limp wrappers which could have been made by less skilled hands than a professional binder's, and the craft is one which can be learned and practised part-time if it does not have to be done too frequently. It was quicker to bind a large medieval manuscript than to write and decorate it, and the arrival of multiple copies of big printed books in London, Oxford and Cambridge at least must have changed the scale of the binding trade there.

I have not reported or researched any of the places and cases I have mentioned as thoroughly as they merit or as I might if I had had more time to do so. I have offered only easily-found fragments of information from which you may get an impression of the extent of our ignorance and the need for more study, especially of surviving books and their relationships to the writing and decoration of localised documents, not just references to book-crafts in local documents.

NOTES

1. I have not yet seen R McKitterick [ed], *The Uses of Literacy in Early Medieval Europe* (Cambridge, 1990), which may touch on this question, though C P Wormald, 'The uses of literacy in Anglo-Saxon England and its neighbours', *Transactions of the Royal Historical Society*, 5 ser, vol 27 (1977), does not do so. For the most recent and

authoritative survey of the primary evidence see H Gneuss, 'Anglo-Saxon libraries from the conversion to the Benedictine reform' in *Angli e Sassoni al di qua e di la del mare* (Spoleto: Centro Italiano di Studi sull'Alto Medievo, Settimane 32, 1986), vol ii, 643–99.

2. J J G Alexander, *Survey of Manuscripts Illuminated in the British Isles, I: Insular Manuscripts, 6th to the 9th Century* (London, 1978), pp 56–7, no 30.

3. N R Ker, *English Manuscripts in the Century after the Norman Conquest* (Oxford, 1960).

4. O Lehmann-Brockhaus, *Latenische Schriftquellen zur Kunst in England...vom Jahre 901 bis zum Jahre 1307* (Munich, 1956), vol ii, pp 415, 432; vol iii, p 351; R Thomson, *Manuscripts from St Albans Abbey 1066–1235*, 2 vols (Woodbridge, 1982).

5. M T Clanchy, *From Memory to Written Record* (London, 1979), esp p 61.

6. R E Latham [ed], *Revised Medieval Latin Word-list from British and Irish Sources* (London, 1965); R E Latham and others, *Dictionary of Medieval Latin from British Sources* (London, 1975-); T B W Reid and others [ed], *Anglo-Norman Dictionary* (London, 1977-); H Kurath and others, *Middle English Dictionary* (Ann Arbor, 1956-); G Fransson, *Middle English Surnames of Occupation 1100–1350* (Lund Studies in English, 3, 1935), pp 128–30.

7. C M Kauffman, *Survey of Illuminated Manuscripts III: Romanesque Manuscripts 1066–1190* (London, 1975), pp 15–16, 109–11, no 83.

8. The same, p 16. I am indebted to Dr M Michael for letting me see his draft indexes of references to illuminators.

9. Cf Clanchy (note 5 above); for instance in the subsidy roll for the West Riding of Yorkshire, 1379, at Scothorp W Clerke Scriptor et uxor, at Gayregrave, Rob Clerk Scriptor et uxor: *Yorkshire Archaeological Journal*, vol 7 (1882), pp 150, 165; M B Parkes, 'The literacy of the laity', in D Daiches & A K Thorlby [ed], *Literature and Western Civilization*, vol ii (London, 1973), 555–77.

10. G Pollard, 'The Company of Stationers before 1557', *The Library*, 2 ser, vol 18 (1937–8), pp 1–38, esp pp 5–9.

11. Latham and others, *Dictionary*; G Pollard, 'The University and the book trade in mediaeval Oxford', in P Wilpert [ed], *Beiträge zum Berufsbewusstsein des mittelalterlichen Menschen*, Miscellanea Medievalia (Cologne, 1964), vol iii, pp 336–44.

12. Fransson, *Surnames*, p 129.

13. Latham, *Word-list*; Fransson, *Surnames*, p 129.

14. Pollard, 'The University and the book trade'; cf M B Parkes, 'Book provision and libraries at the medieval University of Oxford', *The University of Rochester Library Bulletin*, vol 30 (1987–8), pp 28–43; A J Piper & M R Foster, 'Evidence of the Oxford booktrade, about 1300', *Viator*, vol 20 (1989), pp 155–60; Dr Parkes has also kindly shown me a draft of his chapter for the forthcoming vol 2 of *The History of the University of Oxford*, edited J I Catto.

15. See M B Hackett, T H Aston and R Faith in T H Aston and others [ed], *The History of the University of Oxford*, vol ii (1984), pp 88–9, 274–82.

16. The same, pp 274–5.

17. A Kirchhoff, *Die Handschriftenhändler des Mittelalters* (1853-5, repr New York, 1971), p 139.

18. Pollard, 'The Company of Stationers', pp 14–16.

19. E Potter, 'Graham Pollard at work', *The Library*, 6 ser, vol 11 (1989), pp 307-27, esp pp.313, 315–16, 318–19, 323.

20. Pollard, 'The University and the book trade', pp 336-7; N Morgan, *Survey of Illuminated Manuscripts IV: Early Gothic Manuscripts, i: 1190-1250* (London, 1982), pp 14, 68–73, 114–22.

21. See also F Madan, *Oxford Books*, vol i (Oxford, 1895), p 267, vol ii (1912), pp 502–8, where however the first references were dated rather too early; cf Hackett, *History of the University*, vol i, 88–9; H E Salter, *Survey of Oxford*, vol i (Oxford Historical Soc, new series, 14, 1960), p 84, where the first deed is dated *c* 1210.

22. Morgan, *Gothic manuscripts*, pp 114–22; I have not yet seen C Donovan, *The De Brailes Hours: Shaping the Book of Hours in Thirteenth-Century Oxford* (London, 1990).

23. Dr Parkes will give many instances in his chapter for the *History of the University*.

24. Madan, *Oxford Books*, vol i, pp 269, 281.

25. A G Watson, *Catalogue of Dated and Datable Manuscripts c.435-1600 in Oxford Libraries*, 2 vols (Oxford, 1984), lists a number of instances and Dr Parkes will cite others.

26. British Library, Harley MS 862, f 18r, 8 June 1425, at Tackley Inn, Oxford, by the scribe Gilbert de Doem of Utrecht diocese for Master John de Lipomanis of Venice.

27. J Taylor, *The Universal Chronicle of Ranulf Higden* (Oxford, 1966), pp 90, 106; the commentary is British Library, Royal MS 4.C.VI.

28. G J Gray, *The Earlier Cambridge Stationers and Bookbinders* (Bibliographical Soc. Illustrated Monograph 13, Oxford 1904), esp pp 1–4, 7–11.

29. G Pollard, 'Mediaeval loan chests at Cambridge', *Bulletin of the Institute of Historical Research*, vol 17 (1940), 113–29; M B Hackett, *The Original Statutes of Cambridge University: the Text and its History* (Cambridge, 1970), pp 228–9.

30. M Gullick [ed], *Extracts from the Precentors' Accounts concerning Books and Bookmaking of Ely Cathedral Priory* (Hitchin, 1985).

31. H E Bell, 'The prices of books in medieval England', *The Library*, 4 ser, vol 17 (1937), pp 312–32, esp p 315 n4.

32. J E T Rogers, *History of Agriculture and Prices in England*, vol i (Oxford, 1866), pp i, 141-7, 153–4. There is a fifteenth-century note by an Englishman in Caius College MS 328/715 for a search to be made 'in foro nuncupato Jaudewyn market' to see if five named Latin theological books might be for sale: M R James, *Descriptive Catalogue* (Cambridge, 1907), vol i, p 371.

33. Lehmann-Brockhaus, *Latenische Schriftquellen*, vol iii, p 66, no 5385; Fransson, *Surnames*; and subsequently eg F Collins [ed], *Register of the Freemen of the City of York*, vol i (1272-1558, Surtees Society 96, 1897), pp 1–2, 17, 24, 83; W Brown [ed], *Yorkshire Lay Subsidy...1301* (Yorkshire Archaeological Society Record Series 21, 1896), p 119.

34. J R H Moorman, *The English Church in the Thirteenth Century* (Cambridge, 1946), pp 90–109.

35. J Raine [ed], *The Fabric Rolls of York Minster* (Surtees Society 35, 1858), pp 165–6.

36. J Moran, 'Stationers' companies of the British Isles', *Gutenberg-Jahrbuch* 1962; J W Percy [ed], *York Memorandum Book BY* (Surtees Society 186, 1973), pp 193–7, 206–11.

37. G R Keiser, *Studies in Bibliography*, vol 32 (1979), p 165.

38. J B Friedman, 'Books, owners and makers in fifteenth-century Yorkshire', in A J Minnis [ed], *Latin and Vernacular* (Cambridge, 1989), pp 111–27.

39. Percy [ed], *York Memorandum*, p 195.

40. N R Ker, 'Medieval manuscripts from Norwich Cathedral Priory', *Transactions of the Cambridge Bibliographical Society*, vol 1 (1949–53), pp 1–28, esp 23–8.

41. Fransson, *Surnames*.

42. L F Sandler, *Survey of Illuminated Manuscripts: Gothic Manuscripts 1285–1385*, 2 vols (London, 1986), vol i, p 50.

43. N P Tanner, *The Church in Late Medieval Norwich 1370–1532* (Toronto, Pontifical Institute of Medieval Studies, Studies and Texts 66, 1984), pp 2–5.

44. J W F Hill, *Medieval Lincoln* (Cambridge, 1948), pp 161, 363; Fransson, *Surnames*.

45. Kirchhoff, *Handschriftenhändler*, pp 135, 139–40.

46. G S Ivy, 'The bibliography of the manuscript book', in F Wormald & C E Wright [ed], *The English Library before 1700* (London, 1958), pp 36, 60.

47. Cambridge University Library, MS Gg.IV.19, ff 290v–1r: see P Robinson, *Catalogue of Dated and Datable Manuscripts c 737–1600 in Cambridge Libraries*, 2 vols (Cambridge, 1988), vol i, p 31, no 43; vol ii, pl 212.

48. The same, vol i, pp 11, 33, no 50; vol ii, pl 240.

49. D Keene, *Survey of Medieval Winchester*, 2 vols (Oxford, 1985), vol i, pp 352–3, 367, 394; vol ii, p 1343.

50. W Oakeshott, 'Winchester College library before 1750', *The Library*, 5 ser, vol 9 (1954), pp 14–15.

51. The same, pp 15–16.

52. A I Doyle [intro], *The Vernon Manuscript* (Cambridge, 1987), p 14.

53. I know of these from Dr Michael's index.

54. M Bonney, *Lordship and the Urban Community: Durham and its Overlords 1250–1540* (Cambridge, 1990), p 148.

55. J T Fowler [ed], *Extracts from the Account Rolls*, 3 vols (Surtees Society 99, 100, 103, 1898–1901), pp 126, 209, 213, 266, 271, 277, 385, 401, 411, 473, 486, 517, 536, 546, 550, 614. I owe the 1304 reference to Dr Michael's index.

56. A I Doyle, 'Book production by the monastic orders in England c 1375–1530', in L L Brownrigg, *Medieval Book Production: Assessing the Evidence* (Los Angeles, 1990).

57 R Surtees, *History and Antiquities of the County Palatine of Durham*, vol iv (Durham, 1840), 38–9; cf Bonney, *Lordship*, p 63; Durham Cathedral, Finchale account, 13 February–Pentecost 1451, kindly discovered for me by Mr A J Piper.

58. A J Piper, 'The libraries of the monks of Durham', in M B Parkes & A G Watson [ed], *Medieval Scribes, Manuscripts and Libraries: Essays presented to N R Ker* (London, 1978), pp 213–49, esp 244–7.

59. Fransson, *Surnames;* C M Fraser [ed], *The Northumberland Lay Subsidy Roll of 1296* (Society of Antiquaries of Newcastle upon Tyne Record Series 1, 1968), p 40. Bonney, *Lordship,* p 172, notes John Spycer (ie grocer) of Newcastle supplying quires of paper to Durham Cathedral Priory in 1360–3.

60. R M Clay, 'Further studies on medieval recluses', *Journal of the British Archaeological Association,* 3 ser, vol 16 (1953), pp 74–86 & pl XXII; 'Some northern anchorites', *Archaeologia Aeliana,* 4 ser, vol 33 (1955), pp 202–17 & pll XIX–XXI, esp pp 210–12 & pll XX–XXI; Watson, *Catalogue,* vol i, pp 146–7, no 873, ii, pl 290.

61. L F Sandler, *Gothic Manuscripts,* vol i, p 49; 'A note on the illuminators of the Bohun manuscripts', *Speculum,* vol 60 (1985), pp 364–72.

62. *Bristol & Glos. Archaeol. Soc. Trans,* vol 19 (1895), p 218.

63. A I Doyle, 'English books in and out of court from Edward III to Henry VII', in V J Scattergood & J W Sherborne [ed], *English Court Culture in the Later Middle Ages* (London, 1983), pp 163–81, esp p 173.

64. Oakeshott, p 15 (see note 50).

65. *Bristol & Glos. Arch. Soc. Trans.,* vol 15 (1891), pp 139–82, 254–96.

66. Bristol Public Library MS 11: N R Ker, *Medieval Manuscripts in British Libraries,* vol ii (Oxford, 1977), 204–77.

67. K L Scott, 'Lydgate's Lives of Saints Edmund and Fremund: a newly-located manuscript in Arundel Castle', *Viator,* vol 13 (1982), pp 335–66; N J Rogers, 'Fitzwilliam Museum MS 3-1979: a Bury St Edmunds Book of Hours and the origins of the Bury style', in D Williams [ed], *England in the Fifteenth Century* (Woodbridge, 1987), pp 229–43 & pll 1–17.

68. R S Gottfried, *Bury St Edmunds and the Urban Crisis 1290–1539* (Princeton, 1982), pp 110–13.

69. The Oath Book of Colchester *c* 1400 mentions Parchemin-makers, Bookbynderys and Scriveners: Kurath and others, *Middle English Dictionary* (see note 6).

70. C Revard, *Notes & Queries,* vol 224 (1979), pp 199–202; vol 226 (1981), pp 199–200; vol 227 (1982), pp 62–3; *Studies in Philology,* vol 79 (1982), pp 122–46.

71. See K L Scott, *Survey of Illuminated Manuscripts VI: Later Gothic Manuscripts,* forthcoming.

72. *Philobiblon,* ed M Maclagan, tr E C Thomas (Oxford, 1960), pp 92–4.

73. E G Duff, *The English Provincial Printers, Stationers and Bookbinders to 1557* (Cambridge, 1912).

74. G Pollard, 'The names of some English fifteenth-century binders', *The Library,* 5 ser, vol 25 (1970), 193–218.

The Provincial Book Trade Before the End of the Licensing Act

PAUL MORGAN

I have to admit that I have nothing really new to say, but this twenty-fifth anniversary gives an opportunity to survey what has been done during this period. There have been several surveys[1] in recent years but they have tended to concentrate on the eighteenth century onwards, so I should like to consider work on the two previous centuries and see what can be deduced generally. Oxford and Cambridge will be excluded as they are special cases. Students of particular places naturally have strong local patriotism that sometimes fails to put their study into context as the beloved name is seized upon uncritically whenever it is spotted. Some of the studies published before about 1950 tended to concentrate on printing and bookselling only, but the term 'book trade' in more recent years has become widely accepted and includes all aspects such as bookbinding, chapbook and ballad selling, newspapers, paper- and parchment-making. It has always to be remembered that the provincial book trade was rarely a main occupation, usually combined with other interests, and also of little importance to the vast majority of the population, however essential it may appear to us today. It is curious that book-trade history has received so much scholarly attention; why are not the butchers, bakers and candlestick-makers of particular towns studied with such attention? But that question is not relevant to my topic here.

The most important point to emerge from published work on the provincial book trade in England is the domination of London, properly emphasised by Professors Feather and Isaac[2] for the eighteenth century. The late Graham Pollard pointed it out for earlier centuries in his 1959 Sandars Lectures[3] that the capital was equally important in the sixteenth and seventeenth centuries. Wynkyn de Worde, for instance was associated with York printers and stationers;[4] Gerard Wandsforth also left him and another London stationer bequests in 1510.[5] An Exeter bookseller who died in 1553 named John Walley of London as the overseer of his will, while his son was associated with Thomas Barthelet.[6] This association between the capital and the provinces naturally became stronger after the restriction of printing to London in 1557. Professor D F McKenzie's works on the apprentices of the Stationers' Company of London reveal the wide area whence they came[7] and I have tried to show how men from one county interacted and were related to masters and places.[8] A popular misconception is that rural areas were isolated from the capital, but only a quick glance at John Taylor, the water poet's, *Carriers Cosmographie* of 1637[9] reveals how all parts of England could be reached by wagon or coastal ship, provided speed was not the prime consideration; there were also foot-posts to and from a few places like York.

At the beginning of the printed-book era, in pre-Reformation times, the provincial book trade was determined by the medieval manuscript market, often near a cathedral.[10] There obviously cannot be any clear-cut distinction between printed and manuscript books available for sale; one wonders which was acquired in 1474/5 by the wardens of St Nicholas Church, Hedon near Hull, when they bought a missal for 10s. on the mayor's orders.[11] I have been through the Bibliographical Society's *Dictionaries of Printers and Booksellers*, E A Clough's *A Short-title Catalogue Arranged Geographically...*[12] and other sources for the earliest mentions of book-trade members in particular places with the following result:

before 1557	13
1568–1639	15
1640–1649	9
1650–1659	21
1660–1669	13
1670–1679	21
1680–1689	25
1690–1699	18
TOTAL	135

The steady increase from the Civil-War decade is very noticeable and even more so from the Commonwealth onwards. If these are plotted geographically, the concentration in the area bounded by Mersey, Dee, Trent, Avon and Severn, and another in the south-west from Bristol to Plymouth is very obvious; there are very few places in East Anglia, Wales, the south-east and the northern counties, presumably reflecting the size and spread of the population.

What such geographical description does not reveal is the type of book-trade business involved. It has become increasingly evident that it is necessary to discover what type was carried on by particular individuals, if possible. The types are:

Bookselling, subdivided

(a) Bibles, prayer books, psalters

                (b) school-books, elementary and for grammar
                schools
                (c) scholarly books, Latin and English
                (d) chapbooks, ballads, almanacs
                (e) secondhand and antiquarian
                (f) maps, pictures

Bookbinding
Stationery
Publishing
Printing
Paper- and parchment-making.

In all periods, combinations are, of course, found. It has become a truism that the English provincial book trade was not economically viable on its own and was almost invariably associated with other occupations, which could be anything, though certain ones like patent-medicine selling are frequent. It has to be remembered that in market towns it was necessary for a tradesman with a shop to be a member of a trade company. Only in York and Chester were stationers and booksellers sufficiently numerous to have their own company; in smaller towns they had to join with others; in Hull, for example, stationers and binders combined in a general one with goldsmiths, smiths, pewterers, plumbers, glaziers, painters, cutlers, musicians and basket-makers.[13] In a smaller town, such as Stratford-upon-Avon in 1692, a bookseller, binder and playing-card seller joined the mercers, drapers and haberdashers company.[14] The association of trades, forced by economics, is very varied and references to people following several are found as early as the thirteenth century.[15] How strictly enforcement was possible is difficult to determine; in 1636, for instance, Archbishop Laud was petitioned that certain ironmongers in Exeter 'sell divers sorts of books, being divers times admonished by five lawfull booksellers.'[16] A little-known section in the Act for Preventing Abuses in Printing of 1662 allowed a diocesan bishop to license a person as a bookseller, printer and binder who had not served an apprenticeship, but only one example, in Worcester in 1669, is recorded.[17]

Membership of a trade company was not necessary for market traders and itinerant pedlars. Books were sold in markets from the earliest times; in 1531, for example, the Bishop of Lincoln appointed commissioners to search the stalls at St Frideswides's Fair in Oxford for heretical literature.[18] London printers and stationers, however, stopped going to country fairs as it was found to be more effective and cheaper to sell wholesale to provincial retailers who handled other commodities besides books, and could buy in sheets to be bound locally.[19] At the end of the seventeenth century, Michael Johnson of Lichfield, father of the lexicographer, attended Birmingham, Uttoxeter and Ashby-de-la- Zouche regularly.[20] Itinerant chapmen, ballad and almanac sellers have received much scholarly attention in recent years, notably in Mrs Margaret Spufford's magisterial *Small Books and Pleasant Histories,*[21] and it has always to be borne in mind that the printed word reached and influenced more individuals in those forms than conventional books. But market traders and pedlars like Autolycus in Shakespeare's *Winter's Tale,* were continually thorns in the side of the London Stationers' Company, since with few overheads like rents they had advantages affecting both the London and the country trade. A petition to the Company in 1684 includes that the trade of bookselling had been much impaired by the great number of hawkers and others exposing to sale great quantities of books, both bound and stitched,[22]

> by which meanes greate stocks of Bookes lye dead on the Booksellers hands...The Market Higlers and Pedlers in the Country exposing greate numbers of such Bookes as are before mentioned Destroy greate part of the Trade which otherwise Booksellers would have in this Citty and Country.

Not all itinerant booksellers sold only light literature; Michael Sparke, a prominent London stationer in Commonwealth times, spent the first year of his Apprenticeship, 1603, not in London but in Staffordshire 'binding, vending, and putting to sale Popish books, pictures, beads and such trash.'[23] About 1630, in rural Shropshire, Richard Baxter has recorded how 'a poor pedlar came to the door that had ballads and some good books: and my father bought of him *Dr Sibbs' Bruised Reed'.*[24]

A branch of the book trade which is not so widespread now as in earlier centuries is bookbinding. Frequently booksellers supplied this service as Sparke's master, Simon Pauley, did; inventories of booksellers in wills and legal documents often reveal the presence of tools, although binding was never specified in their trade description. Thus in 1677 the inventory of Richard Mountford, a Warwick bookseller in a small way of business included 'working tooles', wax, pasteboard and parchment,[25] and a successor, George Teonge, also bound.[26] The possibility cannot be excluded, though, that booksellers kept tools to be used by binders who travelled round the country at intervals, as they did in Germany, for example.[27] Some binders in market towns must have achieved a fair degree of prosperity through this one activity; Edward Rogers, for instance, who flourished in Stratford-upon-Avon *c* 1646–88, issued in this last year a trade token inscribed 'Edward Rogers, bookbonder: his halfe penny 1668'.[28]

It is dangerous to make generalisations about what stocks could be found in English provincial bookshops in the sixteenth and seventeenth centuries; they varied as much as they do today judging from surviving inventories. In 1568–70 Robert Scott of Norwich was sued for repayment of a debt of £12 for books supplied from London and an inventory showed he had for sale service, devotional, classical and educational books and theology as well as ballads, almanacs and binding equipment; stocks were replenished twice a month.[29] Roger Ward of Shrewsbury in 1585 had a large stock of some 2500 volumes, including books printed abroad, religion, classical texts, textbooks for both grammar and elementary schools, Bibles, prayer books, catechisms and psalters, but he was unusual as this shop was a branch of his London business and Shrewsbury was the centre for supplying most of Wales.[30] An inventory of John Browne of Manchester, who died in 1612, shows he had two shops with books valued at £60.18s.9d. and that he sold stationery and had binding equipment as well.[31] In 1644 John Awdley had a considerably smaller stock in Hull valued at £17.16s.10d.; he carried 187 titles, mostly London-printed theology, classics, school textbooks but also '3 dozen of mapps and certane old books at the end of the shopp', as well as tools valued at 13s.4d., suggesting binding could be done.[32] Richard Mountford of Warwick in 1677 had a very limited range of books, mostly Bibles, school textbooks and devotional works and 'old bookes' totalling £5.15s.11d.[33] A much larger and wider range of books was available a few miles away at Coventry; John Brooke, whose will was proved in 1679, had books valued at £147.3s.10d. and stationery at £27.3s.5d., but was owed £136.4s.8d. 'booke debts' plus £55.11s.2d. 'book debts desperate' and £121 'debts specially desperate', possibly by chapmen.[34] This large stock is comparable to that of Robert Benson, a Quaker greengrocer, bookseller and stationer of Penrith, valued at £74.17s.3$\frac{1}{2}$d. in 1698, the inventory of which was published last year by Professor Peter Isaac.[35] It is hardly surprising that centres like Coventry, Manchester, Norwich, Hull and Penrith had the bigger bookshops and that buyers travelled to them as for other goods. Examining these inventories, the amount of entries common to several, if not all, is very noticeable, and it is to be hoped that someone will put them all on a computer, as Dr E S Leedham-Green has already done for books mentioned in Cambridge wills of Tudor and Stuart periods.[36]

Customers aimed at would appear to be ordinary people seeking a Bible or prayer book to give as a present on a special occasion like marriage or confirmation; schoolchildren in elementary and grammar schools; a few devotional books and sermons for the local clergy, lawyers and occasional physician. Specialist books were supplied to buyers direct from London, Oxford and Cambridge; thus John Langley, a young schoolmaster in Gloucester about 1622/23, wrote to the Oxford bookseller Thomas Huggins ordering a lexicon and 'Tilenus his Syntagma' to be sent by carrier.[37] In 1637 Francis Harvey, a Bristol bookseller, sent books to and from Oxford by carrier, as well as enquiring about the possibility of getting a theological work by a Cardiff clergyman printed in Oxford.[38] A network of communication for the book trade was available, in existence before 1669 when Lord Arlington wrote to Sir Roger L'Estrange that Robert Cleaver had established 'a correspondence with all booksellers in England, Scotland and Ireland' through the *Term Catalogues*, the most important link between the capital and the provinces.[39] Indeed there is evidence that a little later this organised communication system was sufficiently advanced to get controversial literature distributed in the provinces before being sold in London. In 1682 Sir Roger L'Estrange had said:

> Of my experience of the Stationers' ways and confederacies for dispersing libels, I am more and more confirmed that the certain way of tracing and detecting them must begin from the country, for their course is this: the first thing they do on the printing of any remarkable pamphlet is to furnish the kingdom up and down with an impression or two, before they offer at the dispersing of any here [ie London].

His view is confirmed by the practice of the Friends (Quakers) who in 1673 ordered their printer to send their publications out to the counties before London.[40] This communication between book traders was strong enough to sabotage the efforts of John Fell and his academic friends to administer the University Press themselves; Arthur Charlett, of University College, wrote after Fell's death 'The vending of books we never could compasse; the want of vent broke Bp. Fell's body, public spirit, courage, purse and presse'.[41]

Before the restriction of printing to London as a consequence of the granting of a new charter to the Stationers' Company in 1557, there was hardly any actual printing in the English provinces and it is known in only eleven places.[42] Subsequently, before 1692 printing occurred only in a few places such as York and Chester, mainly for economic reasons[43] and these are receiving the detailed attention of William K Sessions in his series of 'greenbacks', nine volumes of which have so far appeared. Clandestine printing and the university presses are outside my terms of reference. Country booksellers would occasionally share with one in London in publishing a local author; the writings of the Puritan William Whately of Banbury, for instance, usually bore the names of George Edwards of London and Edward Langham of Banbury in the 1620s and 1630s; Edwards, incidentally, came from a village near Banbury, and is an example of the ties between town and country.

Papermaking was mentioned as a branch of the book trade at the beginning of this paper, but I am not qualified to say much about it; the work of A H Shorter seems exhaustive and the History of the Book Trade in the North group is to be warmly commended on the attention it has paid to it in their publications. The relationship between local paper-mills and local stationers and booksellers needs investigation.

To conclude, I will offer a few suggestions to anyone who is proposing to investigate the pre-1692 book trade in a specific place in the English provinces. The first is to bear in mind the importance of London connections, including apprentices from the area; next, to search local archives thoroughly for wills, freemens' registers and trade company records for the persons whose names have been gathered from the Bibliographical Society's *Dictionaries*, local collections in libraries, imprint indexes and so forth. Above all, the book trade in a place must not be treated in isolation, but considered in relation to its neighbour - hood and compared with similarly sized towns or districts whose book-trade histories have been published; if unpublished inventories of individual traders are discovered, they must be put alongside published lists of the same time. Looking at and reading the books in a good local collection often turns up unexpected details.

In 1900, H R Plomer, to whom all interested in our subject are so greatly indebted, wrote 'The history of provincial printing has never yet been written, and the task of tracing out the various printers and their work would be long and arduous'.[44] Before the hundredth anniversary of this remark is reached, perhaps some brave person should attempt to do so, but dealing with all sections of the English provincial book trade.

NOTES

1. See, for example, D Knott, 'Aspects of research into English provincial printing', *Journal of the Printing Historical Society*, vol 9 (1973/4), pp 6–21; P Morgan, 'Changes in studies of English provincial booktrade history since 1958', *History of the Book Trade in the North*, PH 39 (1983), 1–4; J Feather, *The Provincial Book Trade in Eighteenth-century England* (Cambridge, 1985), pp 1–2; P Isaac, 'The provincial book trade from the end of the Licensing Act to 1800', *History of the Book Trade in the North*, PH 46 (1987).

2. The same.

3. 'The English market for printed books (Sandars Lectures, 1959)', *Publishing History*, vol 4 (1978), pp 13–21, 37.

4. E G Duff, 'The printers, stationers and bookbinders of York up to 1600', *Trans. Bibliographical Society*, vol 5 (1899), p 98.

5. E G Duff, *A Century of the English Book Trade* (London, 1905), p 165.

6. H R Plomer, 'An Exeter bookseller', *The Library*, 3 ser, vol 8 (1917), pp 128–30.

7. *Stationers' Company Apprentices, 1605-1640* (Bibliographical Society of the University of Virginia, 1961). And his *Stationers' Company Apprentices, 1641–1700* (Oxford Bibliographical Society Publications, n s xvii, 1974).

8. *Warwickshire Apprentices in the Stationers' Company of London, 1563–1700* (Dugdale Society Occasional Papers, no 25, 1978).

9. STC^2 23740.

10. M Plant, *The English Book Trade; an Economic History*. 2nd edn (London, 1965), pp 80-1.

11. *Et in solucione facta pro j. missal apud Hull...solvente per preceptum maioris, x.s*, quoted in J R Boyle, *The Early History of the Town and Port of Hedon in the East Riding...* (Hull, 1895), pp 155 and clxxxvi. Not noticed by C W Chilton, *Early Hull Printers and Booksellers* (Hull, 1982).

12. London, 1969.

13. J Moran, 'Stationers Companies in the British Isles', *History of the Book Trade in the North*, PH 24, (1975), p 4.

14. P Morgan, 'Early booksellers, printers and publishers in Stratford-upon-Avon', *Trans. Birmingham Archaeological Society*, vol 67 (1951), pp 18-19.

15. H Swanson, *Medieval Artisans* (Oxford, 1988), p 104, etc.

16. H R Plomer, 'More Petitions to Archbishop Laud', *The Library*, 3 ser, vol 10 (1919), pp 135-6.

17. P Morgan, 'A bookseller's subscription in 1669', *The Library*, 5 ser, vol 7 (1952), pp 281-2.

18. H Carter, *A History of the Oxford University Press*, vol 1 (Oxford, 1975), p 17.

19. G Pollard, 'The English market', p 14.

20. H R Plomer and others, *A Dictionary of the Printers and Booksellers who were at Work in England, Scotland and Ireland from 1688 to 1725* (London, 1922), p 173.

21. London, 1981, especially Chapter 5.

22. D F McKenzie, *The London Book Trade in the Later Seventeenth Century* (Sandars Lectures, 1976) (Cambridge, 1976), p 26; C Blagden, *The Stationers' Company; a History 1403-1959* (London, 1960), p 170, describes a further petition in 1687.

23. [M Sparke], *A Second Beacon Fired by Scintilla* (London, 1652), pp 5-6.

24. R Baxter, *Reliquiae Baxterianae* (London, 1696), pp 3-4.

25. P Morgan, 'The Warwick bookseller, Richard Mountford', in N Alcock [ed], *The Past in Warwick; Tudors to Victorians* (Coventry, 1955), p 33.

26. P Morgan and G D Painter, 'The Caxton *Legend* at St Mary's, Warwick', *The Library*, 5 ser, vol 12 (1957), p 238.

27. L Gruel, *La Rose d'Or; une Auberge d'Ouvriers Relieurs au 18e siècle: Calw, 1714-1780* (Paris, 1894).

28. P Morgan, 'Early Booksellers...in Stratford-upon-Avon', p 38; W J Davies, *The Token Coinage of Warwickshire* (Birmingham, 1895), no 1173.

29. H R Plomer, 'Some Elizabethan book sales', *The Library*, 3 ser, vol 7 (1916), pp 318-20.

30. A Rodger, 'Roger Ward's Shrewsbury stock; an inventory of 1585', *The Library*, 5 ser, vol 13 (1958), pp 247-68.

31. J P Earwaker, 'Notes on the early booksellers and stationers of Manchester', *Trans. Lancashire and Cheshire Antiquarian Society*, vol 6 (1889), pp 2-4.

32. C W Chilton, 'The inventory of a provincial bookseller's stock of 1644', *The Library*, 6 ser, vol 1 (1979), pp 126–43.

33. P Morgan, 'The Warwick bookseller', p 33.

34. Public Record Office, Prob 4/17902; I am grateful to Mr Giles Mandelbrote for this reference.

35. P Isaac, 'An inventory of books sold by a seventeenth-century Penrith grocer', *History of the Book Trade in the North*, PH 53 (1989).

36. E S Leedham-Green, *Books in Cambridge Inventories. Book-lists from Vice-Chancellor's Court Probate Inventories in the Tudor and Stuart Periods.* 2 vols (Cambridge, 1986).

37. P Morgan, 'The Oxford book trade; letters, c 1611–1647', in *Studies in the Book Trade in Honour of Graham Pollard* (Oxford Bibliographical Society new series 18, 1975), pp 77–8; G Pollard, 'The English Market', p 17.

38. P Morgan, 'The Oxford book trade', pp 81–3.

39. C Blagden, 'The Genesis of the *Term Catalogues*', *The Library*, 5 ser, vol 8 (1953), p 30.

40. D F McKenzie, *The London Book Trade*, p 28.

41. H Carter, *A History of the Oxford University Press*, p 61, quoting Historical Manuscripts Commission, *Second Report*, p 245[b].

42. E G Duff, *The English Provincial Printers, Stationers and Bookbinders to 1557*. (Sandars Lectures, 1911) (Cambridge, 1912).

43. G Pollard, 'The English Market', p 21.

44. London, 1900, p 246; omitted in the second edition of 1915 presumably because E G Duff's *English Provincial Printers* (note 41 above) had been published in the interim.

Cambridge Bindings in Cosin's Library, Durham

DAVID PEARSON

Cosin's Library is the endowed public library founded by John Cosin for the benefit of the diocese of Durham; it was officially opened in 1669. It is housed in the purpose-built library building on Palace Green which was erected at Cosin's expense in 1668, and today it contains about 6000 books. The great majority of these, a little under five and a half thousand titles, are books which Cosin himself assembled before his death in 1672; the collection has changed relatively little since then, either by augmentation or loss. These five and a half thousand books do not represent the sum total of volumes which passed through Cosin's owner-ship, as he gave about a thousand books to Peterhouse in Cambridge after the Restoration, and the available evidence suggests that many of these were books from his own shelves, not books specially bought for the purpose of giving. He also gave books to Durham Cathedral Library, and to individual friends and colleagues. He was both a user and a lover of books, who began acquiring them at an early age and who continued the habit throughout his life; he was indeed one of the major book collectors of the seventeenth century.

His personal fortunes mean that his collecting career can be divided into three discrete segments. We can assume that he began acquiring books in about 1610, when he began his undergraduate studies, and his library then grew steadily until, by the early 1640s, he had around a thousand volumes. As a rising star of the Laudian wing of the Church, he was identified as an enemy of the puritan and parliamentary forces, and he was forced to flee to France in 1643. He had to leave his books behind, and in 1643 or 1644 they were moved to the library of Peterhouse, where they remained until the Restoration. Meanwhile, Cosin in exile began to amass a new collection of books, and, despite the hardships of a frugal existence in Paris as Anglican chaplain to the court of Queen Henrietta Maria, by the time he returned to England in 1660 he was able to include many hundreds of books in his luggage. This 'French' portion of his library has received some separate consideration in print, as it includes many items of sixteenth and seventeenth century French printing which are now very rare, and many of these books have handsome contemporary Parisian bindings which would repay systematic study.[1] The third phase of Cosin's collecting career comprises the last twelve years of his life, when the sufferings of the faithful and uncompromising royal servant were rewarded with elevation to the episcopate, and to an income which allowed him to fulfill his schemes for bibliographical munificence on a grand scale. His library was augmented throughout the 1660s, partly by encouraging donations from others and partly by using receipts from the renewal of Durham Bishopric leases; his correspondence for this period includes numerous instructions to his agents for the acquisition of books, and their subsequent organisation.[2]

This paper concentrates on the thousand or so books which Cosin acquired in the first phase of his career, before he went abroad in 1643. The exact size of his collection at this time is a little vague, as Cosin himself said that he had 1100 books in Peterhouse, but the manuscript list drawn up there shortly after the collection was sequestrated lists only 814 titles.[3] This part of Cosin's collection includes several groups of books, these groups being of varying sizes, which can be identified as having been bound in Cambridge. Some were bound for Cosin, others were acquired secondhand; the different groups have no direct connection between them, but looked at together they offer a series of snapshots of the changing styles of binding in Cambridge between 1520 and 1640. Most of these styles or tools have been recognised as Cambridge work before, but these particular books have on the whole escaped the attention of binding historians, and they have not hitherto been noted in the standard published works on Cambridge binding.

The presence of Cambridge bindings in Cosin's collection is not surprising, as he had many connections with the University there. He went up to Gonville and Caius College from his native Norwich in 1610, and was resident in Cambridge (at least during term) for the next six years, while he proceeded from BA to MA.[4] In 1616 he became secretary and librarian to John Overall, then Bishop of Lichfield and Coventry and subsequently Bishop of Norwich, but after Overall's death in 1619 he returned to Caius where he held a fellowship from 1620 until 1624. He was rhetoric praelector in 1620-1, and university preacher in 1622. It was during this time that he became chaplain to Richard Neile, Bishop of Durham, through whom he obtained preferments which took him away from Cambridge; in 1624 he became a prebendary of Durham Cathedral, in 1625 Archdeacon of the West Riding of Yorkshire, in 1626 Rector of Brancepeth. His links with Cambridge became visible again in 1635, when he was made Master of Peterhouse, and for the next five years or so he was an active figure in college and University life, beautifying Peterhouse chapel, enforcing new codes of discipline for the unfortunate students, and reviving plans for the erection of a new University Library.[5] He was Vice- Chancellor of the University in 1639-40.

It is unfortunate that we have very little direct evidence to show where Cosin acquired his books. Given the career just outlined, it stands to reason that he will have bought books in Cambridge, some of them already bound and some bound there for him, and we can prove this by looking round the shelves and finding books which are demonstrably in Cambridge bindings. What we do not have are any manuscript notebooks or accounts of Cosin's, referring to his book buying, or even an exact schedule of his movements between 1620 and 1640. It can be shown from the Act Books of the Durham Dean and Chapter, and from Brancepeth parish registers, that Cosin spent much of his time in the Northeast between 1625 and 1635, during which time he attended 165 Chapter meetings and performed 64 baptisms at Brancepeth.[6] After 1635 his attendence at Chapter meetings was much more fitful, and it seems reasonable to assume that his main residence then became the Master's Lodge at Peterhouse. His only documented visit to Cambridge in the decade following his move to the north took place in 1630, when he went up to receive his doctorate in divinity, but this cannot have been an extended trip as he graduated on 29 September, and attended Chapter meetings two weeks before and six weeks after that date.

Although he had no preferments in Cambridge between 1624 and 1635, it seems to me unlikely that he would have had no contact with the place during that time. An active collector of scholarly books would naturally gravitate towards the university towns, where demand for such material was met by a sizeable bookselling community, and by the concentration of other private libraries whose contents circulated on the secondhand market. The centre of the English book trade was of course London, and Cosin certainly spent time there; as Neile's chaplain, he was regularly at the Bishop's London residence, and most of the surviving letters to him throughout the 1620s are addressed to him at Durham House in the Strand.[7] I suspect therefore that the bulk of Cosin's book-buying between 1620 and 1640 was divided between Cambridge and London, but the proportions cannot be ascertained. Just occasionally he noted the cost of his books on the flyleaves, including the separate cost of binding, but never the place of purchase or the name of the supplier. Two extant manuscripts show that he had dealings with the London bookseller Richard Whitaker in the mid-1630s, and it may be that Whitaker was the source of some of Cosin's material.[8]

Bookbinding has been going on in Cambridge since the University took root there in the thirteenth century, although documentary evidence is very scanty for the medieval period. The earliest surviving bindings which can today be identified as Cambridge work date from about 1480, and people like Basil Oldham and Graham Pollard have demonstrated that several discrete workshops were operating there during the last twenty years of the fifteenth century. Cosin's Library does not contain any examples of this very early Cambridge work, but it does contain some Cambridge binding of the succeeding generation, in the shape of two bindings from the workshop of Nicholas Spierinck. Spierinck was, like so many other members of the early English book trade, a native of the low countries, who migrated to Cambridge in about 1505 and who remained there until his death in 1545.[9] His bindings are well known, as about 300 still survive; only half that number survive from the workshop of his commercial rival and fellow university stationer Garret Godfrey.

The two Spierinck bindings in Cosin's Library are close in date and the same tools are used on each. One is a quarto containing two separate works printed at Hagenau in 1519, letters of Johann Reuchlin and a work by St Athanasius, and the other is a folio edition of classical texts edited by Erasmus, printed at Basle in 1518.[10] Both were acquired by Cosin before 1643, as they both carry Peterhouse shelfmarks of the Interregnum period. Each binding is decorated in the same style, characteristic of early Cambridge work, in which a roll is used to create a rectangular frame some way in from the edges of the boards, whose central space is filled with further roll tooling applied vertically. The 1518 Erasmus (Plate 1) has wooden boards covered with mid- brown calf, and the decoration is provided using a roll featuring fabulous beasts, also incorporating Spierinck's initials 'N S' which can be clearly seen, and a diaper roll with stylised flower-heads in a diagonal frame. There were originally two clasps across the foredge, of which only the studs and catches now remain. The book has been rebacked but the original leather has been laid down on the new; there are blind fillets around the raised bands created by the four double thongs on which the book is sewn, but the spine is otherwise undecorated. The original arrangement of the endleaves has unfortunately been lost during repair, but the book originally had plain paper flyleaves, and pastedowns taken from a manuscript of a text of Aquinas written *c* 1400. As usual with a book of this period, the edges of the leaves are not coloured. The other Spierinck binding, on the 1519 Hagenau texts, is very similar in style and employs the same rolls; here, pasteboards were used instead of wooden ones, and the book had ties rather than clasps. The second item in the volume has the sixteenth-century inscription of Thomas Ruddock, who could possibly be the man of this name who graduated BA at Cambridge in 1539 and who became Vicar of Swaffham Bulbeck in 1546.[11]

The decoration of English bindings in the first half of the sixteenth century was dominated by the use of rolls and small stamps, although large rectangular panel-stamps were also used. The use of rolls continued to the end of the century and beyond, but in the second half new styles developed. The idea of decorating boards with a large central stamp of symmetrical abstract design appears to have originated in medieval Islamic culture, whence it travelled to Europe in the middle of the sixteenth century.[12] This centrepiece style is first found in London

2. J Calvin, *In Omnes Pauli Apostoli Epistolas...Commentarii*, f° (Geneva, 1557). Cambridge binding, probably from workshop of John Sheares, *c* 1575 (Cosin B.I.20)

1. *Ex Recognitione Des Erasmi C Suetonius Tranquillus [et al]*, f° (Basle, 1518). Binding from workshop of Nicholas Spierinck, *c* 1520 (DUL S.R.8.C.28)

around 1560, and in Oxford and Cambridge shortly thereafter; it then became established as the dominant pattern for the decoration of leather-covered bindings for several decades. In its simplest form, the style is characterised by books whose boards are decorated only with blind fillets round the outer perimeter, and a large central tool of intricate symmetrical design, sometimes oval, sometimes lozenge-shaped, sometimes a cross between the two. More elaborate bindings have additional concentric frames of fillets decorated with small corner tools, and further still up the scale of sophistication we have those decorated with large cornerpiece ornaments whose design resembles that of the centrepieces.

The centrepiece style was extensively used in Cambridge from perhaps 1565 onwards, although I cannot at present identify many tools as Cambridge ones with any degree of confidence. Going through the published sources on the Cambridge book trade it is possible to name at least 35 individuals who were active between 1560 and 1620, some of whom were certainly binders, others of whom may have been. It is very difficult to tie up particular books with particular binders, for a variety of reasons; the bindings are never signed, and books with contemporary manuscript evidence pointing to the source of acquisition are disappointingly rare. Late sixteenth-century tools are never signed with the binder's initials, in the way that Spierinck had 'N S' cut on one of his rolls. Such college archives as I have so far had the chance to examine have yielded very little help, as few colleges were buying books or having them bound before 1600.

It is nevertheless possible to identify some Cambridge centrepieces, and some of these can be found in Cosin's Library. I have described elsewhere two large oval stamps, of similar design, which were in use in Cambridge in the 1570s and early 1580s.[13] The first of these tools is found on two Cosin books, B.I.17 and B.I.20, and the second on one, K.I.25. B.I.17, a copy of Calvin's *Harmonia ex Evangelistis Tribus Composita*, printed in folio in Geneva in 1572, bound with his commentary on the Acts of the Apostles printed the following year, is a typical example of the genre. The binding is constructed of dark brown calf over pulpboards, sewn on five raised bands. The boards are decorated with the gilt-stamped centrepiece, and otherwise only with a three-line blind fillet round the borders; the spine is decorated with a small flower-head tool applied in gilt in each compartment. The edges of the leaves are uncoloured and the edges of the boards have a blind fillet run round. The endleaves include fragments from a contemporary printed Greek and Latin Bible; the use of sheets or leaves from printed books in the endleaves is very common in these bindings, and K.I.25 uses a fragment from a 1565 Geneva edition of Calvin's commentary on Ezekiel as its front flyleaf. B.I.20 (Plate 2), a copy of Calvin's commentary on the Pauline epistles, folio, Geneva, 1557, is very similar to B.I.17, except that the boards have an additional frame of blind fillets, decorated with small fleurons at the corners.

Another group of centrepiece bindings, where the Cambridge connection seems more obvious, is constituted by two Cosin books which bear large centre-pieces incorporating the arms of Cambridge University. These are A.III.23, Jean Mercier's commentary *In Librum Iob*, folio, Geneva, 1573, and B.I.9, containing two folio Biblical commentaries by Benedict Aretius, printed at Morges and Lausanne in 1580 (see Plate 3). The characteristics of these bindings are very similar to those of the preceding group, with which they are roughly contempor-ary, but instead of the gilt oval centrepieces we have large blind-stamped tools comprising a central oval, containing the University arms, surrounded by a decorative frame. The central section was detachable from the frame, as it is found on other bindings used on its own. Both these bindings have suffered at the hands of the repairer and the original spines have been lost; the endleaves of B.I.9 included fragments from a late sixteenth century Biblical commentary by Calvin, and the hinges were strengthened with fragments from a fifteenth century English manuscript of Gregory the Great's *Dialogues*. Neither book has any clue as to its first owner.

The Cambridge pedigree of these bindings seems obvious, but they do in fact present some problems which have not yet been resolved. Both the Cosin books have the same central oval within the same central frame, but other versions exist; there are three similar oval tools with the Cambridge arms, and three similar but distinct frames, which were all in use in the 1580s and possibly in the 1570s as well. They were first systematically described by John Morris in 1968, who attributed all the tools to the workshop of Thomas Thomas, the University printer who died in 1588.[14] His conclusions were subsequently challenged by Howard Nixon, who doubted the likelihood that one workshop could contain three such similar sets of tools, and he suggested the possibility that some of them may have been in use outside Cambridge.[15] Nixon's argument was based partly on his observation that 'the only Cambridge binder who certainly produced gilt bindings' in the Elizabethan period was John Denys, who died in 1578, but we can now refute this as Cosin K.I.25, mentioned earlier, was printed in 1579 and has a gilt centrepiece. At the time of writing, I know of 41 of these University armorial bindings, which divide more or less equally into the three groups; each group contains books with strong Cambridge connections, and I am inclined to doubt the idea that they are not all Cambridge bindings. The design of the central oval on the Cosin centrepiece is identical with that of the printer's device used on the titlepages of two books printed by Thomas Thomas in 1584 – it has been suggested that the same tool may have been used for both purposes – and both

4. R Bellarmine, *Disputationes*, f° (Paris, 1613). Cambridge binding. *c* 1615 (Cosin H.I.1)

3. B Aretius, *Commentarii in Quatuor Evangelistas*, f° (Morges, 1580) [+ 1 other, 1580]. Binding from the workshop of Thomas Thomas, *c* 1585 (Cosin B.I.9)

John Morris and Howard Nixon were in agreement that this was a tool from Thomas's bindery.

The centrepiece bindings mentioned so far have all dated from the late sixteenth century. A set of Cambridge centrepiece bindings from the second decade of the seventeenth century is found on Cosin H.I.1-4, a copy of Robert Bellarmine's *Disputationes* printed in Paris in 1613 (Plate 4). The decorative style is very little different from that seen 30 or 40 years earlier; the boards are covered with dark brown calf, and decorated with a large blind-stamped centrepiece, with a border of a narrow blind roll run twice round the perimeter. All four volumes have been rebacked, and the original spines and endleaves have been lost, but each volume was sewn on five raised bands. It is possible to identify this as a Cambridge centrepiece for several reasons. Most significantly, it is found on the manuscript account of the University of Cambridge presented to the Master of Emmanuel College in 1617 by the arms painter John Scott. Scott's manuscripts are well known to students of early seventeenth century Cambridge; he apparently gave copies of his account, decorated with hand-painted University coats of arms, to each of the colleges, and at least nine survive today, all in Cambridge bindings, although the Emmanuel one is the only one to carry this centrepiece. [16] It is also found used as late as 1630 on a quarto prayer book and Bible, printed in Cambridge by Thomas and John Buck, which has a contemporary presentation inscription from John Buck to Edward Quarles, who was then a fellow of Pembroke.[17] The centrepiece is found on three bindings in Peterhouse, covering books printed between 1605 and 1616, which may possibly be associated with Cosin; it is also found on a set of de Thou's *Historiarum sui Temporis,* 1609, now in the Cathedral Library in Durham, which carries a Peterhouse pressmark and which must therefore have come via Cosin.[18] The design of the centrepiece is quite a common one, and there were at least a dozen variants on this basic pattern in use in England between about 1580 and 1620.

We can see, therefore, that the centrepiece style of bookbinding was still employed in Cambridge in the second decade of the seventeenth century, but its heyday was by then over, and other styles of decoration had become fashionable. At the bottom end of the market, a tendency which becomes noticeable around the turn of the new century is one towards greater simplicity, using only fillets to decorate the boards. It is unusual to find a leather-covered book bound much before 1600 which has no decorative tooling other than fillets, but from about 1600 onwards it is very common. Bindings like this, undecorated save for three blind fillets round the perimeter of the boards, were certainly produced in Cambridge in the early seventeenth century, but for obvious reasons they are not easy to identify.[19]

There was however a great deal of more decorative binding produced in Cambridge in the seventeenth century, and some of it has already received detailed study. Several articles on the subject have been published in the last fifty years or so, each one contradicting to some extent the conclusions of its predecessor; the most recent and most authoritative account is that by Mirjam Foot in the first volume of *The Henry Davis Gift*.[20] She has identified seven discrete groups of bindings produced in Cambridge between about 1610 and 1680, each group associated with a particular set of tools, although some of the groups overlap in date and have tools in common.

Cosin's Library includes a collection of seventeen very similar bindings all produced in Cambridge in about 1620; to these we might add two bindings now in Durham Cathedral Library, which were originally owned by Cosin and donated by him in the late 1630s.[21] An example of this group is T.IV.4, a copy of J C Scaliger's *Exotericarum Exercitationum Liber Quintus Decimus*, quarto, Paris, 1557. It is bound in dark brown calf over pasteboards, and the boards are decorated in blind using a series of small tools, fillets and a roll. The overall pattern is the same as that employed on the centrepiece bindings already dis-cussed, but here the central decoration comprises a collection of small tools symmetrically arranged, and not one large tool. There are two concentric frames, decorated at the corners with small tools; the inner frame is made up of two narrow fillets, and the outer frame comprises a narrow roll surrounded by two fillets on either side. The spine is smooth, as the book is sewn on four sewn-in bands; it is decorated in a way which echoes the ornamentation of the boards, with the same roll run in blind round the four sides, and small tools applied at the head, foot and centre. It also has the title in small gilt letters stamped directly on the spine. T.IV.4 has plain paper flyleaves and separate pastedowns, which are probably contemporary with the binding, although most of these bindings originally had no pastedowns. A very narrow blind roll is run round the edges of the boards, and the edges of the leaves have been coloured yellow. The headbands are blue and white.

This binding, and the others like it, belong to the second of Mirjam Foot's seven groups, and it can therefore be attributed to the workshop of Daniel Boyse, who was a stationer and bookbinder in Cambridge from about 1616 until at least 1630 (his date of death is not known). Dr Foot lists 67 known bindings belonging to this group (not including any of the Cosin ones); some of these are much more elaborate than Cosin's, such as the green velvet binding on the 1629 prayer book reproduced in the Henry Davis volume, but many are very similar to those here in Durham.[22]

Eight of these nineteen volumes comprise collections of between two and seven individual tracts, and in these cases the edges of the leaves have been deliberately coloured in different shades to help distinguish the separate pamphlets. A.V.8, for example, contains seven tracts printed between 1586 and 1614, and the edges are alternately red and yellow; F.IV.8 contains two tracts of 1618–19, and has edges alternately dark and light yellow; G.VI.3 contains four tracts, 1530–1619, and has edges alternately plain, red, yellow and plain. There can be no doubt that this colouring is contemporary with the date of binding, and it is worth commenting on as it is an unusual practice in seventeenth century England. What is less clear is whether it was applied by the binder, or by Cosin; multicoloured edges are not known on any other Boyse binding, so it must have been a special bespoke feature if, as I suspect, the colours were added before the books left the workshop. It should be added that there are several other books in Cosin's Library of roughly similar date, but in different bindings, which share this feature, so it does seem likely that the initiative came from the owner rather than the binder.[23]

From this group of nineteen bindings, one or two stand out as being slightly different (although the tools used may be the same). N.V.1, Richard Montagu's *Diatribae upon the First Part of the Late History of Tithes*, quarto, London, 1621, is bound in green calf and is gilt-tooled (Plate 5); D.V.20, a 1574 edition of the Latin translation of the Book of Common Prayer, is also gilt-tooled, although here the calf is the usual dark brown variety; Y.V.28, Martianus Capella's *Satyricon* printed in Leiden in 1599, is tooled to a simpler pattern without any central decoration on the boards. Most of the others are strikingly uniform as regards the materials used, the pattern of decoration, the colouring of the edges (usually yellow if not multicoloured), and the construction of the endleaves. It is tempting to wonder whether many of them were bound at more or less the same time. The latest dated item in six of the tract volumes is either 1618, 1619 or 1620. In 1619 Overall died, and Cosin returned to Cambridge to take up his fellowship at Caius in the following year; perhaps this would be a time to carry out some reorganisation amongst his books, and gather together in a more satisfactory form some of his loose unbound pamphlets? This is of course pure speculation, and should be treated as such. When trying to make deductions like this, it is particularly regrettable that Cosin himself left us so few clues to allow us to retrace the growth of his collection. One of the nineteen books has a note in Cosin's hand to say that it cost 5s.10d.; this is Y.III.34, one of the tract volumes, which contains four pamphlets dated 1614–20.

Most of the books described so far have been blind-tooled in dark brown calf, and it has to be admitted that many of them are visually rather unexciting, especially after they have suffered the wear and tear of four centuries. The next group of bindings is more striking, since they are all bound in black morocco, gilt-tooled to an elaborate design (see Plate 6). The boards are decorated with a series of concentric rectangular frames, made up with gilt fillets, with small gilt tools at the corners of each frame, and a central gilt decoration made up from several small tools. The spines are smooth, and decorated to match the boards, with gilt fillets and small tools; some have a design of concentric rectangles, others have a ladder-like pattern with horizontal fillets at close intervals. Each book also has its title tooled directly onto the spine in gilt lettering. The edges of the leaves are gilded, and in most cases they are additionally decorated by impressing tools into the top and bottom edges at the spine end, beside the headbands, which are always double. Both the edges of the boards and the turn-ins are decorated in gilt either with a roll, or with repeated applications of a small tool. Most of these books have pastedowns of marbled paper, with flyleaves of plain white paper. They are sewn on narrow white leather thongs, closely spaced together, a point which I will return to below.

There are seven books in Cosin's Library bound in this way, two of which are in two or three volumes, so there are ten volumes in all. To this list must be added a stray volume now in Ushaw College, which has the inscription of Cosin's eldest daughter Mary, and which presumably remained in her personal possession after her father fled abroad, leaving his books in Peterhouse; it has his distinctive cipher 'p m' on the titlepage.[24] Although each binding is different as regards the tools used to create the pattern, they form an interconnected group, with the same tools used in different places on several books. In all there are about thirty tools which are used in varying combinations to decorate the eleven books. Most of the books were printed abroad and their imprint dates range from 1516 to 1633.

This distinctive style of binding was described by G D Hobson in his book on *Bindings in Cambridge Libraries*, where he likened the books decorated in this way to Chinese boxes, an apt term.[25] He listed nine examples known to him, all on books of the 1630s or 1640s, and mostly with strong Cambridge connections. This led him to assert that 'there can be no doubt that these are Cambridge bindings'. I think that this statement is only partially true, and that Hobson's comments on these bindings are in need of some revision.

Firstly, his list can be augmented. He was unaware of the Cosin books, and of three other books which can be added to the list: a 1638 folio Cambridge Bible now in the National Library of Scotland; an authorial presentation copy of Samuel Ward's *Magnetis Reductorium*, 1637, now in the British Library; and a copy of the Cambridge congratulatory verses printed on the marriage of Charles II in 1662, now in St John's College, Oxford.[26] We can therefore more than double his

6. J Vicecomes, *Observationum Ecclesiastarum...Volumen Quartum*, 4° (Milan, 1626). Apparently bound at Little Gidding, *c* 1640 (Cosin D.IV.32)

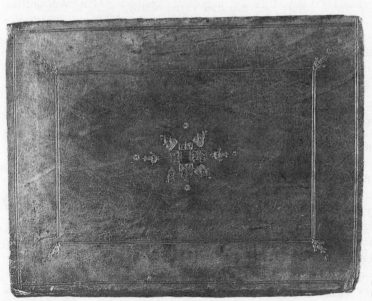

5. R Montagu, *Diatribae upon the First Part of the History of Tithes*, 4° (London, 1621). Binding from the workshop of Daniel Boyse, *c* 1625 (Cosin N.V.1)

list of nine examples. Hobson described his group as though they were all the product of one workshop, and printed the suggestion of H M Davies that they might be the work of Philip Scarlet, a Cambridge binder of the period who is known to have bound books for St John's College in the 1620s and 1630s. As the St John's books look nothing like Chinese boxes, I see no evidence whatsoever to support this theory.[27]

A closer look at the Chinese-box bindings makes it evident that they can be broken down into several discrete groupings, which do not have tools in common. There is a 1634 folio prayer book in St Catharine's College whose binding is identical with that on another copy of the same prayer book in the Bodleian Library, and there are two copies of the 1638 Buck and Daniel Bible with identical bindings, one in Pembroke College, Cambridge, and one in the National Library of Scotland, but there is no overlap of tools between these two pairs.[28] A 1634 folio Bible in Peterhouse is decorated like the 1634 prayer books, including tools of the same pattern (a flaming heart and a central IHS panel), but they are different tools.[29] The binding from Hobson's list which is particularly relevant to the Cosin books is his no V, a Biblical harmony made by the community at Little Gidding, and now preserved in the British Library.

It has long been known that the religious community, founded at Little Gidding by Nicholas Ferrar in 1626, learned the craft of bookbinding from the daughter of a Cambridge binder, and that they exercised their skills in binding the so-called Biblical concordances or harmonies, which they produced by pasting up extracts from printed Bibles, interspersed with appropriate engravings. Some of these were produced on a grand scale for Charles I and members of his court. Having said this, I am inclined to add that the community at Little Gidding has suffered almost as much from the pens of bookbinding historians, as from those of the puritans. A lot of nonsense used to be talked about the embroidered bindings produced by the nuns of Little Gidding, although there is no evidence that the Collet sisters did produce such bindings, or indeed that they were nuns.[30] G D Hobson sought to counter the hagiographical tradition by dismissing the community's work as 'totally destitute of artistic merit', in his unnecessarily waspish account of surviving examples in *Bindings in Cambridge Libraries*, and Howard Nixon, describing one of the harmonies in *The Book Collector* in 1962, felt that there was 'not a great deal to add' to Hobson's account.[31]

I suspect that there is actually quite a lot which can be added to the story of binding at Little Gidding, and some of it is in Cosin's Library. I stated earlier that the Cosin Chinese-box bindings are decorated using a group of about thirty small tools or rolls. The Little Gidding Chinese box, on a Biblical harmony of King's–Chronicles made in 1637, is decorated using five different tools, all of which belong to the Cosin group, and it is uniform with the Cosin bindings in other respects. Other tools from the Cosin group are found on several other known Little-Gidding bindings, including the Acts–Revelation harmony in the British Library, and two copies of Juan Valdes' *Hundred and Ten Considerations*, translated by Nicholas Ferrar and printed at Oxford in 1638, one of which is in the British Library and one in the National Art Library.[32] A common feature of Little-Gidding bindings, which has been noted by several commentators, is a tendency to sew the books on an excessive number of narrowly-spaced bands.[33] As I mentioned earlier, this is a characteristic of all the Cosin Chinese-box bindings.[34] The conclusion seems unavoidable, therefore, if at first sight unlikely, that these books were bound at Little Gidding. It might be thought that we are dealing with a collection of tools which began life in a Cambridge workshop and which subsequently passed to Little Gidding, but I see no evidence to support such a theory.

The production of the harmonies for Charles I and his sons is well documented, but there is evidence which suggests that the family undertook binding work on a wider scale. In 1649 they apparently bound no less than 238 copies of the *Eikon Basilike* for distribution to the American colonies.[35] More pertinently, perhaps, it seems that John Ferrar made some efforts to advertise the community's willingness to undertake work on commission, following the death of Nicholas Ferrar in 1637; we know that he wrote to Isaac Basire along these lines, asking him to circulate the message round 'worthy noble personages', and Basire sent a Gidding-bound book to his wife in 1636.[36] Basire was of course well-known to Cosin, but the work of the community was also familiar to him directly. According to John Ferrar's biography of his brother, the first book presented to the King, in 1635, was sent to him via Cosin as royal chaplain, and it is possible that it was through Cosin that Charles I first heard of the community's concordances.[37] It seems, therefore, that Cosin was a friend, or at least an acquaintance, of the community from an early stage. Given his High-Church inclinations and his wide circle of contacts, it would indeed be surprising if he was not both aware of, and sympathetic to, the activities at Little Gidding.

It is therefore quite plausible that he should have had some books bound there. Some puzzles remain, such as the date of binding, and the choice of books involved. They have no obvious interconnecting theme but include a Sarum missal, a set of Tertullian's works, a collection of French church councils, and a recusant biography of Thomas More; at least three of them were not being bound for the first time, and the latest date of printing is 1633. The other Gidding bindings with which these tools are associated date from *c* 1637–40, and the known community bindings earlier than 1635 use different tools altogether, so a date towards the end of the decade seems most likely.[38] There is some overlap between volumes as regards the watermarks in the endleaves, but there are at least four different marks detectable across the series. One of the books, H.IV.10, has one of Cosin's rare notes on the flyleaf, 'in sheets 19s., binding 8s.', but this is the only clue he has left us. It is not possible, within the confines of this paper, to discuss the Little-Gidding bindery more fully, but I hope I may be able to do so elsewhere. It is possible that the Ferrar papers in Magdalene College, Cambridge, may shed some undiscovered light on the subject, but they are currently unavailable pending their publication on microfilm; they are due to be released towards the end of 1990.

I have described in some detail several types of Cambridge bindings which are to be found in Cosin's Library, but I must stress that this does not exhaust the subject, either as regards the range of styles of bookbinding which were produced in Cambridge in the sixteenth and seventeenth centuries, or as regards the illustrations of those styles to be found in this Library. I would mention in particular several groups of books which appear to have been bound in the 1620s and 1630s, which have very plain bindings in dark brown calf and are sparsely decorated with tiny blind tools. A Cambridge pedigree is highly probable, as very similar bindings occur in most of the Cambridge college libraries and some of the Cosin specimens have tangible evidence; for example, the 1638 set of the works of St Cyril, E.III.14–19, has boards lined with fragments from the 1638 folio Bible printed in Cambridge in the same year by Buck and Daniel, beneath the pastedowns and turn-ins. I do not have space to deal with these books here, and their detailed treatment must wait for another occasion.

I hope to have succeeded in conveying some idea of the valuable material which Cosin's Library holds for the bookbinding historian. I have dealt only with books from the first phase of Cosin's collecting career, as this is the period during which he was most closely associated with Cambridge, but there are many bindings and groups of bindings later than 1640 which are worthy of attention. The collections of single individuals, formed within their lifetime and subsequently kept intact, and not over-repaired, are often the most useful for pursuing this kind of research. I might add that Cosin's Library has recently been thoroughly recatalogued, with notes on the bindings added to the catalogue entries for every individual volume, irrespective of their plainness or finery. This paper is a direct result of that recataloguing exercise, and I hope that the information on the Library and its contents which the new catalogue will make available will stimulate further research on this major collection.

NOTES

1. See E Dubois, 'La bibliotheque de l'évêque Cosin à Durham et sa collection de livres francais...des XVIe et XVIIe siècles', *Bulletin de la Société de l'Histoire du Protestantisme Français*, vol 128 (1982), p 173–88.

2. G Ornsby [ed], *The Correspondence of John Cosin*, part II (Surtees Society vol 55, Durham, 1870); see for example p 259, 268ff.

3. T A Walker, *Peterhouse* (Cambridge, 1935), p 135. The manuscript list of the books is preserved in Peterhouse Library; it has been edited by K J C Hooper, *The Catalogue of Doctor Cosen's Books*, unpublished MA dissertation, University College London School of Library & Archive Studies, 1985.

4. The details of Cosin's university career are set out in J & J A Venn, *Alumni Cantabrigienses* (Cambridge, 1922–54), vol 1, p 400.

5. Walker, *Peterhouse*, pp 55–7; J C T Oates, *Cambridge University Library: a History* (Cambridge, 1986), pp 169–71.

6. The figures are based on the analysis made by J G Hoffman in his PhD thesis *John Cosin 1595–1672: Bishop of Durham and Champion of the Caroline Church*, University of Wisconsin-Madison, 1977, p 99.

7. G Ornsby [ed], *The Correspondence of John Cosin*, part I (Surtees Society vol 52, Durham, 1869), pp 9–105.

8. Durham University Library, Mickleton & Spearman MS 91 fo. 21 (transcribed in D Pearson [ed]), 'Book trade bills and vouchers from Durham Cathedral Library, 1634–1740', *History of the Book Trade in the North*, Working Paper PH45 (1986); Peterborough Cathedral Library MS 20, fo. 32 (deposited in Cambridge University Library).

9. Standard references to Spierinck are G J Gray, *The Earlier Cambridge Stationers and Bookbinders* (Oxford, 1904), pp 43–53; G J Gray & W M Palmer, *Abstracts from the Wills and Testamentary Documents of..Stationers of Cambridge* (London, 1915), p 31–2; J B Oldham, *English Blind-stamped Bindings* (Cambridge, 1952), pp 14–15; H M Nixon, *Five Centuries of English Bookbinding* (London, 1978), p 26.

10. Shelfmarks S.R.8.D.7 (previously Cosin X.3.4) and S.R.8.C.26 (previously Cosin T.1.14) respectively.

11. Venn, *Alumni*, vol 3, p 496.

12. Via Italy; see H M Nixon, *The Development of Certain Styles of Bookbinding* (London, 1963), p 1, and A Hobson, *Humanists and Bookbinders* (Cambridge, 1989), ch 3.

13. D Pearson, 'A Cambridge bookseller's accounts of 1572', *Transactions of the Cambridge Bibliographical Society*, vol 9 (1988), pp 230–47.

14. J Morris, 'Thomas Thomas, printer to the University of Cambridge 1583–8. Part II', *Transactions of the Cambridge Bibliographical Society*, vol 4 (1968), pp 339–62.

15. H M Nixon, 'Elizabethan gold-tooled bindings' in D E Rhodes [ed], *Essays in Honour of Victor Scholderer* (Mainz, 1970), pp 219–70, esp pp 221–3.

16. Emmanuel MS 3.3.1. The other Scott MSS are listed in M R James's various catalogues of the manuscripts in the college libraries; one (the Clare copy) is in Cambridge University Library, MS Gg.V.21.

17. Now Pembroke 1.4.28.

18. Peterhouse D.8.21, K.5.2, O.2.24; Durham Cathedral Library F.II.38-40.

19. An example of a binding in this style, outside Cosin's Library, whose Cambridge origin seems certain, is the Peterborough Cathedral Library copy of J B Bernard, *Seminarium Totius Philosophiae Aristotelicae*, 2°, Lyons, 1599, whose endleaves comprise fragments from sheets of a work printed in Cambridge by Cantrell Legge in 1620 (STC 14371). The inscription on the front stub, '1620 L G 16s.' may conceivably indicate that it was sold by the Cambridge stationer Leonard Greene.

20. 'Two bindings by Daniel Boyse, and some remarks on Cambridge bindings of the seventeenth century', in M M Foot, *The Henry Davis Gift*, vol 1 (London, 1978), pp 59-75; references to earlier work will be found there.

21. Listed in the Appendix.

22. eg Peterhouse F.5.17 (group II no.11), Emmanuel College 326.7.105 (group II no.26), Cambridge University Library Y.4.79 and N*.13.19 (group II nos. 30 and 37).

23. For example, N.V.17 (5 tracts, 1611-17); Y.IV.35 (4 tracts, 1581-99). These bindings are both plain brown calf of early seventeenth-century style (3 fillets round the perimeters of the boards), with gilt flower-head tools in the spine compartments.

24. Ushaw College XIX.G.9.4. See Appendix for a complete list of these bindings.

25. G D Hobson, *Bindings in Cambridge Libraries* (Cambridge, 1929), p 118, plate XLVI.

26. National Library of Scotland L.191.d; British Library C.64.a.20; the St. John's book is described and illustrated in *Fine Bindings in Oxford Libraries* (Oxford, 1968), no 161, where the shelfmark is not given. I am very grateful to Mr John Morris of the National Library of Scotland for sending me details of the first item.

27. The books bound by Scarlet for St John's are covered in mid-brown sprinkled calf, decorated only with two frames of blind fillets, joined by fillets at the corners; examples are St John's D.1.32, F.1.21, G.7.23.

28. St Catharine's E.2.35 (no I on Hobson's list) = Bodleian Library Auct.V.3.16 (Hobson's no III); Pembroke, Cambridge 1.1.18 (Hobson's no VI) = National Library of Scotland L.191.d.

29. Peterhouse K.I.17-19 (Hobson's no II).

30. As acknowledged by C Davenport, *English Embroidered Bookbindings* (London, 1899), pp 103-4.

31. Hobson, *Bindings*, pp 122-4, plate XLVIII; H. Nixon, 'English bookbindings XLII', *The Book Collector*, vol 11 (1962), p 330, reprinted in *Five Centuries*, no 31.

32. The harmony is BL C.23.e.3. One of the copies of Valdes has a contemporary inscription recording that it was bound by Mary Ferrar; it is described by Edward Almack, who once owned it, in *Fine Old Bindings...in Edward Almack's Library* (London, 1913), p 36. This copy was recently acquired by the British Library and has yet to be assigned a shelfmark; the other is L.538-1937 in the National Art Library, Victoria & Albert Museum.

33. Hobson, *Bindings*, p 124; C L Craig, 'The earliest Little Gidding concordance', *Harvard Library Bulletin*, vol 1 (1947), pp 311-31, esp p 328.

34. D.II.11, for example, a folio, is sewn on thirteen bands; G.IV.2, an octavo, is sewn on nine.

35. *Clare College 1326-1926*, vol 2 (Cambridge, 1930), pp 479-80. It is worth noting in this context that there is a copy of the *Eikon Basilike* in the British Library (C.27.d.13) with a note dated 1678 on the flyleaf 'This book was bound at Litle Giding...by...Mary Colet'.

36. J E B Mayor [ed], *Nicholas Ferrar. Two lives* (Cambridge, 1855), pp 361-2; I Basire, *The Correspondence* [ed W N Darnell] (London, 1831), pp 20-2.

37. T T Carter [ed], *Nicholas Ferrar his Household and Friends* (London, 1892), p 186; Mayor, *Ferrar*, pp 117-20.

38. The early bindings are the two earliest concordances; see Craig, 'Little Gidding concordance'.

APPENDIX

Bindings from the Workshop of Daniel Boyse

A.V.8	7 tracts, 1586–1614. 8°
C.III.2	*Certaine Sermons* (London, 1582). 4°
+ELBW.B49Ca (D.IV.23)	2 editions of *The Book of Common Prayer* (London, 1549–52. 2°
D.V.20	*Liber Precum Publicarum* (London, 1574). 8°
E.IV.24	G Massiliensis, *Liber de Ecclesiasticis Dogmatibus* (Hamburg, 1614). 4° WITH J Godefroy, *De Suburbicariis Regionibus* (Frankfurt, 1618). 4°
F.IV.8	J P Moneta, *Duo Tractatus* (Rome, 1618). 4° WITH R Tillesley, *Animadversions* (London, 1619). 4°
G.IV.6	L de Granada, *A Memoriall of a Christian Life* (Rouen, 1586). 8°
G.VI.3	4 tracts, 1530–1619. 8°
G.VI.10	R Niger, *De Contemptu Mundi* (Cologne, 1619). 12° WITH H Oraeus, *Nomenclator Praecipuorum* (Hanau, 1619). 12°
H.I.10	4 tracts, 1584–1614. 2°
H.II.8	N Eymeric, *Directorium Inquisitorum* (Venice, 1607). 2°

H.V.2	J Barclay, *Paraenesis ad Sectarios* (Rome, 1617). 8° WITH Z Boverio, *Paraenesis Catholica* (Lyons, 1618). 8°
N.V.1	R Montagu, *Diatribae* (London, 1621). 4°
P.V.6	J Lydius, *Scriptores duo Anglici* (Leiden, 1615). 8°
T.IV.4	J . Scaliger, *Exotericarum Exercitationum Liber XV* (Paris, 1557). 4°
Y.III.34	4 tracts, 1614–1620. 4°
Y.V.28	Martianus Capella, *Satyricon* (Leiden, 1599). 8°
Cathedral Library D.VII.25–26	St Ambrose, *Opera* (Paris, 1614). 2°
Cathedral Library H.IVA.26–27	Seneca, *Opera* (1621). 8°
Chinese-Box Bindings	
D.II.11-13	J Sirmond, *Concilia Antiqua Galliae* (Paris, 1629). 2°
S.R.8.C.12 (D.III.12)	*Missale ad Usum...Sarum* (Paris, 1516). 2°
D.IV.32	J Vicecomes, *Observationum Ecclesiasticarum...volumen quartum* (Milan, 1626). 4°
F.I.12	G Paleotti, *Archiepiscopale Bononiense* (Rome, 1594). 2°
F.V.6–7	Tertullian, *Opera* (Paris, 1566). 8°
G.IV.2	F de Mendoça, *Viridarium Sacrae ac Profanae Eruditionis* (Cologne, 1633). 8°
H.IV.10	F Collius, *De Animabus Paganorum* (Milan, 1622). 4°
Ushaw College XIX.G.9.4	*The Life and Death of Sir Thomas Moore* [Douai?, 1631?] 4°

'Calculated upon a Very Extensive and Useful Plan' The English Provincial Press in the Eighteenth Century

JEREMY BLACK

The culture of print has played a central role in the increasingly contentious debate about the nature of English society, in the widest sense, in the eighteenth century. The two most important works in this debate are Jonathan Clark's *English Society 1688–1832: Ideology, Social Structure and Political Practice during the Ancien Régime* (Cambridge, 1985) and Paul Langford's *A Polite and Commercial People: England 1727–1783* (Oxford, 1989). Clark argues that England was a Church-State in which the ideological formulations of society, and in particular deference and popular Anglicanism, go far towards explaining the strength of the system. Clark argues that the principal opposition to the monarchical, aristocratic, Anglican regime came not from political radicals, whom he treats as a small and inconsequential group, but from religious radicals, in particular Unitarians. He claims that the collapse of the Anglican-aristocratic establishment in the early nineteenth century was in no way inevitable, was resisted with vigour and owed much to the failure to protect the position of the Church of England. Langford, in contrast, centres his study on the middling orders and sees their preoccupations and influence as crucial to the development of a commercial society with a morality and culture of polite behaviour and judicious Christianity. He writes of the 'enrichment and influence of a broad middle class whose concerns became ever more central to Georgian society and whose priorities determined so much both of debate and action'. Langford advances the bold claim that 'the polite and commercial people of the 1730s...did not, in any fundamental sense, inhabit the same society' as their successors in the 1780s, that indeed 'Englishmen themselves were hardly the same people.'

Langford's stress on change and the middling orders might suggest that he would devote greater attention to the press. In fact although both Clark and Langford discuss the writings of the period at considerable length, they fail to consider newspapers, especially the provincial press, adequately. This is unfortunate, as one of the great areas of development in the eighteenth century was the growth of the press. The English Licensing Act lapsed in 1695. The annual sale of newspapers in England was about 2.5 million in 1713, 7.3M in 1750, 12.6M

61

in 1775 and 16M in 1801. Such expansion was not of course restricted to England. There were 57 German newspapers published in 1701, 94 in 1750, 126 in 1775 and 186 in 1789. In Europe the press both increased in circulation and number of titles in countries where it was already established, such as France and the United Provinces, and spread to other states.

At the present moment it is not possible to present any firm conclusions based on a comparison of the English press and that in other countries; work on eighteenth-century newspapers commonly lacks a comparative element and a valuable article published in 1981 that looked at the English and the French press has not been followed up. Nevertheless, it is reasonable to suggest that one characteristic feature of the English press, especially in the provinces, was that its commercial purpose was central and that advertising played a crucial role in this. There is no doubt that in comparison it was less central to the French press of the period.[2] This reflects an essential feature of the English press that still characterises it today: its capitalist or commercial nature, in marked contrast to the official or semi-official newspapers of some other countries. A similar distinction existed in the eighteenth century. On the continent publishing and printing were generally activities taking place in the context of a society and economic system characterised by privileges, privileges to print news or to sell newspapers being crucial. In this context it is not surprising that most newspapers had an official or semi-official character, a development encouraged by the extent to which there was not an autonomous political world separated from government. Governments were crucial sources of news, understandably so when developments in foreign countries were followed so closely and the nature of censorship regulations ensured that a good relationship between newspapers and the relevant authorities was sought.[3] Thus, for example, the bi-weekly *Mannheimer Zeitung* was both founded in 1767 and transformed into a four-times-a-week paper in 1792 with the backing of the Elector Palatine.

In contrast, in Britain, the press was essentially independent of government and lacked official support. The principal exception was the political essay paper. These were subsidised newspapers, produced for specific political purposes and generally without advertisements. Though of political importance, and a source of items for other newspapers, they were not generally high-selling papers and they were a feature of the metropolitan press, rather than its provincial counter-part. In the provinces the press depended for its viability on sales and advertisements, not on political subsidies, and the expansion of the provincial press can be taken as a measure of the growing wealth and sophistication of provincial society, or at least of that section of it that purchased newspapers.

Thus, the provincial press is an indicator of the same process that can be seen at work in the development of the book trade.

The provincial press developed in a number of ways. Four important changes were the growth in the number of titles, the increase in sales, the improvement in distribution and the development of the newspapers in terms of greater size and more varied content. In 1723 there were about 24 provincial newspapers, in 1753 32, in 1760 35, in 1782 about 50 and in 1805 over 100. Towns where no paper was founded in the first two decades of expansion, such as Hull and Newark, acquired one. Other towns, such as Leeds, saw more newspapers founded. The improvement in distribution networks helped to increase sales and to ensure that the newspaper printer, who stood at the centre of a commercial network, was better placed to sell the other goods, principally books and medicines, that he advertised and sold. At the same time the number of words printed in the average newspapers increased, a process that led to smaller typefaces, more columns per page and larger pages. This process can be seen in the *Bristol Chronicle, Or, Universal Mercantile Register,* a Bristol weekly launched on 5 January 1760. On 3 May 1760 the paper added a list of named agents at Wells, Bridgwater and Taunton; on 23 May 1761 the list was expanded to include Haverfordwest and Pembroke and, on 20 June 1761, agents in Exeter, Chepstow, Caerleon, Newport, Pontypool, Abergavenny and Raglan were added. Distribution to Pembrokeshire was presumably by sea, the Bristol Channel serving as an economic unit, but the expansion into south-east Wales was due to the journeys of a man on horseback, the paper noting in its issue of June 1761

> this paper will, for the future, be constantly vended through...Chepstow, Newport, Ragland, Abergavenny, Pont-y-pool and Carleon, by John Powell...will deliver any message or small parcel if properly directed and left at the Printing-Office.

The *Bristol Chronicle* also increased in size. In 1760 it was an eight-page, two-column-per-page newspaper, but on 27 December 1760, the paper carried an announcement

> ...shall begin our Chronicle for the next year in three columns, after the manner of the London and British Chronicles, as we apprehend it will thereby contain a greater quantity of news than either of the other papers. We have, after much trouble and expence, established as extensive a correspondence for it as any in this city; and can assure the public that

more were sold in neighbouring counties than any other British paper. On 11 July 1761 the paper announced that 'the proprietor...being advised...to alter the form...on account of making the advertisements inserted here more conspicuous' had decided that from the following issue it should appear in 'four folio pages and four columns in the page, after the manner of the Public Ledger...in which form it will contain as much intelligence as at present, and rather more'. A similar process can be seen at work in other newspapers. In the case of the *Bristol Chronicle* it was somewhat accelerated because the paper first appeared in the by-then unusual eight-page format. If other papers are consulted a similar picture of greater content and improved distribution can be discerned. The *Gloucester Journal* of 13 April 1756 named agents in Bristol, Salisbury, Brecon, Hereford, London and Carmarthen. The issue of 16 June 1766 announced 'Advertisements for this paper are taken in by Mr. Morgan Bevan in Swansea, by whom all persons in the counties of Carmarthen, Brecon, and Glamorgan, may be supplied with grocery goods'. At the beginning of 1773 *Drewry's Derby Mercury* named agents in Wirksworth, Chesterfield, Rotherham, Burton-upon-Trent, Ashbourne, Uttoxeter, Winster, Bakewell, Ashby-de-la-Zouch, Loughborough and London and announced that it was 'dispersed by Joseph Housely, through the towns of Alfreton, Higham, Chesterfield, Dronfield, Sheffield and the numerous intermediate villages'. That summer the *Cambridge Chronicle and Journal* named agents in London, Stamford, Leicester, Lincoln, Boston, Newark and Retford, Grantham, Gainsborough, Caistor, Louth, Bedford, Peterborough, Norwich, King's Lynn, Downham, Ely, Bury St Edmunds, Bungay, St Ives, Huntingdon, St Neot's, Wisbech, Spalding and Newmarket. It also offered an account of its distribution network.

> This paper is despatched northwards every Friday night, by the Caxton post, as far as York, Newcastle, and Carlisle; through the counties of Cambridge, Huntingdon, Bedford, Buckingham, Rutland, Leicester, Nottingham, Lincoln, Northampton, Norfolk, Hertford, Essex, and the Isle of Ely, by the Newsmen; to London the next morning, by the coach and fly; and to several parts of Suffolk etc. by other conveyances – persons living at a distance from such places as the Newsmen go through, may have the paper left where they shall choose to appoint.

The *Bristol Journal* was by January 1777 listing named agents in London, Liverpool, Marlborough, Sherborne, Exeter, Taunton, Bridgwater, Wells, Bath, Chippenham, Haverfordwest, Brecon, Carmarthen, Abergavenny and Gloucester. Such papers can be termed provincial if that is taken to mean regional rather than local. The same is especially true of the Newcastle press, which circulated widely in the four northern counties, and of such widely-distributed papers as those published in York and Sherborne. The provincial, rather than local, nature of the press is in part explained by the extent to which the news published was national or international, rather than provincial, however defined. People read the paper to discover news of the outside world and this world was one that was essentially defined by the metropolis and foreign countries, rather than by other parts of provincial England, near or far. It is true that the space devoted both to local news and to news from other provincial parts of England increased, the latter derived substantially from other provincial papers. The *Leeds Mercury* of 18 August 1775 included in its local news items from Thirsk, Wooler, Newcastle and Selby. However, the press at the end of the eighteenth century was still dominated by national and international news, although a strongly local character was provided by the advertisements: both notices and details of items or services for sale. The relative absence of concerns providing services on a national scale helped to ensure that individual advertisements (except those for medicines and books) were generally specific to particular newspapers or to papers published in a single town. Economic news of regional interest was also inserted. *Drewry's Derby Mercury* of 8 October 1773 carried details of the price of cheese at Nottingham fair, and of the willingness of the principal inhabitants of Wolverhampton to accept Portuguese coins.

It was the advertisements that would have provided possibly the principal difference between reading London and provincial newspapers. The news carried by provincial papers derived substantially from the London press, understandably so while the focus remained metropolitan and international. There is no doubt that London papers were read outside the capital in large numbers. The majority of London papers reached the provinces through the Post Office, though near London newsmen were used, as was the case more generally with provincial newspapers. The London press circulated throughout Britain. In January 1775 John Campbell wrote from his seat at Stackpole Court in Pembrokeshire to his grandson John, then in London, 'I read in the Publick Advertiser of Tuesday the 3rd inst. that you had lost at Drury Lane playhouse a fine enamelled gold watch with your crest cypher and motto on the back'.[4] Campbell, who had been an MP for forty years, rising to be a Lord of the Treasury, was scarcely a typical reader, but clearly the London papers had much to offer provincial readers. At present it is not possible to establish the degree of overlap between the reading of London and provincial papers and it is unclear how widely London papers were read outside the Home Counties, where their readership was presumably greatest.

The provincial press can be discussed in terms both of the notion that England was a commercial society, a suggestion in which the role of newspaper advertisements plays a major role, and with reference to the idea that a political world was being created in which public discussion and consideration between equals, rather than personal relationships with reciprocal links of obligation, deference and patronage, was crucial. It is of course by no means clear what readers sought in the press. An item by 'Papyrus Cursor' entitled 'A New Method of reading

Newspapers' published in the *Gentleman's Magazine* of 1766 suggested that not all readers studiously followed the leading stories of the day

> For several months past I have resided in the country, with a very agreeable family, about forty miles from London, where we had plenty of shooting, fishing, walking, and riding. But as the weather was frequently such as obliged us to keep within doors, we then endeavoured to amuse ourselves with cards and news papers. Cards, for those who love play, are a vast fund of amusement, but this is by no means the case with regard to newspapers; for when you have once read the pages of unconnected occurrences, consisting of politics, religion, picking of pockets, puffs, casualties, deaths, marriages, bankruptcies, preferments, resignations, executions, lottery tickets, India bonds, Scotch pebbles, Canada bills, French chicken gloves, auctioneers and quack doctors, this abrupt transition from one thing to another, is apt to overload and confuse the memory so much, that after reading two or three news-papers, people generally throw them down, with the usual complaint of, *Not a syllable of News*; to silence this complaint, and to show that newspapers, as well as cards, are capable of entertainment, I shall just mention one improvement, which we practised in the country with great success; and that was, after we had read the paper in the old trite vulgar way, i.e. each column by itself downwards, we next read two columns together onwards; and by this new method, found much more entertainment than in the common way of reading, with a greater variety of articles curiously blended, or strikingly contrasted.

Numerous humorous examples were provided.[5]

Accepting that papers were read for a number of reasons, including the fact that it was increasingly fashionable to do so, it is, nevertheless, reasonable to speculate over what the impact of the publication of so much news and comment was. Newspapers offered a new means for the dissemination of opinion that was not linked to the corporate ritual of urban life, with its heavy stress on group activities, the importance of anniversary celebrations and the role of religion in defining groups and their values. In addition, provincial newspapers provided another link between the worlds of town and rural hinterlands, links that were already strong economically but which were far weaker politically. Newspapers offered, instead of the hierarchical world of different social orders in town and country, a sphere in which all readers were equal. They were also surprisingly open to the expression of different opinions. This owed much not only to the fact that individual papers generally sought to maximise sales and advertisements by avoiding excessively partisan stances, but also to the need that undercapitalised newspapers lacking reporting staff had for free items.[6] This was especially serious in the parliamentary recess and in peacetime. As the Seven Years' War neared its close, the *Bristol Journal* prepared to fill the likely gap by offering its readers another version of the war, the issue of 15 January 1763 announcing that

> As in times of peace a scarcity of news must consequently ensue, it is presumed a state of England, from the famous Peace of Aix-la-Chapelle to the Declaration of War against Spain in the year 1762, will not be disagreeable to our readers, as it will include many interesting and curious particulars relative to this nation since that time: including The History of the Present War. To be continued weekly.

In fact the political agenda shifted quite considerably in the post-war world. Whereas British politics had been dominated by war or the prospect of war since 1738, after 1763 it was domestic disputes that came to the fore. This was ably demonstrated by the press reports of the celebrations for the proclamation of peace in 1763 which occurred as agitation over the new cider excise was sweeping the West of England

> On occasion of the proclaiming of the peace last week at Stroudwater, an Apple-Tree, which had been cut down for that purpose, was carried in the Procession, together with an Effigy as large as life, with a B inscribed on the back: At the closing of the Cavalcade, the Effigy was put into the Stocks, then hung up by the common Hangman, and afterwards burnt to Ashes: The same ceremony, we hear, was observed at Dursley, and other Parts of the county of Gloucester.[7]

The 1760s brought the issues and disturbances that are often summarized as the Wilkesite movement. The 1770s might seem to suggest a shift back to foreign affairs, with the outbreak of the War of American Independence and the widening of the conflict to include the Bourbons, but, although this was indeed true to a certain extent, that war was in part a civil war that aroused considerable dispute within Britain, and these divisions were covered in the press.[8] The *Leeds Mercury* of 31 October 1775 carried under the Leeds byline, an account of a general meeting in Newcastle over the American crisis. Not all items of American news came through the London press. The *Leeds Mercury*, for example, printed items in late 1775 derived from a letter received by a gentleman at Berwick from his friend at Boston (18 July), a letter from Boston to someone at Halifax (1 August), a ship from Boston arriving at Liverpool (19 September), a letter from a soldier at Boston to his father in Chester (10 October) and a letter from Virginia to a correspondent at Whitehaven (24 October). In the period between the Peace of Paris in 1763 and Britain's entry into the Revolutionary War in 1793, the press was pulled towards a consideration of domestic affairs by two factors: first their intrinsic importance and secondly the fact that the press needed more copy. Most newspapers had expanded in size during the period 1739–63; the return of peace was not to be accompanied by any reduction in size. The absence of documentary evidence on this point necessarily makes it conjectural but it appears that newspapers welcomed the rise in contentious 'public' politics in the 1760s. Dramatic political events provided not only points of reference in terms of public activity that could serve to explain, or rather provide an explanation for these developments, but also types of political activity that produced material for those who wished to report them.[9] The appeal to a public wider than that customarily involved in political activity had to be striking and dramatic, comprehensive and swift, and this led both to the use of print and to the demonstrative politics of petitions, addresses, instructions, demonstrations and riots that could be reported readily. The extent to which the provincial newspapers rose to the challenge can be debated. As with most reporting of the period, of indeed any period, there were accounts of events but little in the way of serious analysis. The analysis was provided largely by partisan anonymous or pseudonymous contributions that tended to make moral points. Indeed, the extent to which the press of the last decades of the century adopted a programme of social improvement can be related to the manner in which politics was generally discussed. There was little difference between upbraiding rioters or food hoarders in 1766 and declaiming against drunkenness or slavery. Political discussion, thought and reflection were not divorced from their ethical context and a reading of the provincial press would offer an account of English society in which politeness was definitely seen as a goal. Under the Derby byline, *Drewry's Derby Mercury* of 8 October 1773 claimed 'The frequency of all kinds of felonies is complained of by all degrees of people, and some counties have (in order to lighten the burden from an individual) laudably formed associations for apprehending and prosecuting all offenders, within their several districts', and urged that the same be done in Derbyshire. A different aspect of culture was catered for in the *Leeds Mercury* of 26 December 1775 'The present appearance of the grand planet, Jupiter, upon the meridian, at midnight, excites the curiosity of astronomers; we insert the following for the perusal of those less conversant in that science'. The *Cambridge Chronicle* of 22 July 1775 informed its readers how to deal with drownings.

However, rather than presenting this as a triumphant example of the transformation of English society, it is necessary to note also a number of qualifications. Whatever the irritation with individual practices, there was little sign, whether in the press or in society of a rejection of hierarchical norms. Even the possibility of radically different arrangements was discussed very rarely. An anonymous essay 'Thoughts on Levelling, with an Account of the insurrection of Wat Tyler', published in the *Bristol Journal* of 5 April 1777, claimed

> A consciousness of primitive equality is strongly impressed on the heart of every man; and a desire of recovering their original consequence, joined to the pressure of present incoveniencies, has at different times roused the populace of every nation to arms.

Such bold suggestions were, however, rare and newspapers campaigned for moral improvement rather than radical political reform. This conclusion appears less surprising in light of a detailed recent study of the electoral system which argues that the 'need' or desire for reform was limited and that electoral politics, although lively, were centred on specific grievances, rather than on any fundamental disaffection.[10]

Secondly, and more significant, is the social location of the press. Langford admits that by concentrating on a 'broad middle class' his work introduces an element of 'bias'[11] and it is certainly true that he gives less than proportionate weight to the bulk of the population. This is also true of the press as can be noted in many ways. For example, a lengthy notice of over a column in the *Gloucester Journal* of 10 April 1780 announced the prizes offered by the Glamorgan Society for the Encouragement of Agriculture. The item noted the problems facing agricultural improvement

> The form and situation of this county, as well as the illiterateness of the generality of small farmers make us near half a century behind some parts of England in the art of agriculture...The gentlemen of this county, from their observations in travelling, and from books, and their own experience, discover many improvements as to mode of tillage, different kinds of manure, succession of crops, artificial grasses, implements, etc. which they cannot prevail upon the farmers to adopt so speedily, any other ways as by pecuniary rewards, and an honorary distinction among the gentlemen will dispose them the more to make experiments, and to instruct and convince their respective tenants and neighbours by the superior force of example.

Detailed modern studies have indeed led to a sceptical view of the value or use of the press as a medium for the diffusion of agricultural information.[12] Newspapers were not inexpensive and the cut-price London papers of the second quarter of the century were not matched in the provinces. Even though per-caput consumption of newspapers rose during the century, there was no massive growth in popular readership, especially outside London. An examination of the literary or theatrical news or the advertisements does not suggest much of an effort to cater for and thus create a mass readership, and the bulk of the claims made for its existence related to London. Advertisements were usually not for generally consumed products, but for goods or services that were either new to the area or, more commonly, luxury or occasional, in effect visitors from the outside world and frequently products of the metropolitan world and its fashions.[13]

Similarly, the frequent attacks on popular superstition, drunkenness and a range of activities that were held to characterise a distressingly wide section of the population, such as profanity and cruelty to animals, scarcely suggests that the press was asserting values shared by all. In a comparable fashion one might doubt the extent to which slavery was widely abhorrent outside the circles that pressed for its limitation or abolition. Items appeared urging petitions to Parliament for action, as in the *Derby Mercury* of 23 February 1792, but newspaper agitation suggests as much a sense of desperate prodding of apathetic opinion and hostile interests, as it does any control of priorities for debate and action by a broad middle class. The press could also serve to repeat popular superstitions. *Drewry's Derby Mercury* of 10 September 1775, reporting a fatal accident in Staffordshire, noted, 'it is very remarkable that a bird hovered over the head of the deceased for a considerable time'.

To suggest that the press needs to be seen as at best a limited guide to provincial opinion does not mean that it was without consequence. Part of its importance was negative. The provincial press did not serve to foster feelings of regional identity. There were occasional items, especially at election time, in which preference was voiced for local individuals or interests, but, in general, a striking feature of the provincial press was its absence of a strong sense of place and of accompanying hostility, towards either London or other regions. This offers a parallel to the general 'enlightened' character of most of the European press, provincialism and parochialism clearly being dismissed alongside popular superstition. The English provincial press helped to create a national awareness of public politics, so that issues resonated through the political community. That may, however, have been less important than the role of the provincial press in spreading interest in issues that were not so obviously partisan. The didactic and educational nature of the press was expressed in a letter from J W of Bradford published in the *Leeds Mercury* of 21 November 1775 that began

> When any public alteration is to be made, or a new law proposed the nature
> and use thereof ought to be explained, in order to inform the judgements of
> such as will of course be affected thereby; so that every person for himself may
> determine how far he ought to assist in obtaining or opposing the same. The
> intended application for an act to establish a Court of Requests, for an easy and
> speedy method of recovery of debts under Forty Shillings, within a few
> parishes round this town, is now become a general topic of conversation...

In particular, the press played a major role in disseminating and sustaining fashions among those who possessed the interest, knowledge and funds to pursue fashions, but were otherwise removed from the world of the metropolis. Fashions entailed not only clothes, items on which appeared in provincial newspapers, but opinions and ideas, fads and hobbies. There was a growing appetite for fashions in this wider sense in the middling orders Langford writes about, and this appetite was facilitated by their growing wealth. The provincial press helped to keep these people informed, to ensure that the metropolitan world did not appear remote, and in this respect news and advertisements performed a complementary function. If this does not amount to a suggestion that the press performed a similar role for the whole of society, the conclusion reflects both the extent to which the newspapers were socially circumscribed and hesitation about endorsing the notion of a vertically integrated society in which ideas and practices were readily disseminated down the social hierarchy.

NOTES

1. The quotation at the head of this article comes from the *Bristol Chronicle*, 5 January 1760.

2. S Botein, J R Censer, and H Ritvo, 'The periodical press in eighteenth-century English and French society: a cross cultural approach', *Comparative Studies in Society and History*, vol 23 (1981), pp 464–90. Recent work can be approached in and through G Feyel, *La 'Gazette' en Province à travers ses Réimpressions, 1631–1752* (Amsterdam, 1982); J R Censer and J D Popkin [ed], *Press and Politics in Pre-Revolutionary France* (Berkeley, 1987), see esp p 20.

3. J D Popkin, *News and Politics in the Age of Revolution: Jean Luzac's 'Gazette de Leyde'* (Ithaca, 1989), pp 36–45.

4. Dyfed Record Office, Carmarthen: Cawdor Papers Box 128.

5. *Gentleman's Magazine* (1766), p 587.

6. J M Black, *The English Press in the Eighteenth Century* (London, 1987); J M BLack, 'The Beinecke Collection of late eighteenth century English newspapers', *Yale University Library Gazette* (1990).

7. *Bristol Journal* 23 April 1763; for the situation in Exeter, 14 May 1763. On the background see P Woodland, 'Extra-parliamentary political organization in the making: Benjamin Heath and the opposition to the 1763 cider Excise', *Parliamentary History*, vol 4 (1985), pp 115–36.

8. J Honey, *Experience and Identity: Birmingham and the West Midlands, 1760–1800* (Manchester, 1977), pp 199–206; J E Bradley, *Popular Politics and the American Revolution in England* (Macon, Georgia, 1986), pp 99–107.

9. For similar comments in the reporting of the French Revolution see J M Black, 'The British press and eighteenth-century revolution: the French case', in P Dukes and J Dunkley [ed], *Culture and Revolution* (London, 1990), p 111.

10. F O'Gorman, *Voters, Patrons and Parties: the Unreformed Electorate of Hanoverian England, 1734–1832* (Oxford, 1989)

11. Langford, *Polite and Commercial People*, p xi.

12. S Macdonald, 'The diffusion of knowledge among Northumberland farmers, 1780–1815', *Agricultural History Review*, vol 27 (1979), p 32; J R Walton, 'Mechanization in agriculture', in H S A Fox and R A Butlin [ed], *Change in the Countryside* (London, 1979), p 34; P Horn, 'The contribution of the propagandist to eighteenth-century agricultural improvement', *Historical Journal*, vol 25 (1982), p 317.

13. J J Looney, *Advertising and Society in England, 1720–1820: a Statistical Analysis of Yorkshire Newspaper Advertisements* (PhD thesis, Princeton, 1983); P S Brown, 'The vendors of medicine advertised in eighteenth-century Bath newspapers', *Medical History*, vol 20 (1976); R Porter, *Health for Sale: Quackery in England 1660–1850* (Manchester, 1989), pp 71, 115–22.

Mobility and Innovation in the Book Trades
Some Devon Examples

IAN MAXTED

In 1506 an inventory of Exeter Cathedral Library listed among its more than six hundred volumes about half a dozen which were described as 'impressorie artis', that is to say printed books.[1] An important technological revolution was just beginning to make itself felt in the South-West of England. The twenty-six soldiers of lead which were in the vanguard of this revolution caused a series of innovations in the way in which information was distributed. The resulting changes were spread over a period of several centuries and in Devon a select group of individuals was responsible for their local introduction.

The first area requiring innovative thought and action was that of the publication and sale of the printed materials which could now be produced in such relatively large quantities. The Devon pioneer in that field is Martin Coeffin, whose name first appears in the imprint of two schoolbooks printed for him in Rouen. The earlier in date is the vocabulary known from its first three words as *Os, Facies, Mentum* which was printed by 'Laurentij Hostingue et Iameti Loys' in about 1505. The whereabouts of the second is no longer known so identification is uncertain. It is probably the *Tractatulus Verborum Defectivorum* and was printed by Richard Goupil around 1510. Nicholas Orme[2] has located 32 references to Coeffin in Exeter documents between 1511 and 1538 but his trade, where it is given, is always stated to be that of a bookbinder. His publishing activities, although pioneering, appear to have been shortlived. In the Exeter military survey of 1522 he was stated to be a native of Normandy and was assessed for a sallet, a bill and as being worth twenty marks. He had a servant, also born in Normandy, named as John Bokebender, who was assessed for 20s. On 28 April 1524 he was granted letters of denization and was then described as a 'bokebynder'. He was admitted a freeman of Exeter on payment of £2.0s.0d. only in 1531/2, perhaps 25 years after he had first begun to trade in the city.

Coeffin and the booksellers who succeeded him were dealing in books printed in London or abroad. Not until 1698 was the first permanent printing press established in Exeter. It was set up by Samuel Darker who had previously worked in Bull's Head Court in the parish of St Giles Cripplegate in London where he is recorded in 1695, and a number of London imprints can be ascribed to him.[3] He was born in about 1665, the son of Samuel Darker of London, fishmonger, and was apprenticed to Robert Roberts, citizen and stationer, in 1679, becoming a freeman of the Stationers' Company in 1686. He married in 1685 and several children are recorded incuding one, John, who was apprenticed to Samuel's widow and later became a master printer in London, binding his own apprentice in 1710. Samuel's career in Exeter was a short one. He died in March 1700 in London of stopping of the stomach and was buried in St Giles Cripplegate. There was no will; his widow swore to administer his estate at the London Court of Orphans. An inventory dated 23 September 1700 includes two presses. He does not seem, therefore, to have relinquished his London business and never took out the freedom of Exeter. His Exeter business seems to have been largely run by Samuel Farley, whom he had taken as partner in 1698, within a year of setting up his Exeter press.

Farley's origins are uncertain; nobody of that name is recorded in the Exeter baptismal or marriage registers before 1699[4], nor is the family recorded in seventeenth century Exeter inhabitant lists transcribed by Professor Hoskins.[5] He continued Darker's business after his death in 1700. It was quite an ambitious printing office with a steady flow of titles including several large-scale works, notably John Prince's *Damnonii Orientales Illustres*, a biographical dictionary of eminent Devonians whose 600 pages were illustrated by woodcut coats of arms and which occupied the printers for several years, until its eventual publication in 1701, and Ellis Veryard's *An Account of Divers Choice Remarks...Taken in a Journey through the Low Countries, France, Italy and Part of Spain...*, a folio of almost 400 pages published in 1701.

Farley was responsible for an innovation of his own in about 1704, when he established the first recorded newspaper in Exeter *Sam. Farley's Exeter Post Man*.[6] He remained in Exeter at a series of addresses until September 1715, when he moved to Salisbury to establish the *Salisbury Post Man*. He remained there for only about one year, perhaps leaving to concentrate on *Sam. Farley's Bristol Post Man*, the newspaper he had established in February 1713. Before his death in 1730 he had returned to Exeter to set up *Farley's Exeter Journal* in 1723, but he seems not to have stayed for long as Edward Farley was running this newspaper from 1725.

The earliest recorded periodical in Devon was published in Plymouth by Orion Adams, who was active there between 1758 and 1764. The first issue of *The Plymouth Magazine: or, the Universal Intelligencer* appeared on 23 October 1758 and the publisher announced his intention to continue it fortnightly. It contained the freshest advices foreign and domestic with the prices of corn, stocks, lottery tickets, bills of mortality and similar intelligence as brought in Tuesday's and

Friday's posts. While waiting for Sunday's post Adams set 'The Fairring' and 'Friendship', two new songs as sung at Vauxhall and Ranelagh. There were five advertisements, all for sales by the candle and all placed by Francis Fanning. Set in an identical measure to the main text are two supplementary pages of 'Memoirs of Frederick iii, King of Prussia' which breaks off abruptly and is followed by the first sixteen pages (signatures A and B) of Romeo and Juliet with the imprint: 'London: Printed for Fr. Cooke,...1758'. The whole seems a cross between a cut-down weekly newspaper and an apology for one of the London monthly magazines.[7] It does not seem to have survived for long, perhaps because of the narrow advertising base. In 1759 Adams appears to have founded a more traditional newspaper, perhaps called the *Plymouth and Exeter Gazette*, but this seems to have ceased before 14 January 1760, when the *Western Flying Post* names Adams as the late printer of the Plymouth paper. In the issue of the 18 February of the same paper Adams thanked his readers for their support but regretted that he had been obliged to cease publication. No copies of the Plymouth newspaper are known to survive.[8] Adams remained in Plymouth until at least 1763 when he printed *Observations on that part of a late Act of Parliament which lays an Additional Duty on Cyder and Perry* by Thomas Alcock, but had moved on by 1765, in which year William Andrews moved from Exeter to Plymouth 'there then being no printer there'.[9] Orion Adams had been born in 1717 in Manchester, the son of Roger Adams, printer of the *Manchester Weekly Journal* and later of the *Chester Courant*. He was even more of a wandering printer than Samuel Farley. Daniel Prince described him as 'an old itinerant type' in a letter to John Nichols dated 8 October 1795. He had worked as a master in Manchester where he had started a short-lived newspaper *Orion Adams's Weekly Journal* and a fortnightly periodical modestly entitled *The Humourist: or the Magazine of Magazines* in 1752, and also in Chester, Plymouth and Dublin. He worked in London and other provincial offices as a journeyman. Soon after leaving Plymouth he was a prisoner in the King's Bench Prison, Surrey, and applied in the *London Gazette* of 16 August 1766 to take benefit of the Act for the Relief of Insolvent Debtors. His fortunes soon improved. In Birmingham he became partner with Nicholas Boden, with whom he published, in 1769, a folio Bible, part of which was printed in Baskerville's office. In that year he was distinguished as a brilliant character in his own carriage at the Shakespeare jubilee in Stratford, but a few months later he was distributing playbills for an itinerant company. He, or a printer of the same name, appeared in Exeter in August 1775 when he applied for a licence to marry. He died in poverty near Chester in April 1797 at the age of 80. Biographers[10] comment on the instability and eccentricities which made the last fifty years of his life 'a lamentable scene of chequered events'. It is as well that his heart was 'as light as his pocket; for, under all adversities his temper was cheerful, obliging and friendly'.

On 8 March 1813 a new type of newspaper appeared in Exeter to compete with the more traditional *Exeter Flying Post* and *Exeter and Plymouth Gazette*. These were both four-page broadsheets with five columns to the page and closely set text. The mastheads were modest affairs, typical of the provincial press of the time. The newcomer was of a much smaller format with eight pages in each issue and had only three columns to the page, generously separated by double rules. It had a splendid engraved masthead depicting an eagle and a decorative engraved rule at the foot of the first page. Its title confirmed that it set out to appeal to a broader range of readers: *Flindell's Western Luminary : the Family Newspaper of the Nobility and Gentry, Farmers & Traders*. Its pages were numbered sequentially and it may be that Flindell intended to produce an index. None has been traced and sequential numbering was dropped after the first volume. Similar experiments with new forms of newspaper were being undertaken elsewhere in the country at this period. One example, recently described by Michael Perkin[11] was the *Liverpool Mercury*, established in 1811 by Egerton Smith, which was provided with a title-page and index to each annual volume. In 1815 a list of subscribers to the *Western Luminary* was included, a most unusual occurrence for a newspaper, and the list of 1900 names indicates that the printer and many of the readers regarded the *Western Luminary* as something different from the normal newspaper. Besides its advertisements (which included one for Caslon's types on the front page of the first issue), and the commercial, foreign, domestic and local intelligence, there was a prominent section on fashion, literature and the arts, soon to be entitled the 'Literary and Fashionable Repository' and, set in a larger type, the 'Review', an opportunity for the editor to make utterances on matters of the day, often in outspoken terms.

The proprietor of this newspaper, Thomas Flindell, was born in Helston in 1767 and apprenticed in Falmouth, probably to Philip Elliott. It may have been Elliott's death in 1787 which set Flindell on his years of travel. This period took him to Bath, Edinburgh, London and Doncaster, where in 1790 he became editor of the *Doncaster Gazette*. In 1798 he returned to Helston to found the Stannary Press, where he began the publication of the Bible in fortnightly parts. In 1800 he moved to Falmouth, where he founded the *Cornwall Gazette and Falmouth Packet*, the first newspaper in Cornwall. His partners in this undertaking failed in business and Flindell himself was imprisoned for debt in Bodmin gaol. A subscription was raised on his behalf which enabled him in 1803 to relaunch his newspaper in Truro as the *Royal Cornwall Gazette*. It was vigorously conducted but tended to fall into the hands of the Tory party, a factor which led to the launching in 1810 of the Whig *West Briton*. Two years' warfare with the rival editor resulted in Flindell's move to Exeter to establish a newspaper on his own principles.

While in Exeter he was a partner with George Simpson of Devizes, printer and publisher of the *Devizes and Wiltshire Gazette*, a partnership which was dissolved in 1819. His outspokenness, to which he had admitted in his prospectus for the *Western Luminary*, landed him in trouble on several occasions, the most serious of which resulted from intemperate language on the subject of Queen Caroline of whom he wrote in July 1820 'Shall a woman who is as notoriously devoted to Bacchus as to Venus – shall such a woman as would, if found on our pavement, be committed to bridewell and whipped, be held up in the light of suffering innocence?' On 19 March 1821 he was found guilty of a libel on the Queen and sentenced to eight months imprisonent in Exeter gaol. There was an appeal for funds to meet the expenses of his libel trial organised by an alderman of Exeter and advertised in local newspapers. Within little more than a week more than sixty people raised about £160. His health had been badly affected by his imprisonment and he died on 11 July 1824.[12] The *Western Luminary* passed into the hands of the Dewdney family, who were still conducting it in the 1850s.

While the occasional illustration had appeared in Devon books since the first years of the eighteenth century, it was not until the second decade of the nineteenth that the first publisher appeared in Devon who was to make a feature of the publication of engravings and illustrated books, and he set up business not in Exeter but in the infant coastal resort of Sidmouth, where he established the Marine Library on the beach in 1809. The first publication of John Wallis, the proprietor of this establishment, dates from 1810 and was a guidebook entitled *The Beauties of Sidmouth Displayed* by the Rev Edmund Butcher. It contains a folded aquatint after J Nixon of the 'View of the Beach and Peak Hill, Sidmouth' and was a modest foretaste of the publications to come. The second edition published in about 1820 contains eight aquatints and the third published a year or two later boasts no fewer than thirty-one, mostly by the Londoner Daniel Havell after the Sidmouth artist Henry Haseler. In the guidebook it was stated that he had 'expended in excess of £900 in engraving, coloring, &c'. The most magnificent single print was a panorama of the sea front at Sidmouth with Wallis's library proudly centre-stage. This was aquatinted by Havell after H Cornish and was about nine feet long. Besides many individual prints, including views from his library, Wallis was responsible for several other books profusely illustrated with coloured aquatints. He used the earliest lithographic illustrations in Devon in *Sketches from Nature of Sidmouth and its Environs*, published in 1819 and 1820. The twelve lithographs in these albums, of which only 100 sets were issued, were produced by Rudolph Ackermann in London. In 1826 he issued the first lithographs by the Exeter artist George Rowe in *Forty-eight Views of Cottages and Scenery at Sidmouth, Devon*.[13] There was considerable rivalry with similar establishments in Sidmouth which can be amusingly traced in the guidebooks that each published. John Marsh's *The Sidmouth Guide* says of the Marine Library in 1818 'the views from it are good, but rather inferior to those from the library of Mr. Marsh.' It must have been a source of great satisfaction to Wallis that Marsh was declared bankrupt in 1819, the year in which Wallis was appointed bookseller to the Duke of Kent after a visit fawningly commemorated in the guidebook he published the following year.[14]

Wallis's origins are revealed in the illustration of his circulating library in the panorama published in 1815. Its signboard reads 'Wallis's, the original circulating library & reading room, and at no. 42 Skinner's Street, London'. In fact the London business was at that time being run by John Wallis senior and his son Edward. John junior was born in about 1780 and apprenticed to his father on 4 March 1794, becoming a freeman of the London Stationers' Company on 4 February 1806. He ran his own business at 186 Strand for a short period before moving to Sidmouth. Wallis senior had been in business since 1775 with premises at Yorick's Head, 16 Ludgate Hill, and at 54 Cornhill, before moving to 13 Warwick Square in 1804, and 42 Skinner Street in 1812, where his son Edward joined him as partner in 1813. Edward and John were joint publishers of the 1815 panorama. They built up an extensive trade as sellers of maps and prints, publishing maps by John Cary among others, and were also active in the field of juvenile publishing, producing many jigsaw puzzles and games. These were the skills that the son John learned and developed, in Sidmouth, to such effect.[15]

We have now considered the careers of half a dozen individuals who were responsible for innovations in the Devon book trades and there are a number of common features. The first is that they were not normally natives of the place where they made their innovations. Coeffin came from Normandy and Wallis from London for example. While innovations must inevitably be introduced from outside, it is surprising that they are not more frequently brought in by natives of the place, who had previously left to be apprenticed or who invited partners from outside to bring new skills to a local enterprise. Secondly, the innovators did not always survive for long periods, frequently moving on to other areas. The second feature is that they often seem restless spirits; indeed in the case of Orion Adams this is specifically mentioned by contemporary writers. Innovation is not always synonymous with success.

If we are looking for success stories, for those who brought the practice of the trade to its highest and most successful state and who set up long-established businesses, we more often have to look to natives of the town in question or to individuals who were more completely settled there.

In the early period there is often insufficient evidence to draw many conclusions on the success or otherwise of individuals. Coeffin does not emerge as a major bookseller, although his fines as a non-freeman for permission to trade are considerably higher than normal, suggesting a measure of success. It is not until the following century that other Exeter booksellers began to emulate him in having books printed on their behalf in London. At the end of the sixteenth century Michael Harte appears to have run a large and successful business in Exeter. He was the son of John Harte of Exeter but left his native city to learn his trade, being appenticed to John Windet, citizen and stationer of London in 1581 and turned over to Andrew Maunsell and to Robert Dexter, when the latter succeeded Maunsell at the Brazen Serpent in about 1590. He became a freeman of the Stationers' Company in 1592, but left London soon afterwards to return to Exeter where he became a freeman by succession on 31 December 1593, operating as a bookseller there until his death twenty years later. His former apprentice John Moungwell, took an inventory of his master's goods after his death in 1615. It shows a stock of at least 3500 volumes. Unfortunately few are listed individually, but those which are show a wide-ranging and up-to-date stock.[16]

But perhaps the most notable bookseller in Exeter before 1800 was Gilbert Dyer who ran a bookshop and circulating library in the High Street from about 1785 until his death in 1820. He was born in Widecombe in the Moor in 1743, the son of a schoolmaster whom he assisted before moving to Exeter to become schoolmaster at Tuckers Hall in June 1767. He served more than fifteen years as a schoolmaster in Exeter before becoming a bookseller; indeed when his book *The Most General School-Assistant* was published in Exeter in 1770 his name did not even appear on the imprint. In the 1780s he opened a bookshop opposite Guildhall, in premises probably formerly occupied by Walter Dight. He was a learned man, the author of several works.

Dibdin paid tribute to him in his *Bibliomania*

> Mr G Dyer of Exeter is a distinguished veteran in the book-trade: his catalogue of 1810 in two parts, containing 19 945 articles, has I think never been equalled by that of any provincial bookseller, for the value and singularity of the greater number of volumes described in it.

Hone's *Yearbook* mentions 'the erudite Maister Dyer, the collector of a circulating library, the choicest and perhaps the most extensive, of any in the whole kingdom, except in the metropolis'. Hone also comments on Dyer's collection of theology as being 'astonishing; it was stacked on manifold shelves to the angle point of the gable of their huge upper warehouse.' His enterprise proved the foundation of two successful businesses in Exeter. His library was taken over by

Maria Fitze and remained in her family until the 1850s, while the bookshop was continued by Dyer's son, also called Gilbert, from 1821 to 1829, by William Strong from 1829 to 1837, and by Edwin Jeanes from 1837 to 1843.

Among the early printers perhaps the most famous and longest surviving was Andrew Brice.[18] He was born in Exeter in 1690 and claims that he was originally intended for the ministry but his father was too poor. He was apprenticed to the Exeter printer Joseph Bliss but absconded. He never became a freeman of Exeter. From the time he established his first newspaper *The Postmaster* in 1717 he enjoyed a chequered career of more than fifty years in Exeter. Because of its longevity his series of newspapers became known as *Brice's Old Exeter Journal*. He appears to have left Exeter only once, when he set up Cornwall's first shortlived printing press in Truro in 1742. He spent many years working on his *Grand Gazetteer*, a folio of almost 1500 pages issued in 44 monthly parts between 1751 and 1755, and in a collected form in 1759. He took Barnabas Thorn into partnership in 1769 and seems to have lived in semi-retirement until his death at the age of 84 in 1773. Brice's business, including his newspaper, was continued by Barnabas Thorn and then by his son Richard until the latter's death in 1787. In his introduction to *The Mobiad*, written in 1770, a few years before his death, he writes of his love for his native city[19]

> Born, bred, brought up, and having always dwelt, in the City, I have a natural inclination to love her, as my mother, and wish sincerely for her welfare...During my poor remains of life I shall heartily wish a continuance of prosperity, and growing reputation, in all respects, to this my beloved Exeter – from which no endeavours have prevail'd to draw me away.

But these outline biographies are only examples, perhaps not chosen entirely at random, and not sufficient to prove a more general pattern. Elsewhere the closed structure of the Exeter book trades in the sixteenth to eighteenth centuries has been charted by reference to artisan dynasties constructed from freedom records.[20] Of equal interest would be the examination of a control group from a later period. The fullest listing of book-trade personnel in Exeter during the period covered by the British Book Trade Index is provided by the Census of 1851; indeed the closing date of BBTI was chosen in order that the wealth of information available from this source could be included. The Census is the only source always to give the place of birth, so that it should be possible to correlate this factor consistently with the type of business that the individuals were running.

The schedules of the census enumerators' returns for 1851 reveal 504 individuals associated with the book and paper trades in Exeter, Topsham, and the suburban parishes out of a total population of 45 388. This total included 164 papermakers employed in four mills. Apprentices are included as well as other employees; indeed 147 individuals (29 per cent) were aged under 21. There were 139 women (27 per cent of the total) employed, largely in the paper mills, where they made up well over half of the workforce. Those born outside Exeter totalled 292 (58 per cent), but many came from elsewhere within the county, only 130 (26 per cent) originating from outside Devon. Clearly it would be irrelevant to investigate all 504 individuals, most of whom, being employees or apprentices, would be in no position fundamentally to affect the nature of individual busi-nesses.

To ascertain those of the trade who were masters the names were checked against trade directories for the early 1850s. This produced 87 names, a smaller group which could be examined more closely. Of these 87 49 were born in Exeter, 16 came from elsewhere in Devon and 22 originated outside the county.

It is difficult to establish what constitutes innovation and then to identify those individuals who could be said to match the criteria, especially when all are not equally well documented. As already mentioned, success does not in itself imply innovation; an individual in 1851 could be simply benefitting from the business built up by previous members of the firm. Innovation must involve the intro-duction of new fields of book-trade activity into a locality or the application of new techniques within an existing field of activity. As most major areas of the book trade had been developed by the mid-nineteenth century, evidence of innovation would not be so striking and would normally be confined to refine-ments of an existing field of activity, frequently by the introduction of new technology.

Some degree of consistency of documentation is afforded by the fact that a newspaper for this period *Trewman's Exeter Flying Post* has been indexed in some detail by a Job Creation Project in the 1970s. The index entries were checked to see whether there were any references which could be considered out of the ordinary in any way. Using these admittedly subjective criteria certain individ-uals attracted attention.

Among printers and booksellers Thomas Howe emerges as an interesting entrepreneur, although he is not listed as a printer in the census schedules. He had begun his career as a printer and bookseller at 217 High Street in 1827, but in 1831 he moved his premises to 207 High Street, where the rapid development in his business began. He designated his emporium as the 'Exeter Bazaar' and experimented with a variety of means of attracting customers to his premises, which now included a wide range of stationery and fancy goods, such as work boxes, writing desks, dressing cases, tea caddies, cabinets, and toys. The January sale was one means of enticement and an advertisement for the 1837 sale on 26 January includes the postscript 'the Chinese juggler continues to attract attention and is universally admired'. But Howe's main attraction, the Cosmorama, was open gratis only to those who spent more than one shilling at the Bazaar. In the middle of March 1835 the newspapers announced the opening of this permanent exhibition of panoramas at Howe's Bazaar. It included initially the House of Lords on fire, Calais Pier, Cowes, the Needles, Tintern Abbey, and St. Michael's Mount. Howe changed the selection every few months, and the Cosmorama remained a feature of Exeter life until his death in 1856, from 1836 being known as Howe's Gothic Gallery.[21]

Thomas Latimer was the most progressive Exeter newspaper editor in the mid-nineteenth century. Not only had he built up the *Western Times* to be the leading radical newspaper in Exeter, but shortly after being placed in charge of it in 1835 he introduced a steam-driven machine constructed by Dryden and Sons of London which was able to produce 1400 copies per hour. This innovation was a major factor in the newspaper's increasing its circulation by 1850 to almost 4000 copies a week, a figure sixty per cent above its nearest rival.[22]

Among printers perhaps Besley was the most innovative in Exeter during the 1840s. It was he who became the only significant Devon publisher of small steel-engraved vignette views. The earliest major publisher in this field was J Harwood of London, who between 1851 and 1854 published well over one thousand views in his numbered series *Scenery of Great Britain*, about 40 of them covering Devon. He was followed by Kershaw and Son, who published a similar number of vignettes between 1845 and 1860. The most successful national publisher in this field was William Frederick Rock, a Barnstaple man who sought his fortune in London, and began his series in 1848. This would eventually include some 7000 views, 260 of them of Devon scenes.

In 1848, the same year as Rock began his series, Besley began to publish a series of larger vignettes, mainly by the local artist George Townsend. In the years to 1871 this ran to about 100 views of Devon and Cornwall. A smaller series was introduced in 1853 and by about 1875 the numbering had reached 215. These vignettes were sold individually or in albums, and were also used as letter headings. Besley also experimented with tinted versions of the plates, often used in his 'Route Books', a series of guidebooks of Devon and Cornwall which he began to publish in 1844, the year when the railway reached Exeter. Each guidebook included an account of the sights to be seen from the recently con-structed railway lines and here too Besley was innovative in promptly meeting a new local demand.[23]

James Bannehr was born in London in about 1810 according to the 1851 census. He is not recorded by Twyman in his directory of London lithographic prin-ters,[24] but Bannehr takes pains to stress his London origins in an advertisement in *Trewman's Exeter Flying Post* on 28 July 1836. Directories list him as a law stationer, a lithographer and share broker trading in Bedford Street, Exeter, from about 1835. The directory entries and advertisements suggest that he was probably one of the first in Exeter who used the relatively new technique of lithography for legal forms rather than for illustrations. The first lithographer in Exeter had been Thomas Bayley whose shortlived establishment seems to have been mainly used for illustrations in 1827.

In the early 1850s Owen Angel was experimenting with a new form of illustration, photography. He is first listed in trade directories as an engraver and printer, but on 26 March 1846 an advertisement in *Trewman's Exeter Flying Post* notes that he had added lithography to his skills, and on 4 January 1855 another advertisement in the same newspaper tells us that photographic portraits were being taken daily. On 22 November 1855 he was advertising stereoscopic prints of local views, which he had taken during that summer. At about this time he established the West of England Photographic Institute and photography came to play an increasingly important part in his business. Newspapers report his winning several prizes and in the 1880s he opened a gallery. Beginning as an engraver he became one of Exeter's earliest and most successful photographers.

Of these five only one, Besley, was born in Exeter. Two were born elsewhere in Devon, Howe in Tiverton and Angel in Totnes; the other two were born outside the county, Bannehr in London and Latimer in Bristol. Of another ten who seemed to emerge with some individuality from the newspaper references around the time of the 1851 census only one was born in Exeter, five coming from outside Devon. It is not possible here to examine the careers of these and other members of the Exeter book trades in detail, and this investigation does not lay claim to any scientific accuracy, being subjective and impressionistic in many ways. Nevertheless it is striking that, while over half the persons listed in both the 1851 census of Exeter as well as in trade directories were born in the City, only two of the fifteen identified as innovative were natives of Exeter. It should be added that, although the census had been transcribed before the biographical details were analysed, a full correlation of places of birth as given in the census was not undertaken until after the analysis to avoid being influenced by the available data.

The image of the wandering printers who set up their presses in a hundred towns across fifteenth-century Europe is one that is fixed in the consciousness of all who study the history of printing. In the very earliest years printing was spread by Germans, not locally born individuals who visited Germany to receive instruction. Germans were responsible for the introduction of printing into Italy in 1465, Switzerland in 1468, France in 1470, and Spain and Poland in 1473. This was in part because of the secrecy in which the black art was shrouded in its infancy, but even later migrant workers were instrumental in spreading new ideas in the book trades. This is particularly true in England where aliens accounted for two-thirds of the book-trade personnel in the years to 1535, Exeter's Martin Coeffin being one of them. William Caxton is unusual in being a native of the country to which he introduced printing and there is no other native English printer recorded with certainty until Robert Copeland, twenty years after Caxton's death. What is equally remarkable is to see the importance of mobility for innovation in the book trades surviving into nineteenth-century provincial England. The effects are not so dramatic or easy to quantify, because it is not normally completely new practices that are being introduced but refinements of existing ones. Nevertheless it does underline the importance of tracing links and movements between one locality and another within the book trade. The realisation of this should influence the type of information to be given priority in the all-too-brief notes field in the British Book Trade Index record. The place of birth, the name and residence of the master to whom the individual was apprenticed and a note of other localities where he or she is recorded, all these are crucial to charting the development of the book trade.

It is a major function of the British Book Trade Index to look across local boundaries and reconstruct this network of connections. In doing so it is making an important contribution towards understanding the processes involved in the spread of print culture.

NOTES

1. George Oliver, *The Lives of the Bishops of Exeter* (Exeter, William Roberts, 1861), pp 323–74.

2. Nicholas Orme, 'Martin Coeffin, the first Exeter publisher', *The Library*, 6th ser, vol 3 (1988), pp 223–30.

3. Ian Maxted, *The Devon Book Trades: a Biographical Dictionary* (Exeter, Maxted [forthcoming]). The entries on Darker and Farley owe much to Professor Michael Treadwell.

4. *International Genealogical Index*. Microfiche index of baptisms and marriages produced by the Church of Jesus Christ of the Latter Day Saints.

5. *Exeter in the Seventeenth Century: Tax and Rate Assessments 1602–1699*, edited by W G Hoskins (Exeter, Devon and Cornwall Record Society, 1957).

6. G A Cranfield, *The Development of the Provincial Newspaper 1700–1760* (Oxford, Clarendon Press, 1978), pp 56–61. R M Wiles, *Freshest Advices* (Columbus, Ohio State University Press, 1965).

7. Copy in Westcountry Studies Library which may be incomplete.

8. Wiles (see note 6).

9. John Ingle Dredge, *Devon Booksellers and Printers in the 17th and 18th Centuries* (Privately printed, 1885-91).

10. For example see C H Timperley, *Encyclopedia of Literary and Typographical Anecdote* (London, H.G.Bohn, 1842), p 795.

11. Michael Perkin, 'Egerton Smith and the early nineteenth century book trade in Liverpool', in *Spreading the Word: the Distribution Networks of Print* (Winchester, St Pauls Bibliographies, [forthcoming]).

12. R A J Potts, 'Early Cornish Printers, 1740-1850' *Journal of the Royal Institution of Cornwall*, new ser, vol 4 (1963), pp 307-9. Timperley (see note 10), p 893.

13. J V Somers Cocks, *Devon Topographical Prints 1660-1870: a Catalogue and Guide* (Exeter, Devon Library Services, 1977), pp 12, 238, 244-5 etc.

14. Edmund Butcher, *The Beauties of Sidmouth Displayed*, 2nd edition. (Sidmouth, Wallis, [1820?]).

15. Ian Maxted, *The London Book Trades 1775-1800: a Preliminary Checklist of Members* (Folkestone, Dawson, 1977), p 237.

16. Devon Record Office, Exeter City Archives (Court of Orphans) book 144, p 129.

17. There is an entry for Dyer in the *Dictionary of National Biography*.

18. T N Brushfield, 'Andrew Brice and the Early Exeter Newspaper press', *Transactions of the Devonshire Association*, vol 20 (1888), pp 163-214. This is outdated on the earliest newspapers in Exeter.

19. Andrew Brice, *The Mobiad; or, Battle of the Voice* (Exeter, Brice and Thorn, 1770), p xviii.

20. Ian Maxted, 'Work in Progress on the Provincial Book Trades', in *Report of Seminar on the Provincial Book Trade, University of Loughborough 12 July 1983* (Newcastle upon Tyne, History of the Book Trade in the North, 1983), pp 5-8.

21. Samuel Smiles, 'Panoramas in Exeter 1816-1864', *Newsletter of the International Panorama and Diorama Society*, new ser, vol 5, no 2 (1989), p 6-9.

22. Richard S Lambert, *The Cobbett of the West: a Study of Thomas Latimer and the Struggle between Pulpit and Press at Exeter* (London, Nicholson and Watson, 1939), pp 97-8, 123-4 etc.

23. Somers Cocks (see note 13), pp 9-11, 304-8.

24. Michael Twyman, 'A directory of London lithographic printers 1800-1850', *Journal of the Printing Historical Society*, 10 (1974-75), pp 1-55.

Cross-Regional Connexions

P J WALLIS

This paper intends to investigate the claim that 'the whole structure of the trade had evolved to take books from London to the provinces, and not in the opposite direction'. This statement emphasises the predominance of the London trade and suggests that there can be no independent provincial trading and that any provincial initiative has necessarily to finish up in London.[1] It also neglects the fact that some London tradesmen migrated from the provinces and maintained their home roots, but this factor will not be explored here.

It is very easy for a local historian to become familiar with local sources and records and not look elsewhere. This preliminary study will consider some of the connexions away from the home base. Clearly it would be inadequate to consider towns like Newcastle and Gateshead, just on opposite sides of the river, as different, although they are in different counties (in this study the recent county changes will be neglected). Local studies often quote connexions within the same county between towns such as Birmingham and Coventry, Leeds and Bradford, or Liverpool and Manchester. The title 'cross-regional' indicates that consideration is being given to tradesmen living further afield, although no precise definition of the regions considered is attempted. A few examples from Ireland, Scotland and Wales will be included, without wishing to deny these countries their national status; it would also be possible to consider America in a similar way.[2]

A few words about London may help, as our study is considering the differing importance of the metropolis and the provinces. If two tradesmen, say B and X in different regions, were each connected with L in London, it would be possible to argue that these latter connexions through L were more important than the direct B–X, so such cases will be excluded. It would also be possible to distinguish between local and national London tradesmen and so include, say, Hampstead and Guildford. Further the London connexion could be merely token and some such examples wil be mentioned later, but the study will be kept simple by largely excluding London cases.

Both personal biographical relations and subsequent commercial relations, as shown by imprints and other bibliographical features, will be considered. An interesting example is provided by John Clay of Daventry (1713–1775). Like many others he moved from his home at Derby into another region for his apprenticeship to a Daventry bookseller, whom he succeeded. His customers came from a wide area, including Lutterworth in his home region, where he opened a branch shop; there were also branches at Rugby and Warwick, in a third region, where he was helped by his three sons, Samuel (1744–1800), William and Thomas (1758–1781), who succeeded briefly at Daventry. The story affords an interesting example of cross-regional connexions of a firm, which were strengthened, as is often the case, by the participation of more than one generation.[3]

The so-called 'eccentric' Market Harborough bookseller and printer, William Harrod, was responsible for partly editing and publishing local histories at Stamford, of which town he became an alderman, Mansfield, and his home town. His first publication, a poem, even suggests that he moved to Sevenoaks after his journeyman service in London. There seems enough evidence to consider his career as cross-regional, whatever definition of the regions is favoured.[4]

Let us now consider Samuel Terry, known as the founder in 1712 of the first but short-lived Liverpool newspaper, the *Courant*, and so a subject for the Liverpool group. It records his move to Cork for a year or two and then to Limerick for 1722–5, quoting Plomer and Lancastrian sources. Munter gives a similar account with more detail, but surprisingly does not quote from Robert Herbert's standard work for the Limerick book trade, although this is used for other biographies. Herbert had suggested that Terry was apprenticed at Limerick, receiving his Freedom in 1680, but had no facts for the intervening period 1680–1710 nor for after 1727. Clearly more work is necessary, particularly to confirm the apprenticeship (and so his birth just before 1660), and whether Terry died about 1727 or moved elsewhere, but enough is known to call him a cross-regional tradesman.[5]

The reader anxious for other examples of such tradesmen will find many in our *NE Book Trade*. The printer of the Ostervald Bible, John Harrison, moved from Carlisle to Newcastle and on to London while the book was in progress. Robert Perring (1787–1869) was a younger Carlisle man, who had a spell at Leeds before coming to Newcastle, like his partner John Hernaman; the former moved to London but returned to Carlisle and was best-known as a newspaper editor and proprietor. It seems that editors were more mobile than ordinary tradesmen and it is worth noting that Boase often gives biographies of cross-regional men; a similar example was W W Fyfe (1817–1867) who moved from Berwick to Paisley, Dorchester and Glasgow. William Fordyce came to Newcastle after experience in London and Paris; he had considerable influence in Newcastle and had branch shops at North Shields and Hull. David Bass and Gilbert Gray both came to Newcastle from Scotland, and John Soulby came from Ulverston to Barnard Castle. Lewis Pennington (1755–1826) went from Kendal to York and on to

Durham where he died; his example illustrates the importance of records of local freedoms, many of which have been published, in recording migrating trade- smen. John Blackwell (1792–1872) was a newspaper publisher in Sheffield and Newcastle. The final example illustrates some of the difficulties inevitable with migrations, as it is not certain that the *York Gazetteer* agent at Richmond (North Riding) in 1743 was the same Mr Bainbridge who was a Barnard-Castle booksel- ler in 1765. It will be noticed that most of the examples given are of men moving into the region, possibly because of its attraction, but partly because the deaths of many trademen are unknown, so the last-known date might simply reveal ignorance of removal to another region. In any case there are enough examples to indicate the frequency of cross-regional migrations.[6]

On the bibliographical side of this study, investigation of a particular book can be described under the following heads:

(*a*) the title-page, particularly the imprint and sometimes date;

(*b*) the title-page verso, colophon or other details supplementing (*a*);

(*c*) contemporary advertisements, including proposals and newspapers;

(*d*) additional material from the text, including preface;

(*e*) any subscription list(s), hereinafter abbreviated as SL;

(*f*) external material such as letters about publication, publishers'/printers' ledgers

This study is largely concerned with (*e*),information from subscription lists, indicating how they show concretely and in detail the books reaching the reader.

Before discussing particular subscription lists it will be helpful to make a few points. Forenames are often omitted or reduced to initials. The ordering of a list is often not strictly alphabetical, so care is necessary in searching for an entry, which could be in a list of additions at the end of the main list or elsewhere, possibly with the errata. Sometimes there are ordinary misprints and often spelling variations. In our catalogue we use the initials A and J to indicate that the entries in the subscription lists sometimes contain the subscriber's address and job or vocation, with A+ and J+ when many entries contain this information. Sometimes local addresses are to be taken from the imprint, with or without any indication. Addresses are more common than jobs, and not all booksellers are so indicated. Subscriptions for multiple copies are not always given, but should be studied when available, as they often refer to book tradesmen. Some lists have minor differences in variant issues. Sometimes lists appear in a later edition or volume of a set. Finally it must be remembered that subscription lists may take some time to complete and may include dead subscribers, and more positively that the list can be used to estimate a date omitted from the title-page.[7]

The rest of this paper will consider a number of subscription lists chosen to show how they supplement the imprint indication of the distribution process. The mentioned restriction to imprints not including London excludes many music lists and most sale catalogues (eg that for Charles Hutton in 1816 held by Leigh and Sotheby, printed by Wright and Murphy of Holborn, indicating that 1s. catalogues could be obtained at 12 booksellers all round the country).[8] Nonetheless many additions could be given to the following examples, each of which starts with the indicator and author, a short title and imprint followed by relevant points taken from the subscription list.[9]

740TRAvers,Henry *Miscellaneous Poems* York: by C Ward & R Chandler

Nearly all the 364 subscribers were from Yorkshire, like the only tradesman mentioned, the York bookseller John Hildyard, apart from Ward & Chandler described as booksellers at York and at Temple Bar, London. As there had been a 1731 London edition it is not surprising that the SL suggests that the London branch had little effect on the sales, but it draws attention to one of the few cases of London and provincial shops of the same firm rather than the usual cooperation between independent firms.

734SHOrt,Thomas ...*Mineral Waters of Derbyshire, Lincolnshire, Yorkshire* Sheffield: by John Garnet for author

The local appeal suggested by the imprint is put in perspective by the 456/602 SL which rather naturally includes many medics from places as far apart as Chester and Liverpool, Worcester, Nottingham, Ipswich and Norwich. The distribution system is indicated by John Haxby helping at Sheffield, Lord at Wakefield, Potter[7] at Chester, Jeremiah Rowe at Derby, Martin Bryson[7] at Newcastle and by two London booksellers – John Whiston took only two copies but Fletcher Gyles with 40 was clearly more important.

767DUPont,John *Second Volume of Miscellanies* York: by N Nickson

At first glance the local Yorkshire SL is supported by the York bookseller Etherington taking three copies (Nickson the printer took only one), but there is another named bookseller, Alexander Donaldson of Edinburgh. His influence is indicated by one-tenth of the 370/385 list being from Scotland, chiefly Edinburgh, and is one of many Yorkshire-Scotland connexions, not hinted at in the imprint.

746BROwn,Christopher *Itinerarium Totius Sacrae Scripturae* York: by Thomas Gent for author

This typical imprint hides the less common topographical arrangement of this 600/626 SL. Unfortunately the local agents are not specified, but are presumably included in the list. The towns mentioned include York (54), Newcastle (53),

Scarborough (36), Halifax (26), Hull and Sunderland (24), Stockton (20), and 43 with fewer subscribers, all from Yorkshire and the north.

766CUNningham,John *Poems, Chiefly Pastoral* Newcastle: by & sold T Slack (25) for author, and sold W Charnley (12) & J Barber (6)

The strong Newcastle concentration suggested by the imprint is belied by the SL. Apart from the three Newcastle booksellers mentioned in the imprint with the indicated subscriptions, there are those at Berwick – C Buglass (28) and Alnwick – A Graham (2) with four in Co Durham each subscribing for 6 copies – Darlington: T Darnton; Durham: R Manisty; Stockton: J Pickering; and Sunderland: James Graham. At Kendal occurs James Ashburner and in Yorkshire, Bedale: C Jackson; Richmond: William Tunstal; and York: W Tesseyman and C Etherington. Further south are Cambridge: Fletcher & Hodson (6) and four at London: J Almon (25), Richardson & Urquhart (15), H Baldwin (12) and T Davies (6), not represented in the imprint and with few subscribers, perhaps because of a separate London edition. There were also few Scottish and Irish subscribers.

787BURns,Robert *Poems, Chiefly in the Scottish Dialect* Edinburgh: for author and sold William Creech

This large 1526/2876 list clearly has to be considered in relation to the contemporary London and Belfast editions, so it naturally reflects the distribution in Scotland. The leading role of Creech is indicated by his large subscription of 500 copies; he was helped by seven other book tradesmen in Edinburgh and two at Glasgow. Morison & Sons of Perth took 50 copies with others at Dumfries, Stirling, Kilmarnock and Kelso. The only two English booksellers were S Crane[6] at Liverpool and William Charnley at Newcastle; no Londoner was mentioned, and the coffee-houses listed were probably given as postal addresses.

797LLoyd,Evan *Plain System of Geography* Edinburgh: by Mundell & Son for author

These two Scottish books have similar imprints but had quite different appeals, as the Lloyd had hardly any subscribers from Scotland. Apart from the Newcastle printer Solomon Hodgson there were only four centres mentioned – Workington; William Ekford (12) and John Richardson; Whitehaven: William Reed; Wigton: Thomas Hudson; and Carlisle: Francis Jollie. One wonders how much the Northwest booksellers were aided by the author's fellow schoolmasters and former pupils, but it is clear that the Edinburgh imprint was largely token as regards distribution.

776ETHerington,Christopher *Subscribers to the York Chronicle*

This long 2230 list occurs in the 14 & 21 June issues of the paper. Unfortunately the list consists of names only (often surnames only), without addresses or jobs, but next to it is an analysis of the circulation with several town and villages grouped round the main centres: York 273, Boroughbridge 265, Sheffield 204, Stockton 128, Gainsborugh 89, Richmond 88 and Lincoln 75...finishing with Durham & Sunderland 36 and Newcastle and further north 14. The close connexion between newsagents and booksellers has often been emphasised, but much work will be necessary to analyse this long list before it can be concluded how much this was the case with this largely Yorkshire list, with some readers from the neighbouring counties of Lincolnshire, Nottinghamshire and Durham.[10]

770BROoks,Jonathan *Antiquity; or the Wise Instructer* Bristol: by S Farley for editor

773BROoks,Jonathan   (2) York: by N Nickson for editor

It is convenient to take together these two similar but separate lists, 1937/1957 and 1785/1909, for the first two editions of this popular collection edited by the Bristol Quaker, because they both exhibit many, but different, cross-regional connexions. The preliminary analysis made so far could be greatly strengthened by researchers with Quaker knowledge and the conclusion confirmed by pro-pinquity analysis (see later). Meanwhile the following towns are represented by tradesmen subscriptions to 773BRO: Alnwick: Alex Graham (6); Carlisle: Alexander Campbell (6); Carmarthen: J Ross; Daventry: John Clay (see above); Durham: Richard Manisty (2); Halifax: William Edwards; Market Harborough: Mrs Mary Ratten; Hull: John Ferraby; Kendal; William Pennington (2); Lancaster: Anthony Ashburner (3); Liverpool: John Gore (6) and John Sibbald (6); New-castle: David Akenhead (6), Joseph Atkinson, Joseph Barber (6) and William Charnley; Nottingham: Samuel Cresswell; Penrith: Anthony Soulby (2); Preston: William Street (2); Ripon: Richard Beckwith; Scarborough: Thomas Craven; Spalding; John Albin; Stockton: Richard Christopher (2); Sunderland: Henry Beighton (6) and James Graham (6); Whitehaven; John Dunn (6), Matthew Little (6), John Ware & Son; and York: William Tesseyman (25). London has only John Millan (6), John Rivington (6) and William Trickett (3), with comparatively few other subscribers. While there was concentration on Yorkshire (note the large Tesseyman subscription), subscribers also came from a distance, Scotland, Lancashire, even a few from Wales and some from Bristol despite the 1770 Bristol list. That list covers the West (Bath, Bristol, Cirencester, Exeter, Salisbury & Sherborne), South and Midlands (Walsall & Wolverhampton) areas and as far north as Manchester (John Prescott); booksellers are not indicated in the list but some have been identified. Topographically the lists have a small overlap and they show similar patterns for the Southwest and Northeast.

771EVAns,William *New English-Welsh Dictionary* Carmarthen: for John Ross & Richard Rhyobro; sold Raikes (Glocester); D Lewis (Bristol); Jones (Brecon); Beadles (Pontypool); D Morgan (Neath); D Evans (Swansea); Samuel Evans (Lanwenog); J James (Aberystwyth); W Jones (Bala); & Allen (Haverfordwest).

This long imprint contrasts with, but supplements, the short SL, which indicates the subscriber's address but not his job, so other booksellers may not have surfaced; the subscribers come from all over Wales, including one at Salisbury and the Bristol merchant in the imprint, David Lewis.[11]

A similar Scottish subscription list is

805WITherspoon,John *Works*, vol ix Edinburgh: for Ogle & Aikman, J Pillan & Son, J Ritchie & J Turnbull

There are two London booksellers, Robert Ogle(25) and T Williams(25), in this list, but all the other nineteen are from Scottish towns, as are nearly all the other subscribers. Clearly this list is useful for connexions between Scottish booksellers, but for little outside.

782HOOd,Robert *Fourteen Sermons* Newcastle: by T Saint, sold E Humble; also Graham (Sunderland); Thorne (Durham); Christopher (Stockton); Binns (Leeds); Smith (Bradford); Spence (York); Brown (Hull); Clark (Whitby); Roddam (N Shields); W Pennington (Kendal); & R Baldwin (London)

The SL of this book by the Newcastle unitarian minister mentions that the subscribers were from Newcastle except when stated, so there is less doubt than in most topographical analyses. Apart from Newcastle there are only three towns with more than five subscribers out of the total 199, all less than 10% of those at Newcastle, viz Leeds (14), Brampton (12) and Wakefield (8), where sales were possibly promoted by the unitarian ministers. The SL does not suggest that the London Baldwin was an effective salesman. The dominance of the Newcastle subscribers is very obvious and the West-Riding shops seem to have been more successful than those in Co Durham – perhaps because readers there could get copies quite easily from Newcastle after the SL was closed.

A)793 – A *Anthologia Hibernica i* Dublin: for Richard Edward Mercier

In this case, as for many Dublin SLs, it is probable that subscribers without a stated town were from Dublin. The Irish towns in the list are given below and special reasons seem to account for the Perth (Morison & Son) and Utrecht (Wild & Altheer), as for the two London shops, Faulder and Robinsons.

B)793MALlet,David *Works of... Viscount Bolingbroke* Dublin: by P.Byrne

C)794PAyne[X],John *Universal Geography* Dublin: by Zachariah Jackson

D)799GAHan,William *Sermons and Moral Discourses* Dublin: by T M'Donnel

The main subscribers were: at Dublin Hugh Fitzpatrick (150), Richard Cross (25), and Pat Wogan (25); at Clonmel Thomas Gorman (25); and at Cork James Haly (25).

E)800CRUttwell,Clement *New Universal Gazetteer, or, Geographical Dictionary* Dublin: by & sold John Stockdale

These five subscription lists all have a single tradesman in the imprint, but the many booksellers in the SLs, summarised below, refute the suggestion that they had 'a very restricted local circulation'. The letters indicate that booksellers from the specified town appeared in one or more of the above SLs indicated A, B, C, D, E and the figures show when there was more than one shop. Athlone A; Belfast A, 3C, E; Carlow E; Clonmell D, E; Coleraine B, C, E; Cork C, D, 2E; Derry A, B, E; Downpatrick 2A; Drogheda E; Dublin 18A, 11B, 27C, 4D, 20E (total 44); Galway A, E; Kilkenny A, B; Limerick 2A, E; Mullingar C; Newry A , B, C, E; Portarlington A; Sligo B, C; Tralee C; Waterford B, E; Youghall C.[12]

The Dublin 1807 edition of Thomas Ward's *Errata of the Protestant Bible*, printed by Richard Coyne, has a subscription list of less than 400 subscribers, many with Dublin addresses and a number from Maynooth, the Catholic college. It includes a hundred from the Catholic bookseller Hugh Fitzpatrick and 50 copies for James Hely, the Cork bookseller. These are insignificant compared with 1000 copies for [P] Keating, [R] Brown & Co, who appear in the imprint with their address, Duke Street, Grosvenor Square. It would be interesting to have details of the English network which enabled them to sell twice as many copies as in Ireland; it would seem likely that priests were more responsible than booksellers. The 1810 Belfast edition of Andrew M'Kenzie's *Poems and Songs* has a long list of over 2000 subscribers mainly with Irish addresses, but few vocations. It surprisingly finishes with two pages from Scotland and one from Jamaica. The link is not obvious and more work is needed to assess the significance of these unexpected cross-country connexions.[13]

813YOUle,Joseph *Arithmetical Preceptor, or...Arithmetic* Sheffield: by J Montgomery for author; and Longman, Hurst, Rees, Orme & Brown (London)

Once again the London names in the imprint are not supported by entries in the SL. The large number of multiplicities is headed by three entries, one of 50 to a local bookseller, Thomas Orton, and the other two of 50 and 80, like many of the smaller multiplicities, are to teachers of mathematics. It seems probable that many of them bought copies for their students – the title-page explained that the book was designed for the scholars. The more usual arrangement was for individual students to subscribe for books. As nearly all the subscribers were from Sheffield and south Yorkshire, with only a few from the neighbouring counties of Nottinghamshire and Derbyshire, Longmans played only a token role. There were two personal subscriptions from Philadelphia but no evidence of American promotion.

Job Orton's *Short and Plain Exposition of the Old Testament*, 6 vol, 1788–91, with an imprint 'Shrewsbury: by & sold J & W Eddowes, sold also [named booksellers in] London', has been quoted as an example of a country book with a wide distribution through subscription publication. The distribution of subscribers to the first volume is described verbally and analysed according to the eleven regions in a table giving the number of subscribers from 180 different towns in the regions. Omitting the two northern regions with few entries the figures are given in Table 1.

The third line shows the spread of subscribers around the regions with the highest in the West Midlands, the region containing Shrewsbury, and less than half elsewhere – the West region is dominated by Bristol, and the London figures are exaggerated by including eight other counties with London and Middlesex.[14] Similar tables could be constructed for other subscription lists, but comparison by inspection would be difficult. It is much easier using a *propinquity index*, measuring the regional distribution of readers and showing how close the readers were to the 'home' region, in this case West Midlands. The index would give a result of 1 if all the books were sold in the home region, and is reduced as the readers live further and further away. The key to the calculation is given in line 4 with the inter-regional coefficients. These form a geometric series 1, 0.5, 0.25, 0.125 etc (the common ratio being arbitrarily taken as 0.5) descending from 1 for the home region, with adjacent regions being 0.5, and those further away and adjacent to these 0.25, and so on; thus the coefficient for the West Riding is half that for Nottingham (East Midlands). The last line is obtained by multiplying these coefficients by the number of subscribers. Finally the total of the products is divided by the number of subscribers to give the weighted average or index, 298.1 divided by 557 giving 0.54. The claim that the 'excellent…London publishers' were more responsible than those of the West Midlands, doubtful from the table, is not confirmed by a smaller index of 0.31 calculated using London as the 'home' region.[15]

These results can be compared with those for another provincial/country book, the *Treatise on Mensuration* by the Newcastle mathematician and later FRS, Charles Hutton, issued in parts 1768–70 with a final imprint 'Newcastle: by T

TABLE 1

Region	London	West Midlands	East Midlands	South Midlands	East Anglia	West Riding	Lancs Cheshire	West	Wales	Total
No of towns	22	44	18	12	12	11	13	24	22	174
Subscribers	76	191	26	40	26	48	41	75	34	557
Coefficients	0.25	1	0.5	0.5	0.25	0.25	0.25	0.125	0.5	—
Products	19	191	13	20	6.5	12	10.25	9.375	17	298.1

Propinquity Index is 298.1 divided by 557 = 0.54

Saint for author; sold J Wilkie and Richard Baldwin (London)'. Neglecting entries with unknown addresses, sales of 539 copies were made over twelve regions ranging from Dundee to Penzance. It is not surprising to find a larger index (of 0.63) than for Orton, the dominance of Newcastle being even greater than that of Shrewsbury in the Orton list. Again the London influence was less, 32 sales out of 539 compared with 3 out of 23 for Orton. An obvious difference between the two lists was the presence of many schoolmasters and the absence of booksellers (only C Etherington of York) in the Hutton list. The inclusion of the Pelman Street Mathematical Society and the knowledge of Hutton's later leadership of the philomathic movement suggest that wide circulation of the book was partly due to these teachers.[16]

In conclusion, it is hoped that enough subscription lists have been briefly discussed to see how much care is necessary to avoid misleading interpretations of imprints in considering distribution of sales. In many cases 'London' in an imprint has been shown to be only token. The importance of provincial/country imprints has been examined and it is clear that there was a flourishing provincial trade encompassing more than one region. To facilitate comparison between different subscription lists the theory of a propinquity index has been sketched and some preliminary results obtained.

NOTES

NB If a work is referred to more than once the full details are given in the Bibliography, which includes all the PHIBB items with short references like B75 and its revision P370.

1. The Durham Jubilee Seminar seems an apt occasion not only to look at develop-ments in different regions, but also to assess the significance of the activities of the many groups taken together and in particular to relate provincial and metropolitan developments. There is a 'hidden agenda' which needs to be made clear, a problem which is also met in other studies including mathematics and medicine (P350 & P360). The textual quotation is taken from John Feather's recent book (p 75, but cf pp 61, 115, 120), a well-researched wide-sweeping survey which can be consulted for a fuller exposition of some points below.

2. Cole has assembled much material about Irish emigration to America. One of his examples, Robert Bell, born in Glasgow, practised in Berwick, went to Ireland in 1759 and then in 1767 to Philadelphia until his death in 1784 (*DAB*). Plomer notices Mesphet Fleury who moved from France to London to Philadelphia and Montreal. John March of Yarmouth and Norwich went to America and died in Washington (Fawcett). Joseph Gales (1761–1841) of Newark, founder of the reforming *Sheffield Register* fled to Germany and on to Raleigh, North Carolina, where he founded the *Raleigh Register*, before moving to Washington (Timperley p 761, *DAB*).

3. Professional, political, religious and social relations will all appear (Wiles, Feather p 93). John Feather, 'John Clay of Daventry' *Studies in Bibliography*, vol xxxvii (1984) pp 198-209; P260, P369. For printing dynasties see Cranfield p 56. Many studies like Adams have shown how booksellers supplemented their business by acting also as postmasters, grocers, patent-medicine sellers, &c.

4. *DNB*, Timperley p 869, Pendred, Feather pp 80, 112-13, P369.

5. Liverpool Bibliographical Society. Robert Herbert, *Limerick Printers and Printing*, Limerick Public Library, 1942. Munter, Feather. Since the last sentence was drafted the Limerick City Library has kindly informed me of the birth in Cork in 1657 and the death in Limerick in 1729 of Samuel Terry.

6. Christopher J Hunt, *Book Trade in Northumberland and Durham* (Newcastle, 1975), with *Supplement*, (P269) and P268. F Boase, *Modern English Biography*, 6 vol (reprint 1965). J H E Bennett, *The Rolls of the Freemen of...Chester* (Birkenhead, 1906-8). P H Hartopp, *Register of the Freemen of Leicester*, 2 vol (Leicester, 1927-33). C H Jenkinson, *Surrey Apprenticeships from...the Public Record Office, 1711-1731* (Surrey Record Society, 1929). A M Oliver, *The Register of Freemen of Newcastle...of the Eighteenth Century* (Newcastle, 1926). Gertrude Thrift, *Roll of Freemen. City of Dublin*, 4 vol *1575-1770 (Dublin, 1919)*. C C B Watson, *Register of Edinburgh Apprentices 1701-1755* (Scottish Record Society, vol lxi, 1929). C C B Watson, *Roll of Edinburgh Burgesses...1701-60* (and *1761-1841*) (Scottish Record Society, vols lxii, lxviii, 1930-3). Marguerite Wood, *Register of Edinburgh Apprenticeships 1756-1800* (Scottish Record Society, vol xcii, 1963).

7. The simplest introduction to subscription lists is still P196, but many other items are included in P356, which has a brief subject index. Each list is identified by a brief indicator of three figures giving the date (omitting the 1 of the thousand), followed by three letters, usually the first three of the author's name – to make the identification unique occasionally the last letter is altered (eg 794PAX below). The catalogue of lists in B75 is shortly to be greatly supplemented by P370. P350 & P368 and P360 contain mathematical and medical subscribers and subscription-list titles, and P369 includes subscriptions for book tradesmen.

8. Plomer includes many tradesmen who in 1749 sold sale catalogues of Thomas Warren, a Birmingham bookseller, and Fawcett (p 7) quotes Richard Beatniffe's 1787 catalogue of four individuals.

9. Plomer, Feather, Cole and Munter, and publications of the various regional groups give details of many tradesmen mentioned; older books like Timperley often have useful information. Details of many York tradesmen are in W K & E M Sessions, *Printing in York* (York, 1976). Entries like 456/602 indicate the numbers of subscribers and subscriptions, different when multiplicities are recorded; it may be useful to remember that the average subscription list had just over 300 subscribers, but a few had ten times as many. Imprints are not verbatim but organised in the form 'by X, for Y, sold Z' with printers, publishers and booksellers in order but with combinations shown; semi-colons separate tradesmen from different (indicated) towns.

10. eg Cranfield, Feather, Pendred, Wiles.

11. Eiluned Rees, *Libri Walliae*, 2 vol in 1 (Aberystwyth: National Library of Wales, 1987), has useful book-trade appendices/indexes pp 845-923, which have been

published in the same author's *The Welsh Book-Trade before 1820* (Aberystwyth: National Library of Wales, 1988).

12. Feather p 110. The five Dublin lists included are only a small sample of those known (P370), so that the summary could easily be extended in period and quantity. Even so, only about half the Dublin tradesmen occur in Cole; Pollard p 183 gives the totals from 1760 rising to 40–50 in the last decade of the century, and about as many printers. Few of the other centres are noticed by Cole, who has only the last list (E) in his incomplete listing. Adams discusses a few Belfast lists, but space precludes their discussion here.

13. A start could be made with some quite high multiplicities recorded by American booksellers. Pollard pp 152-3.

14. Feather (pp 114–5, 140) bases his analysis on the subscription list in vol i, not on the complete list in the final volume, so our figures for 791ORT differ.

15. For such a calculation the important first two figures in lines 4 & 5 would change as follows: the coefficients in line 4 would simply reverse, and the products in line 5 would be 76 and 48 in place of 19 and 191.

16. Compare 813YOU above. B52 outlines briefly the philomathic movement.

REFERENCES

J R R Adams, *Printed Word and the Common Man* (Belfast, 1987)

Birmingham Bibliographical Society, *Working Papers for an Historical Directory of the West Midlands*, nos 1–7 (in progres), 1975–87

H Carter, *Guildford Freeman's Books 1655–1933* (Guildford, 1963)

Richard Cargil Cole, *Irish Booksellers and English Writers 1740–1800* (London, 1986)

F Collins, *Register of the Freemen of..York, vol ii 1559–1759* (Surtees Society vol cii, 1900)

G A Cranfield, *Development of the Provincial Nnewspaper* (Oxford, 1962)

DAB Dictionary of American Biography, 20 vols (London, [1928-36]), edited by A Johnson and others

DNB Dictionary of National Biography, 22 vols (London, 1901–09), edited by L Stephen & S Lee

Trevor Fawcett, 'Eighteenth-century Norfolk booksellers: a survey and register', *Transactions of the Cambridge Bibliographical Society* vol 1 (1972), pp 1–18

John P Feather, *Provincial Book Trade in Eighteenth-Century England* (Cambridge, 1985)

Liverpool Bibliographical Society, *Book Trade in Liverpool to 1805* (Book Trade in the North West Project Occasional Publications, 1981)

Robert Munter, *Dictionary of the Print Trade in Ireland 1550–1775 (New York, 1988)*

John Pendred, *Earliest Directory of the Book Trade...1785*, edited by Graham Pollard (Bibliographical Society, 1955) (contains much material besides the directory)

Project for Historical Biobibliography (PHIBB)

B52 'British philomaths – mid-eighteenth century and earlier', *Centaurus*, vol xvii (1973)

B75 *Book Subscription Lists: a Revised Guide*, 1975;   with 4 Supplements (see P370)

P196 *Book Subscriptions – Progress and Plans   –1972–1975–197– , 1979*

P260 *Eighteenth-century British Books: an Author Union Catalogue*, 5 vols (Folkestone, 1981)

P268 *North-east Book Trade to 1860: Imprints and Subscriptions, 2nd edn, 1981*

P269 *Book Trade in Northumberland and Durham to 1860: a Supplement to C J Hunt's Biographical Dictionary* (Newcastle, 1981)

P350 *Biobibliography of British Mathematics and its Applications*, Part II, 1701–1760

P356 *Publications in Historical Biobibliography*, 3rd edn (replacing P215), August 1987

P360 *Eighteenth Century Medics (Subscriptions, Licences, Apprenticeships), 2nd edn, 1988*

P368 *Index of British Mathematicians*, Part III, 1701–1800

P369 *Eighteenth Century Book Trade Index of Imprints and Subscriptions*, 2nd edn, 1977

P370 *Book Subscription Lists Guide* (to replace B75 & 4 Supplements)

H R Plomer, *A Dictionary of the Printers and Booksellers...1668 to 1725* (and *1726 to 1775*) (London, 1922, 1932)

Mary Pollard, *Dublin's Trade in Books 1550–1800* (Oxford, 1989)

C H Timperley, *Dictionary of Printers and Printing* (London, Edinburgh, Glasgow, Dublin & Manchester, 1839)

Roy McKeen Wiles, *Freshest Advices: Early Provincial Newspapers in England* (Ohio, 1965)

The Welsh Printing House from 1718 to 1818

EILUNED REES

On first sight, the choice of dates, 1718 and 1818, may appear arbitrary. 1718 is, however, a vital date in the history of the Welsh booktrade since it witnessed the advent of commercial printing to Wales and 1818 rounds off the first century of printing.[1] In 1718, a press was set up in the village of Trefhedyn in Cardiganshire by a literary man, Isaac Carter. By 1818, every town in Wales had at least one printing-establishment and they were run by professional printers. Carter's motivation for setting up a press was concern for the souls of his fellow-countrymen who were inadequately supplied with edifying literature. The printers who were in business in 1818, although they too produced many religious books, were primarily commercially-minded businessmen.

Although printing had reached Wales in 1718, the number of books produced in the country during the first half of the eighteenth century was minimal compared with the output of Welsh books in Shrewsbury and London. The first generation of Welsh printers were amateurs, men who learned just enough of the craft to get by. The presswork was poor, the inking erratic, a sense of design non-existent. Nevertheless, their efforts are to be admired; it was no mean achievement for someone like Carter to print books of over 300 pages.

Carter moved from Trefhedyn to Carmarthen in 1725, where Nicholas Thomas, who had encouraged him in his printing venture, had established a press of his own. Printing continued uninterrupted in Carmarthen, but elsewhere in Wales printing enterprises sprang up only to wither when the founders died or lost interest. The antiquary, Lewis Morris, had ambitious schemes for printing, but all that materialised was one issue of a periodical *Tlysau yr Hen Oesoedd* (*Gems of Ancient Times*), printed in 1735 on the press he had at his home in Holyhead, Anglesey. In 1759, John Rowland, a schoolteacher, set up a press in Bodedern, also in Anglesey, which he moved to Bala, Merioneth, a couple of years later, and which was abandoned on his death.

In the 1740s, the early Methodists set up a press in Pontypool, operated by Samuel and Felix Farley of Bristol and the London bookseller, Samuel Mason. In this instance, the printers were professionals, but the venture still lasted barely two years.

In the second half of the eighteenth century, printing became a familiar feature of Welsh life. People became accustomed to having their printing needs met

101

locally. In 1762, a Scotsman, John Ross, came to Carmarthen, to join Rhys Thomas, who had been printing there since 1760. Their partnership did not last long; Thomas moved to Llandovery and later Cowbridge. Ross, however, stayed in Carmarthen, proclaiming himself the only printer in the area who had been properly brought up in the craft.[2] The professional had arrived and the mere fact that a man who had spent seven years as overseer of a printing-house in London chose to move to a country town in Wales shows how prospects had improved.

Once a professional had come on the scene, the days of the amateur were numbered, though the transition did not take place overnight; the first printers in Wrexham (1772) and Trefriw (1776), Richard Marsh and David Jones respectively, were booksellers, while the first printer in Dolgellau (1798), Thomas Williams, was a drover and the first in Machynlleth (1789), Titus Evans, an exciseman. John Theophilus Potter, first printer in Haverfordwest (1779), originally came to the town with a company of comedians. Unlike the first generation of printers, however, these men established printing traditions, indeed dynasties.

The impression one gets of the amateur printing-houses is that they were 'one-man bands' and yet the mechanics of printing render it highly unlikely that one man could operate singlehanded if he was printing anything more ambitious than a small pamphlet. The low standard of presswork rules out the likelihood of employing journeymen printers and one can only assume that local labour was recruited. In contrast, by the end of the eighteenth century, evidence of well-staffed establishments may be deduced from the advertisements for both apprentices and skilled workmen which appear in newspapers.

Most, though by no means all, of the books printed in Wales in this period were in the Welsh language. The native printers tended to be Welsh-speaking but the influx of non-Welsh professional printers at the beginning of the nineteenth century raised the problem which had dogged printers of Welsh books in England and on the Continent since 1546, unfamiliarity with the language. John Ross, when advertising his business, stated that he had an overseer for the Welsh work. His most illustrious overseer was Evan Thomas, a compositor who had worked in printing offices in Shrewsbury and Chester, and who was a poet and almanacker to boot. The press established in Bala by Thomas Charles, a leading proponent of the Calvinistic Methodist cause and a founder member of the British and Foreign Bible Society, was run on a thoroughly professional basis. He had succeeded in getting as his printer Robert Saunderson, who been apprenticed to William Collister Jones in Chester, and as overseer of the Welsh work John Humphreys, who had performd the same task for the above W C Jones.

Incidentally, it seems that in due course both John Ross and Robert Saunderson learned Welsh themselves.

Wrexham was already anglicised by the eighteenth century. John Thomas had his textbook for young people, *Annerch Ieuengctyd Cymru*, printed there in 1795 by the Marsh sisters. He makes the extraordinary statement in his apology for misprints that the book had passed through the hands of eight or nine printers, of alien race, who understood not a word of Welsh.[3] The statement is extraordinary on many counts: it implies that there was a staff of eight or nine in the establishment; the term *'o estron genedl'* seems to suggest that they were English by birth rather than merely English-speaking; there was obviously no overseer for Welsh work. The Marsh business was taken over by John Painter and he had occasion to remind one of his clients, Walter Davies, in 1802 that 'for all Works printed in a Language different from the English it is a Rule in our Trade to charge 2*s.* per Sheet extra'.[4] Painter used Daniel Jones as 'corrector of the press' for Welsh work, but it is not clear from correspondence whether Daniel Jones was employed in his office or whether it was an ad-hoc arrangement.[5] Anna Tye was another woman printer in Wrexham and in 1799 she was announcing in Welsh to her friends in Wales that she could undertake printing in their own language correctly and on reasonable terms.[6]

Certain printers offered a translation service. Amongst the Cardiganshire Quarter Sessions Records is an account of the disbursements of Herbert Lloyd, Clerk of the Peace, in connection with a 'special order concerning Robberies and Burglaries' in 1786. In addition to paying John Ross £2 for printing two hundred in English and £2 for printing two hundred in Welsh, he gave Ross £1 'for having such translated into Welsh'.[7] In 1818, Samuel Williams, the Aberystwyth printer, charged three shillings for translating into Welsh 'Advice respecting the Fevers' and the following year a shilling for the Welsh version of 'Cautions to Innkeeper'.[8] In the imprint of T Collier's *Enwaediad a Bedydd* (1790), Titus Evans of Machynlleth advertises that anything can be translated from English into Welsh with care at a reasonable price.

Amongst the first of the native printers who received an apprenticeship in his own county was John Daniel. He was a Carmarthenshire farmer's son and he was taken on as apprentice by John Ross. After serving his term, he went to London to work with the King's Printers, returning to Carmarthen in 1784 to set up his own very successful firm. He, in turn, sought apprentices locally and an advertisement of his is the first relating to printing as yet unearthed in Wales. It is found in a book printed in 1787:[9]

> Wanted, as an apprentice to a printer, a smart active youth, from the country. Preference will be given to one who can read the Welsh language. Letters

directed, post paid, to J Daniel, Printer, in King-Street, Carmarthen, will be duly answered.

Three newspapers were founded in Wales at the beginning of the nineteenth century: *The Cambrian* (1804), *The Carmarthen Journal* (1810) and *The North Wales Gazette* (1808), and members of the booktrade were able to advertise more widely for staff, although they did not abandon the practise of using their own publications; John James and Samuel Williams, within a year of setting up in Aberystwyth, were seeking an apprentice by means of a note at the end of their edition of Bunyan's *Gogoniant y Deml* (1810).

The advertisements are not standard. Sometimes knowledge of Welsh is specified, as in advertisements placed by John and Charles Broster of Bangor in their *North Wales Gazette* in January 1808, 'for an apprentice to a printer...one understanding the Welsh Language grammatically will be preferred', and by Thomas Ridd of Cardiff in *The Cambrian* in October 1811

> Wanted immediately, Three Young Men, as apprentices to the printing and bookselling business. Young men who have had a classical education, and understand the Welsh language, would be preferred. They will be taken without a premium.

One wonders whether he had difficulty in attracting the right kind of young men, because when he had placed an advertisement for 'a sober, steady, active young man, as an apprentice' the previous March, he had stated that 'as he will be taken in the house as one of the family, a premium will be expected'. Thomas Jenkins of Swansea, proprietor of *The Cambrian*, also requested a premium for taking on 'a lad of a good family, and liberal education', adding that 'any lad, whose parents or guardians will advance a few hundred pounds in the business, shall immediately take a share of the same, answerable from 5 to 10 per cent. per annum'.[10] In a subsequent advertisement, he echoed John Daniel's sentiments in a rider, 'one from the country will be preferred'.[11] By 1815, he too was waiving a premium: 'premium not so much a consideration as respectability of connexion'.[12] Charles Broster of Bangor was happy with 'a moderate premium' for 'a youth of rather superior education, as an apprentice to a lucrative and respectable business'.[13]

Most apprentices were assured that they would be treated as 'one of the family'. The ages specified varied slightly: John Cheese Watkins of Abergavenny wanted his lad 'from 12 to 14',[14] while Edward Carnes of Holywell preferred one a bit older, 'a youth of about 14 or 15 years of age',[15] and John Davies of Llandeilo sought one still older, 'from 14 to 16 years of age'.[16] The average age does, however, appear to be fourteen.

Obviously, printing establishments were expanding as well as becoming professionally organised enterprises. Nevertheless, it is surprising to find someone like Thomas Ridd, who is not regarded as a major printer, taking on three apprentices in his first year. The newspapers have provided insight too into the efforts of the printers to recruit workmen who were already skilled. Wrexham printers used the pages of the *Chester Chronicle*: Anna Tye in March 1796 'Wanted immediately, a journeyman printer, that can work at case and press'; in April 1799, Richard Taylor 'Wanted immediately, two journeymen printers, who can work at case and press. Good workmen will meet with suitable wages and constant employ'. There is more uniformity in advertisements for journeymen that in those for apprentices; there was always a sense of urgency, 'wanted immediately', they were often required to work at case and press and a sober man was guaranteed constant employ and good wages. Knowledge of Welsh was sometimes stipulated: John Voss of Swansea asked for a journeyman who 'understands the Welsh language',[17] while William Williams of Brecon took no chances and advertised for 'a steady, sober man, who understands both the English and Welsh languages'.[18]

Thomas Jenkins in 1810 expressed the need for a pressman 'who perfectly understands his business, and can occasionally assist at case'.[19] Daniel and John Evans, also of Swansea, stated that they wanted 'two compositors who understand the Welsh Language' in 1806,[20] while in 1813, David Jenkin of Swansea advertised for 'two active Welsh compositors'.[21] Advertisements for pressmen or compositors occur less often than those for journeymen who could turn their hand to case and press. Rarer still are references to other members of a printing establishment; the Brosters included in an advertisement in January 1808 for a journeyman printer 'used to work at case and press' and 'an apprentice to a printer' a plea for 'a clerk who understands book-keeping and accompts'.[22] The latter post must have been a vital one in the larger establishments. John Daniel was one of the printers who prospered; he even has the rare distinction of having a street named after him in Carmarthen, John Street, and a glimpse into his life-style is provided by an advertisement in *The Cambrian* in the autumn of 1808 for 'a young man to take care of two horses, to wait occasionally at table, and who will otherwise make himself useful in the house'.[23]

Travellers in Wales sometimes commented on printing-houses but they did not give the kind of information which would delight the book-historian, such as how many presses there were and what the work-force consisted of. Edward Williams, 'Iolo Morganwg', was in Carmarthen in 1796 and in his diary he notes that[24]

> the printing office, and bookselling shop of Mr. Daniel would appear respect-
> able even in London, he prints Welsh Bibles, and many other Welsh books. Mr
> Ross another printer and bookseller, prints Welsh Bibles and other books, with
> a Welsh Magazine, &c.

We are none the wiser about the about the average size of an establishment. Although it was decreed in 1799 that presses had to be licensed, the only declaration within our period so far found is that of Thomas Roberts of Caernarfon, dated 4 November 1799, who declared 'a printing press and types for printing'.[25] The presence of press figures in certain books printed in Carmarthen by John Ross and John Evans complicates the picture instead of clarifying it. John Ross used figures 0 to 4, with 3 in different sizes or inverted. John Evans used the figures 0, 2, 3, 4, 5, 6, 7 and 9. It is unlikely that the figures were linked with presses. They could conceivably be linked with pressmen, but why use 0 and what pressman would choose the symbol of an inverted 3?

It is possible that work was farmed out to other printers if the undertaking proved too much for existing resources. Theophilus Jones's *History of the County of Brecknock* taxed the resources of the North brothers in Brecon to such a degree that he was trying to get two journeymen from Bristol for a period of at least six months to hasten the printing of the second volume in 1806.[26] Three years later, the author was complaining bitterly about one of the Bristol workmen, saying that [27]

> he drinks on one or two days in the week, and not only sins himself, but like his brother or his uncle Beelzebub seduces the other black boys; and now that the work is near a conclusion, not having employment in view, he absolutely keeps away on purpose to prevent its completion.

In the early days, printers had only one press. In South Wales, one assumes delivery would be by sea from London; in Anglesey, the links with Dublin were stronger. Lewis Morris issued in March 1732 'Proposals for erecting by subscription, a Printing Press at Lannerch-y-medd, in the Isle of Anglesey'. He specifies that the press would be new, 'after the *Dutch* fashion'. His original intention was that profits of the press would be applied towards the maintenance of John Rhydderch, a Welshman who had been a printer in Shrewsbury and who 'is now, in his old age, reduced to very low circumstances'. Presumably, John Rhydderch was to operate the press. Nothing came of the proposals but Morris got his press nonetheless, from Dublin, and a Dublin printer, J Powell, allowed one of his men to go over to Anglesey to instruct the proud proprietor in its use.[28] Reference had already been made to *Tlysau yr Hen Oesoedd*, printed on this press in Holyhead, whither Morris had moved by 1735. The press lay idle for many years. In January 1762, John Rowland had considered buying it, as letters from William Morris to his brother Lewis testify. However, he found the type too large, it was small pica he was after, but he offered to buy the wood- and stone- and iron-work without the type. He pointed out when asking what the owner would take for it that he could have a brand new press for twelve pounds.[29] Eventually, the press was bought by David Jones of Trefriw, a poet, publisher, bookseller and collector of manuscripts, who started printing in 1776. His son, Ishmael Davies, continued the business and his son John Jones transformed it. John Jones decided to get a modern press and fancied the model patented by Alexander Ruthven in 1813. It seems he built most of his Ruthven press himself, utilising the expertise he had acquired as apprentice to a smith.[30]

John Rowland had used a Blaeu press and it was apparently the one used by Saunderson, after some restoration; Thomas Charles wrote in October 1806 to Joseph Tarn of the Religious Tract Society to report that[31]

> the press is at last set up, and seems to be a good one. A few articles are wanting which belonged to it – one screw, the sheep's foot, two wrenches, still, brazer – what would amount in all to about half a guinea to buy them.

Secondhand presses were highly prized. John Bird of Cardiff might not have branched into the printing business had he not been able to buy in 1791 the press and types which had belonged to Henry Walters of Cowbridge for seventeen guineas, which he was committed to pay in six months: he writes in his diary[32]

> nothing of that sort could be had here but at an extravagant rate for Carriage etc. either from Bristol or Swansea...The greatest temptation to me was that offered by the owner of letting me have it and pay as above.

The story of how Henry Walters started printing is worth a digression.

In 1760, Rhys Thomas started printing in Carmarthen. Four years later, he moved to Llandovery and in 1770 took his brother Daniel into partnership. He heard that John Walters, Rector of Llandough and Vicar of St Hilary, was seeking a printer for his magnum opus, *An English-Welsh Dictionary*, and duly offered his services. The reply he received from Walters has survived and will be quoted later in this article. Walters expressed reservations about the press being in Llandovery, which is probably why Thomas moved to Cowbridge when he got the commission, leaving the Llandovery business in the hands of his brother. The first fourteen parts of the dictionary were duly printed between 1770 and 1783, but relations between author and printer became strained when progress ground to a halt. Thomas was involved in a complicated lawsuit, which absorbed much of his time and energy, but there is no doubt too that his resources had been taxed to the limit in his attempt to print such a mammoth tome. Inevitably, the small jobs and jobbing printing which brought in regular revenue could not be executed on the same scale while parts of the dictionary were in press. Poor Thomas was imprisoned in Cardiff gaol for debt in 1783. Difficulties arose in 1777: John Walters's son Daniel records in his diary on May 13[33]

> The bailiffs came to the printers to seize their goods. Mrs. Thomas, after sending Caleb [their son] backwards and forwards many times, came with tears in her eyes to intreat my father to come to Cowbridge. He went; and the goods being appraised he bought them.

In 1783, John Walters found himself owner of a press but without a printer and so he sent for his seventeen-year-old son Henry, who was being apprenticed that year to Robert Raikes of Gloucester. With limited experience and the help of Thomas's assistant, Sion Morgan, he assumed charge. He could not. however, be expected to cope with the dictionary and his father had to invoke the help of the London-based philanthropist, Owen Jones, to get the remainder of his manuscript printed in London. John Walters was probably bitterly regretting that he had not carried out his original plan of having the work printed in Bristol. He had been partly swayed by a desire to have the printing done by a Welsh-speaking fellow-countryman.

Henry Walters was unsuited to the business and after Bird had bought the press, he became a recluse, dying in 1829. Edward Williams related a sad episode to his son Taliesin in August 1813[34]

> In Cardiff on my return home, I was told by Mr. Bird that Henry Walters
> (against whose goods & property an execution had been brought) had leaped
> out of his window last thursday night and had ran down to Gileston, but not
> finding me at home, had gone nobody knew where, and was supposed to have
> made away with himself, that they were every where searching for him but
> could not find him: this induced me to take Cowbridge in my way home, it was
> late last night when I arrived, and going to the Eagle was told by T. Rees that
> Henry had returned.

The press which Bird bought from Walters had to be assembled by a printer and the type could not have been up to standard as he was receiving delivery of new type from London in six months.[35]

The most flamboyant of the Methodist reformers in Wales was Howell Harris, who established a 'family', a religious commune, in Trevecka, Breconshire, in 1752. One Methodist, Barbara Parry, complained of persecution to the Court of King's Bench and she donated the money she received in compensation to the 'Family'. Harris put it towards the purchase of a printing-press. He despatched Evan Roberts and James Prichard to London in 1756 to see about a press and to learn what they could about operating it. Evan Roberts produced some handbills and advertisements for the Brecon Society in the 1750s but no books were printed until 1770. In 1806, Maurice Hughes, who had been a bookbinder and printer at Trevecka, moved the press to Talgarth and printed there until 1814. The press and type were subsequently purchased by an apprentice of William Williams in Brecon.

John Ross boasted of a press made in London by a well-known carpenter.[36] The sale catalogue of David Oliver of Wrexham's business in 1822 listed a 'printing press, of the Demy size'.[37] Printers were only too anxious to take advantage of any stock being disposed of locally. John Evans bought the stock of John Daniel in Carmarthen, even though he was already well-established and presumably had well-equipped premises. For someone setting up business, the purchase of a running concern was a godsend and John Painter of Wrexham was one such beneficiary. The Marsh sisters had inherited the business from their brother John, who had succeeded his father Richard. They had been in business less than two years when in November 1796 they were advertising 'the whole stock in trade of the late Mr. Marsh of Wrexham' in *The Chester Chronicle*. The stock included books, stationery, bookbinding materials, 'together with a complete printing-office, consisting of types of every description, most of which are nearly new'.[38] John Jenkins bought in 1818 the press of Zecharias Bevan Morris, printer in Swansea and Carmarthen, and in partnership with Thomas Williams set up Argraffdy'r-beirdd (the poets' printing-house) in Merthyr Tydfil in 1819.

The earliest reference to copperplate printing in Wales is an advertisement placed in *The Cambrian* on 8 December 1810 by Jonathan Harris, Carmarthen, in which he announces 'Letter-press and Copper-plate printing neatly executed'. (There is an earlier reference, in 1807, to 'Copper-plate copies of Hebrew letters and words' being available for 1s. at J Evans and Jonathan Harris, Booksellers, Carmarthen, but there is no certainty that they themselves printed them.) Thomas Ridd of Cardiff and John Cheese Watkins of Abergavenny offered copperplate printing in 1811, Samuel Williams of Aberystwyth, John Davies of Llandeilo, John Powell Davies of Carmarthen and John Painter of Wrexham by 1820.[39]

Mention has already been made of the three newspapers which circulated in Wales in this period. *The Cambrian* was printed by Thomas Jenkins in Swansea, *The North Wales Gazette* by the Brosters in Bangor and *The Carmarthen Journal* by John Daniel in Carmarthen. *Seren Gomer* started as a weekly newspaper in 1814 but it was not a success and the printer, David Jenkin of Swansea, was selling the equipment used to print it at the end of 1815[40]

> To Printers and others, disposed to establish a Welsh newspaper. To be sold by private contract, the following new type, and other printing materials, formerly used in publishing that well-known and widely circulated newspaper, called Seren Gomer, viz.
>
> An excellent double-crown Press.
> One pair ditto Chases.
> Ten brass Gallies, four Composing Sticks, and a set of Brass Rules.
> 260 lb Long Primer.
> 250 lb Minion.
> 220 lb Brevier.
> 10 lb Bourgeois two lines.
> 30 lb Leads, various thicknesses.
> 1 dozen ornamented Dashes.

2 dozen Thin Brass Rules.

2 Wood Cuts.

David Jenkin disposed only of the newspaper equipment and he remained in business for another twenty years. *Seren Gomer* became a periodical and its founder, Joseph Harris, a Baptist minister, started his own printing business in Swansea in 1816.

From the above advertisement, it is obvious that printers had to invest in a good selection of types as well as presses. Secondhand type in good condition was always welcome but the purchase of new type was always announced with great flourish. Within a year of printing, Nicholas Thomas was issuing proposals for a publication which, he said, would be printed with new type shortly to be delivered from London.[41] The new type appears in books printed in 1723 onwards. He seems to have acquired a third fount around 1725–7. The demands of the Welsh language with its preponderance of 'y's, 'd's, 'w's, etc could not be met from a normal fount of letters and, as the words were more important than the aesthetic appearance of the page, printers had few qualms about mixing type founts and sizes. David Jones of Trefriw had yet another method of dealing with the problem, adjusting the spelling; he apologises in his edition of William Smith's *Histori yr Iesu Sanctaidd* (1776) for substituting 'v' and 'u' on account of a shortage of 'y's. When he set up as he printer, apparently he had to pawn his library to buy type.[42]

John Walters insisted on a high standard of typography for his dictionary and in replying to Rhys Thomas's tender to print his dictionary, he pointed out that inelegant and ugly typefaces would no longer be acceptable after seeing the craftsmanship of Caslon and Baskerville.[43] Caslon type was used in Trevecka and Bala. A fount of diamond type was specially cast for the pocket-sized Welsh Bible printed at Trevecka in 1790. Morgan John Rhys had planned on having new type for his periodical *Y Cylch-grawn Cynmraeg*, and there were frantic letters from Trevecka to William Owen-Pughe, conveniently based in London, begging him to try and procure the founts required, as there seemed little prospect of a supply arriving through the normal channels after an announcement of Caslon's bankruptcy had appeared in the papers.[44]

Robert Saunderson got his types from Mrs Caslon in 1803, including Greek and Hebrew.[45] Hebrew type was used in Wales as far back as 1773 and 1776, brought in by John Ross for printing two works *A Plain Grammar of the Hebrew Language* and *The Hebrew and English Lexicon Improved* for William Higgs Barker. John Evans used Hebrew type for a second edition of the former in 1814. Evans already had it in stock for the benefit of one his good customers, Thomas Burgess, Bishop of St Davids, for whom he printed, amongst other works, the *Rudiments of Hebrew*

Grammar in 1813. Although no books printed entirely in Greek have come to light, Greek type was used in quotations and there is an example on the title-page of Joseph Harris's *Galarnad...Titus Lewis*, printed by Evans in 1811 and in Thomas Burgess's *A Letter to the...Bishop of Durham, on the origin of the Pelasgi, and on...the Aeolic Digamma*, printed by Evans in 1815.

Edward Carnes of Holywell in 1799 was offering for sale 'a good assortment of new type by Fry and Steel'[46] and the sale catalogue of David Oliver of Wrexham, 1822, included 'types...in good condition, well selected...various fonts and sizes of Roman and Italic from Nonpareil to Fourteen-line Pica'.[47]

Since materials had to be sent from London, there were frequent panic letters despatched from Welsh printers when the necessary supplies were not forthcoming. *Y Cylchgrawn Cymmraeg* was printed in old type because the promised new type did not arrive. Thomas Charles of Bala in 1806 asked William Owen Pughe to call on Beale Blackwell to find out whether he intended sending the ink which had been ordered twice; 'I wish to have it immediately, or my press must stop'.[48] It would not be Pughe's first visit to Blackwell's; in 1783 he had been asked by John Walters 'to get from Mr Blackwell...a cask of ink, of the value of 15s., and send it down by the Swansea Coach, directed to Mr. Rees Thomas, Printer, Cowbridge.'[49]

Paper was expensive and the cost rose steadily as the government increased paper taxes. John Painter was involved in a lengthy correspondence[50] with Walter Davies prior to printing his translation of a work by Thomas Gisborne under the title *Eglur Olygiad o'r Grefydd Gristionol* in 1801. Painter estimated that 26 reams of paper would be required to print 500 copies of 350 8vo pages. Painter had a stock of paper at 26s. a ream, which he recommended in preference to a cheaper paper at 21s. per ream. He said that the Government was about to double the Duty on printing and writing papers, which would bring the price to 30s. were he to order it now. Within a mere week, he wrote again to Davies 'A Paper Maker has informed me that paper of the quality of the sample I sent you will not in future be afforded for less than 34s. per ream – he says that Duty will be mostly treble on those kinds of paper.' Painter was one of the few printers who used local paper. He tried, unsuccessfully, to get the contract for printing Walter Davies's *General View of the Agriculture...of North Wales*, using the argument 'It can be printed quite as well at Wrexham and cheaper – labour being lower and having a paper-mill within a mile of the town'.[51] The watermark of the paper on which *Eglur Olygiad* was printed takes the form of the initials 'EB' and it is more than likely that it was manufactured in Edward Bozley's papermill at Esclusham, near Wrexham. Other initialled watermarks appear in publications associated with Painter: 'E Wilding 1796' and 'Joseph Coles 1810'. In 1795, another Wrexham printer, John Marsh, used paper with the watermark 'W Elgar'.[52] William Wilmot of Pembroke printed *A Catalogue of Books Belonging to the Pembroke Society* (1791 on paper from the mill of Lloyds of Prendergast, a mill also patronised by Jonathan Harris of Carmarthen; 'T Lloyd 1810' is clearly marked in the paper of one of his broadsides.[53] North of Brecon used paper from the Llangenny Paper Mills for printing Theophilus Jones's *History of the County of Brecknock* (1805–9). There were at least fifteen papermills in Wales in 1816 but their production was geared more to brown paper than printing paper.[54] The printing paper they did produce was of good quality, possibly too good, too expensive for general use. Paper was usually imported and, being bulky, it had to be carried by sea. There are several graphic accounts of publications being held up because ships carrying supplies of paper had been delayed by storms.[55] Bristol served the major ports in South Wales, while Dublin, Liverpool and Chester catered for the ports in North Wales.

Paper was the subject of criminal proceedings on one occasion; Zecharias Bevan Morris was committed to Cardiff gaol in 1806 for stealing 30 reams of paper, valued at £30, the property of Dr William Turton. Morris had been one of the Swansea printers engaged in printing Turton's translation of Linnaeus, and the paper concerned was intended for another of Turton's works, *British Fauna*, printed by John Evans in 1807.[56]

The multi-volume translation of Linnaeus, *A General System of Nature*, was printed in Swansea between 1800 and 1806 by John Voss, Zecharias Bevan Morris and David Williams. It was a work which made considerable technical demands of printers and it is unlikely that the publishers, Lackington, Allen & Co, would have farmed it out to Swansea printers were it not for the fact that the translator lived there and was conveniently at hand for proofreading. On the other hand, the firm retained links with Wales, its name appearing with regularity in imprints, prefixed by 'and sold by'. A less common form of trade link was forged when Lackington, Allen & Co subscribed to a hundred copies of Thomas Heywood's *Life of Merlin*, printed by John Evans in Carmarthen in 1812, which were subsequently issued with a new title-page bearing the imprint 'London: Printed for Lackington, Allen & Co, 1813'.

Ambition...by Beppo Cambrienze was another work printed in Swansea for a London publishing firm, Thomas Jenkins for Cadell and Davies. William Davies, Thomas Cadell's partner, was a Montgomeryshire man. Cadell and Davies, like Lackington & Allen, appear in Welsh imprints, though they did nor specialise in Welsh books as did E & T Williams. Evan and Thomas Williams were from Cardiganshire and their premises in the Strand, London, were one of the haunts of the Welsh literati, although they did not aspire to the conversazione of the house of Longman, Rees, Hurst and Orme, another firm found in Welsh imprints. Owen Rees, the highly respected partner in the firm, could be said to have influenced the course of Welsh antiquarian publishing. Vaughan Griffiths was yet another Welshman who had joined the ranks of the London printers and he found it useful to have outlets in his native land; the imprint to *The Will of God* (1793) reads 'London: Printed and sold by V Griffiths...sold also by J Mathews, Strand; and J Ross, Carmarthen'.

When the British and Foreign Bible Society published a Welsh Bible in 1814, Thomas Charles persuaded Robert Saunderson to lease one of his assistants, Evan Evans, for 5s. a sheet, to Thomas Rutt in London.[57] Thomas Charles was a friend of William Owen Pughe and at one time he was almost persuaded to adopt the idiosyncratic type devised by Pughe to cater for his unorthodox views on Welsh orthography. Fortunately for the future of Welsh printing and the Welsh Bible, Charles remained in the traditional mainstream. As well as being a founder member of the British and Foreign Bible Society, Charles was involved with the Religious Tract Society. After Charles died, Saunderson continued the assocation, printing Welsh material for the Society.[58]

Supplies of books from London seem to have arrived with less hassle than printing supplies. All the Welsh printers were booksellers and by the beginning of the nineteenth century they were priding themselves on the speed of the arrival of new publications. David Jenkin of Swansea placed notices in *The Cambrian* in September 1810 to the effect that 'having established a regular correspondence with Booksellers in London' he 'begs to inform Ladies and Gentlemen, that their orders for any description of books will be executed with the greatest expedition'. London and Bristol booksellers found it worth their while to advertise their catalogues in the *The Cambrian*. North-Wales booksellers could take advantage of the proximity of Chester and Shrewsbury for supplies. Within Wales, printers exchanged publications, allowing trade discounts, and subscribed to one other's publications.

In addition to running shops, printers had stalls at local markets and at fairs. Richard Marsh's career as a bookseller was given a boost in 1757 when Thomas Durston, the prolific Shrewsbury printer, gave up attending the Wrexham Fair, nominating Marsh his local agent.[59] Fairs were convenient meeting-places for author and publisher and John Painter, after moving into a more commodious house, is in a position to offer Walter Davies and his wife a bed when they came to the Wrexham Fair.[60] The markets and fairs were part of the distribution network system involving itinerant booksellers. They secured trade discounts for bulk purchase; in the words of John Ross 'Shopkeepers and others, who buy a quantity, to sell again, will have a good allowance made them'.[61] Without the services of itinerant booksellers, publishers and printers could not have coped with subscription publishing, which was by far the most common method of publication in Wales.

The secondhand book trade was flourishing at the beginning of the eighteenth century. Crispianus Jones was selling secondhand schoolbooks in the market and from his home in Carmarthen in 1723.[62] A common addenda to many an advertisement was a phrase such as that used by Thomas Ridd in *The Cambrian* on 26 January 1811 'Libraries or parcels of second-hand books bought or taken in exchange'. Printers supplemented their secondhand stock by attending auction sales, which were duly advertised in newspapers. An annotated sale catalogue of the Peterwell estate (1791) shows that John Ross bought £25 worth of books.[63] The antiquarian book trade is normally associated with sales of country-house libraries and those of well-known collectors but the Brosters are found in June 1812 selling four Welsh manuscripts, two of which were written on vellum. They appear in a column in the *North Wales Gazette* 'The following small collection of books, in Ancient British Literature, are to be sold, at this Office'. In addition to the manuscripts, old and new Welsh printed books are listed.

Booksellers' catalogues evolved in a predictable manner: an announcement of a future publication became augmented by a list of other publications printed by the printer or written by the author, the lists growing longer as the book trade developed. John Daniel's lists became eight-page catalogues, which were appended to the almanacks of John Harris from 1797 to 1800, and they listed his general stock and not exclusively publications associated with him or the almanacker. In 1801, Thomas Williams of Dolgellau issued a catalogue as a separate work *Cofrestr o Lyfrau Cymraeg (A Register of Welsh Books)*. It cost 2*d.* which would be deducted from the cost of any book purchased if the catalogue was returned in a fit state. Thereafter, catalogues became a familiar part of the Welsh book world. Ann Scott was the daughter of John Ross and she took over her father's business briefly after his death in 1807. Her catalogues have an extra dimension as the main one contains a list of fruit and forest trees on sale; her husband Walter Scott was a market gardener. John Evans, Carmarthen, published several catalogues, the ones dated 1822 and 1825 being detailed enough to be used as checklists for current Welsh publications. In 1812, he produced a 24-page catalogue of books published by subscription *Cofrestr of Lyfrau Gwerthfawr, yn Cael eu Cyhoeddi Trwy Ragdaliadau, yn Rhanau*. He guaranteed delivery of part issues to the house of the subscriber, carriage paid. In the same year, Richard Jones of Dolgellau produced a catalogue of current books *Cofrestr o Lyfrau Cymraeg ag Sydd ar Werth*, and he notes the binding, blue wrappers, bound and half-bound. The most attractive of the catalogues is that of Jonathan Harris, Carmarthen, dated

1818. Harris's Catalogue of Welsh books is a good example of functional typographical layout.

Presswork in Wales was greatly improved by this time and compares favourably with provincial printing generally. Indeed, William Ouseley had nothing but praise for the Brecon firm responsible for printing his *Travels in Various Countries of the East* for the London publishers Rodwell and Martin between 1819 and 1823. Henry and Priscilla Hughes had a nephew in their Brecon office, Evan Prosser, who subsequently became a master printer in Pontypool. Ouseley pays him tribute[64]

> For...woodcuts I am indebted to Mr. Evan Prosser, a young artist whose typographical ingenuity is sufficiently evinced in the numerous quotations from Arabick, and Persian, as well as other languages, foreign and ancient, by him alone arranged for the press.

The early Welsh books tended not to be illustrated; the crude woodcuts which accompanied chapbooks and ballads scarcely merit more than a passing reference. Books were decorated with headpieces, tailpieces and ornamented initials, though at first they were in such poor condition that they must have been the discarded stock of some English printers. Nicholas Thomas's ornaments continued in use by his successors in Carmarthen, Samuel Lewis and Evan Powell, betraying increasing signs of wear and tear as time went by. Since most Welsh books were religious in content, the need for illustration was minimal, until literacy gained ground through all ranks of society and the range of publications was extended. People's taste became more sophisticated. Professional printers brought with them not only ornaments of a better quality, but also the expertise required to use them to good effect.

Book illustration was in its infancy in Wales before 1820 and some of the early attempts are endearing. Was it John Daniel, the printer, or Owen Hughes, the author, who was responsible for the illustrated alphabet in *Allwedd Newydd, i Bobl Ieuangc i Ddysgu Darllain Cymraeg* (1801)? It had originally been designed for English children, which is why many a Welsh child must have been puzzled as to why the letter A (for Ape) should have a picture labelled 'Eppa'!

John Painter was aiming at a more discriminating audience with *The Twenty Tribes of Wales*, which he proposed publishing by subscription in 1802. The proposals indicate that the octavo edition, price 10s.6d., would contain 'the Arms of the tribes, at the head of each, beautifully engraved on wood, by Hole, (from the school of Bewick)'. Moreover, 'A few copies will be printed upon large paper, with the first impression of the Arms. Price one guinea'. His proposals failed to attract enough support.

Theophilus Jones showed enterprise in illustrating *The History of the County of Brecknock*. He secured the help of fine artists as illustrators, including Richard

Colt Hoare, Charles Norris and Thomas Price. Price did the armorial and archaeological drawings for Theophilus Jones and when Jones 'brought an engraver to
Brecon to execute the plates...Thomas Price used to observe his method, and
watch his artistic processes, with the attention of a pupil emulous of excellence.[65]
The engraver was James Basire. Even so, the plates had to be printed in London,
and they remained in the possession of John Booth, the London bookseller
named in the imprint until they were sold at five shillings apiece.[66] Thomas Price,
cleric and antiquary, learned the technique of engraving when he was a young
man from an engraver in Builth, William Davies,[67]

> who chiefly practised that branch of his art, which includes marking letters
> and devices upon silver and other metals. This man, being ingenious, versatile,
> and poor, was accustomed to undertake the execution of any little works of
> taste and skill which occasions chanced to call for, such as lettering placards,
> flags and banners for festivals, or painting heraldic pennons and hatchments.
> Thomas Price soon found him out, and frequenting his workshop, acquired by
> observation all that the practice of its master could teach.

Apparently, Price would stand chatting to a shoemaker neighbour, 'working
away with a graving tool upon a small block of wood in his hand'. He corre-
sponded with the great lithographer Hullmandel in 1827.

Peter Williams, when publishing his edition of the Welsh Bible in 1770, welcomed a gift of two maps from Richard Morris. The maps had been produced for
the 1746 Cambridge-printed edition of the Welsh Bible and Morris despatched a
consignment of 18 000 to Carmarthen before the last part issue of the Bible was
distributed.[68]

When proposals were issued, two prices might be quoted, for unbound and
bound copies. A great many printers offered a bookbinding service. A bookbinder could either be part of the establishment or a freelance binder who had an
arrangement with the printer. Crispianus Jones advertised his bookselling and
bookbinding business in Nicholas Thomas's books, which suggests that he did
the binding for the printer when he was not repairing and rebinding old books.[69]
Samuel Williams of Aberystwyth kept a bookbinder on the premises but also sent
out work to other binders in the area.[70] Rhys Thomas had a bindery in Llandovery and Cowbridge: he was paid 2s.6d. 'for binding ye Bible & Psalm book'
in Llandovery in August 1771[71] and a book with an ownership date 1778 bears a
label stating 'This book was bound at the Printing-Office, Cowbridge'.[72] John
Marsh of Wrexham had a bindery on the premises; the notice in the *Chester
Chronicle* for the sale of his stock in November 1796 refers to 'bookbinding
materials of every kind'. In March 1816, Edward Carnes, Holywell, was advertising in the *Chester Chronicle* for 'A Journeyman Binder who perfectly
understands the business, particularly the finishing department'. John Painter

in his correspondence with Walter Davies over *Eglur Olygiad* goes into considerable detail when estimating for the binding, prices being quoted for the different
kinds of materials and degrees of tooling.[73]

Bookbinders could get their supplies from shops attached to the printing-
houses. The Sales-book of Samuel Williams[74] abounds with records of sales of
millboard, pasteboard, skins of leather and parchment, marbled paper, plain
paper. Paper was in demand universally and the Brosters opened a 'Wholesale
stationary warehouse for shopkeepers' in Bangor in 1808.[75] Shops must have
been colourful for books, stationery and bookbinding materials were by no
means the only items on sale. John Ross in 1787 offered in addition to[76]

> Great variety of Bibles and Common Prayers, Testaments, Spellings, Primers,
> Child's Guides, and Children's little Books; SCHOOL BOOKS in Greek, Latin,
> or with Translations, Lexicons, Dictionaries, Gazetteers, Grammars, &c. &c
> And all periodicals and other publications, as cheap as in London
>   STATIONARY...Writing paper, plain, gilt, or black-edged, vellum, parch-
> ment, cyphering and copy books, shop-books, Champante's best sealing-wax,
> wafers, ink-pots, slates, &c. A neat assortment of Ladies and Gentlemen's
> pocket books from the Maker, in Turky and other bindings, with or without
> instruments. Maps and prints, plain and coloured, drawing-books, watch-
> papers, copies and black lines for writing, Gilbert's pencils, &c. Also sells,
> liquid Japan ink, Walkden's fine British ink powder for records, Bailey's Patent
> Blacking Cakes, fine scented Pomatum, Durham Flour of Mustard, patent
> smelling bottles, pasteboards for binders, fine mill'd boards for clothiers,
> camel hair pencils and water colous in shells, &c &c. And all the patent
> medicines.

Ross may have stocked patent medicines, in common with many printers, but
he did not market them on the scale of John Daniel, who devoted as much space
in the *Carmarthen Journal* to his patent medicines as to his books. Jonathan Harris
was another who described himself as 'a medicine vendor' but he sold 'real and
patent medicines'.[77]

Some indication of the quantities kept in stock may be gathered from an
advertisement for the sale in 1816 of stock belonging to George North of Brecon[78]

> all the genuine, useful and extensive stock of books, prints, paper, and station-
> ary goods, of Mr. George North, a Bankrupt, comprising about five thousand
> volumes, in various languages and branches of literature; many rare and
> curious old books; some valuable modern books; several copies of Jones's
> History of Brecknockshire; near one thousand choice engravings, antient and
> modern; four hundred reams of paper; a select Circulating Library, in one lot;
> English and Welsh Bibles; Prayer Books, &c. furniture and fancy papers, &c.

The general stock in shops would have included examples of the jobbing
printing which kept printers solvent. Jobbing printing was lucrative; there was
a steady demand for forms and documents associated with local-government
administration, law and order, the sale and transfer of land, estate management,

the Poor Laws, the highways and elections. Robert Owen of Welshpool supplied 'Precedents of the most approved Forms, for Justices, Sheriffs, and Attorneys',[79] while Samuel Williams's Sales Book is a useful source for showing the range of items in constant demand in a small country town. Social affairs, from biddings to Assembly Rooms balls, generated printed material, and theatre bills, election posters or anything else considered special could be printed on silk. Tradesmen placed orders for billheads and account books and Charles Heath of Monmouth was prepared to make up 'the books of any society...to the pattern required'.[80]

Specialist services were offered. David Jenkin, Swansea, in 1810 advertised[81]

> Writings neatly and expeditiously engrossed and copied on the following terms:
> Engrossing, or copying on parchment, 2d. per folio
> Ditto   ditto on paper   1d.
> Copying briefs or abstracts   9d. per sheet

Circulating libraries and reading rooms had come into vogue with the rise in literacy. Both John Ross and John Daniel ran circulating libraries in Carmarthen in the late 1780s, while in Haverfordwest the Potters established reading rooms and a circulating library.[82] Such facilities were desirable in seaside resorts, and members of the book trade in Tenby, Aberystwyth and Swansea were swift to answer to the needs of tourists. David Jenkin of Swansea announced in *The Cambrian* in June 1812 that he had

> lately considerably enlarged his Library, and as he is determined henceforth to replenish it with all the popular novels, &c. as soon as they are published, he has no doubt of receiving support adequate to his exertions. He has also lately opened a Subscription Reading Room, where the London and Provincial Newspapers, Magazines, Reviews, &c. are regularly taken in for the use of subscribers.

John Bates, shopkeeper in Holyhead, the terminus of the Irish ferry, set up a circulating library in the early 1790s with 'a variety of new and entertaining books, which prove a very agreeable resource to passengers when detained by contrary winds'.[83]

Like their counterparts in England, Welsh printers pursued interests unconnected with the book trade. Reference has already been made to their role as vendors of patent medicines. Mark Willett, Chepstow, went a stage further, becoming first a chemist and druggist and then a surgeon. R Goodere of Swansea was a perfumer. One or two printers were insurance agents, John Bird of Cardiff for the Phoenix Fire Office and Bristol Tontines, J C Watkins of Abergavenny for the Union and Birmingham Fire and Life Insurance Companies. Richard Jones, Dolgellau, was an auctioneer and John Pugh a solicitor in the same town. Ministers of religion, poets, schoolmasters and a draper are numbered amongst the printing fraternity, while William and George North brothers of Brecon had a somewhat unusual sideline; they ran a waggon service, which must have been a tremendous advantage in distributing publications. They added to Matthew Williams's Almanacks details of 'The Waggons for Carmarthen, &c. which carry goods for all parts of Monmouthshire & South Wales'. Even so, George North went bankrupt.

The relationship between author and printer in Wales is relevant to this article only in so far as it throws light on contemporary publishing practice. Walter Davies was on the whole satisfied with John Painter's work and this is reflected in the letter he wrote to his fellow-cleric John Jenkins in 1818[84]

> As Mr Evans of Caermarthen offers but a scanty pittance for Eos y Mynydd's Psalmody, I shall not give him the offer of my *Huw Morus*: I will have it printed at Wrexham. Painter will risk all chances with me – loss or gain, I shall have only to furnish the copy, he will undertake the whole expense and trouble, and divide the profit.

Such an amicable arrangement is less commonly recorded than disputes – authors claiming that they had not been sent proofs or that the final account did not tally with the original estimate, printers indignantly protesting at accusations of dishonesty and cheating. Printers had to retain the goodwill of the public and the letters which have survived show considerable restraint when they are defending their honour. Authors and societies (useful publishing bodies in this period) had to take costs into consideration when giving custom but some of them at least tried to give work to more than one printer as a matter of principle. Richard Davies was having his *Sermons* printed in Brecon. In the preface to the first part of Volume 1, he explains 'From a wish to employ both the Printers, resident in this town, I had determined to publish the work in two parts, – of two volumes each. – This will account for the difference in the type of those now printed.[85] The printers were George North and Henry Hughes.

Both John Evans and Jonathan Harris regularly printed material for the Society for Promoting Christian Knowledge and Church Union in the Diocese of St Davids (founded in 1804) and the Society seems to have patronised every member of the book fraternity in Carmarthen during the year October 1807 to October 1808: John Daniel received £1.10s.0d. 'for six dozen Welsh Readings', £7.10s.0d. 'for 60 sets of the Rev T Sike's three Dialogues' and £1.0s.0d. for '20 copies of Rev Johnson Grant's Sermon on the reasonableness of the Church of England', Jonathan Harris was paid £54.2s.5d. 'for paper, printing, packing, and carriage of Deanery parcels, &c. as per bill', while John Evans got £88.5s.6d. 'for paper, printing.&c. as per bill'.[86] Even Thomas Jenkins of Swansea benefited through payment of £10.7s.0d. 'for Advertisements in the Cambrian, as per bills'.

Being a regular printer for the above Society, indeed printing anti-Unitarian tracts on its behalf, did not inhibit Jonathan Harris from undertaking work for the Unitarians, a potent force in South Wales at this time. He wrote to Edward Williams, 'Iolo Morganwg', on hearing that the Unitarian Book Society was proposing to print his translation of Belsham's *Calm Enquiry* to say that he would feel 'particularly obliged if you will have the goodness to [give] me the preference to print the same, having printed several tracts before to the Society'.[87]

The Society set up in the Diocese of Bangor to publish religious tracts differed from that of St Davids in that it concentrated on provision of religious literature in the Welsh language. Thomas Roberts of Caernarfon was the first choice of printer but he fell out of favour in 1805 for 'not appearing disposed to assist the Society in the distribution of their tracts' and Thomas Williams of Dolgellau was nominated in his place.[88]

The problems of copyright did not occupy the Welsh over-much. Ballad-writers complained from time to time at their ballads being pirated and Azariah Shadrach issued a warning in verse that anyone who printed his book without permission would be punished:[89]

> Pwy bynna' Breintio'r Drych Gwrthgiliwr,
> Heb gael cenad gan ei Awdwr,
> Fe gaiff boen a chosp yn sicir,
> Am iddo gynnyg dwyn ei lafur.

John Jenkins affirmed his copyright at the end of his work *Gwelediad y Palas Arian* (1811); he explained that the first five parts had been printed by William Williams of Merthyr and the rest by John Evans of Carmarthen, all on behalf of the author, and that the right to reprint lay solely with the author.

An edition of Theophilus Evans's *Drych y Prif Oesoedd*, printed by William Williams in 1803, notes in the imprint that it was published with the consent of Theophilus Jones, the author's grandson. John Painter's proposals for *The Twenty Tribes of Wales* specified that 'Mr. Yorke has given him the copy-right in the Five Royal Tribes, with such corrections and additions as he has since made'.[90]

There was an accusation of piracy when Richard Jones, Dolgellau, brought out a second edition 'carefully corrected' of Walters's *English-Welsh Dictionary* in 1814. Newspapers in Spring that year contain the following notice[91]

> This day is published, in quarto complete, price 2£.5s. unbound, an English & Welsh Dictionary…By John Walters…A very few copies only of the valuable work remain unsold. – This is the genuine edition corrected by the Author's own hands: which is greatly superior in every point of view to a PIRATED EDITION now printing in a remote corner of the country.

As Walters died in 1797, the notice obviously advertises the first edition, but it is strange that the Dolgellau edition is called 'pirated' when its list of subscribers amounts to over six hundred names, including those of printers and booksellers.

Mark Willett, a Chepstow printer, complained that a fellow-printer in the town, William Lambert had literally stolen his work. The episode is related in the preface to *A Survey of the History, Antiquities, and Scenery, of Monmouthshire* (1813). This volume was intended to be published under the title of 'The Beauties of Monmouthshire', but that design was abandoned on account of a catchpenny publication, got up under the same title, by an adventurer of the name of LAMBERT, who surreptitiously obtained a copy of the greater part of it while it was at press. However, this dishonourable dealing soon became notorious, and many of his 'Beauties' which were advertised at 5s. per copy, were at length sold at the reduced price of 7d. each.

Without doubt, the most interesting story of piracy concerns Welsh almanacks.[92] In order to evade Stamp Duty, almanacks were printed in Dublin from 1765 onwards, the word 'almanack' being deliberately omitted from the title in order to avoid arousing the suspicions of the Excisemen. No evidence has come down to posterity of who masterminded a development of the original scheme, whereby the Dublin-printed editions were augmented by versions printed in Wales with a false Dublin imprint. It all became very complicated, resulting in at least three editions of the *Cyfrill* series being issued every year. Ishmael Davies, Trefriw, and Edward Prichard, Machynlleth, were two printers involved in the plot, identified in contemporary sources as well as by their ornaments.

The first century of printing in Wales was a crucial one in the history of Welsh culture. The changes that had led to editions of 200 copies becoming editions of over 8000 copies were a foretaste of the golden age of Welsh publishing which was to follow. The achievements of the great printer-publishers of the nineteenth century, men like Thomas Gee of Denbigh, the Rees family of Llandovery and the Spurrells of Carmarthen, were remarkable and one cannot praise them too highly. At the same time, we should not underrate the difficulties encountered by their predecessors or begrudge the pioneers the credit they deserve for their determination to provide their fellow-countrymen with the printing facilities that were already common east of Offa's Dyke.

NOTES

1. Having written several articles on the Welsh book trade during the last twenty-five years, I am finding it virtually impossible to avoid reusing primary source material, albeit in different contexts. I apologise to those who may have read some of my previous work for inflicting upon them the dubious thrill of recognition.

2. H Evans, *Ymddiddan Rhwng Hen wr Dall a'r Angeu* (Caerfyrddin: J Ross, 1764), Sig A1[v].

3. J Thomas, *Annerch Ieuengctyd Cymru* (Gwrecsam, 1795), p 370.

4. National Library of Wales (henceforth cited as NLW) Add MS 1807E, f 1034.

5. The same, f 1042.

6. *Yr A B C* (Gwrecsam: A. Tye, 1799), advertisement on last page.

7. NLW Cards/QS/08/4/1788–1800.

8. NLW Add MS 2844E.

9. B Francis, *Marwnad ar...John Thomas* (Caerfyrddin: J Daniel dros yr Awdur, 1787).

10. *The Cambrian*, 7, 14 and 21 November 1812.

11. *The Cambrian*, 22 January 1814.

12. *The Cambrian*, 18 February 1815.

13. *North Wales Gazette*, 28 December 1815.

14. *The Cambrian*, 23 July 1808.

15. *North Wales Gazette*, 7 September 1809.

16. *The Cambrian*, 11 March 1820.

17. *The Cambrian*, 13 June 1807.

18. *The Cambrian*, 4 November 1820.

19. *The Cambrian*, 22 and 29 December 1810.

20. *The Cambrian*, 5 and 12 April 1806.

21. *The Cambrian*, 13 and 20 November 1813.

22. *North Wales Gazette*, 5 and 12 January 1808.

23. 24 September and 1 October, 1808.

24. NLW Add MS 13115B, f 363.

25. NLW Add MS 12186C.

26. E Davies, *Theophilus Jones, FSA, Historian: His Life, Letters and Literary Remains* (Brecon, 1905), p 88.

27. The same, p 96.

28. M Jones, *Hanes Trefriw* (Llanrwst, 1879), p 22.

29. I Jones, *A History of Printing...in Wales* (Cardiff, 1925), pp 58–9.

30. G Morgan, *Y Dyn a Wnaeth Argraff* (Llanrwst, 1982), p 9.

31. D E Jenkins, *The Life of the Rev Thomas Charles...of Bala* vol 3, (Denbigh, 1908), p 69.

32. *The Diaries of John Bird of Cardiff...1790–1803*, edited by H M Thomas (Cardiff, 1983), p 66.

33. D J, 'Early printers in Wales', *Bye-gones* (7 September 1881).

34. NLW Iolo Morganwg Letters, f 895.

35. *The Diaries of John Bird*, pp 70–1.

36. See note 3.

37. D Oliver, *A Catalogue of the Remaining Part of the Books, Stationery, Shop-fixtures, &c* (Wrexham, 1822).

38. *Chester Chronicle*, 18 November 1796.

39. E Rees, *The Welsh Book-trade before 1820* (Aberystwyth, 1988), p XXXIII.

40. *The Cambrian*, 2 December 1815.

41. *Cyffes Ffydd...Wedi ei Gyfieithu gan R D* (Caerfyrddin: N Thomas i'r Cyfieithydd, 1723), advertisement on last page.

42. Letter from Evan Evans to David Jones, 30 August 1776, quoted in A Lewis, 'Llythyrau Evan Evans at Ddafydd Jones o Drefriw', *Llên Cymru*, vol 1 (1950–1951), pp 247–8.

43. Quoted in A Lewis, 'Geiriadur Saesneg-Cymraeg John Walters (1770–1794)', *Llên Cymru*, vol 3 (1954–5), p 188.

44. NLW Add MS 13222B, f 375.

45. NLW Add MS 12845B. Photocopy.

46. *Chester Chronicle*, 13 December 1799.

47. See note 37.

48. NLW Add MS 13222B, f 4.

49. Cadrawd, 'John Walters and the first printing press in Glamorgan', *Journal of the Welsh Bibliographical Society* (1910), p 86.

50. NLW Add MS 1807E, ff 1029–44.

51. NLW Add MS 1807E, f 1038.

52. P Yorke, *Tracts of Powys* (Wrexham, 1795).

53. *By Command of the King of Kings* (Carmarthen, 1810).

54. A E Davies, 'Paper-mills and paper-makers in Wales 1700–1900', *National Library of Wales Journal*, vol 15 (1967–8), pp 1–30.

55. E Rees, *The Welsh Book-trade before 1820*, p XXXVI.

56. I Jones, *A History of Printing...in Wales*, p 151.

57. D E Jenkins, *The Life of the Rev Thomas Charles...* vol 3, pp 484–5.

58. The same, p 601.

59. John Prys's Almanack for 1757.

60. NLW Add MS 1807E, f 1035.

61. D Thomas, *Pechadur Noeth* (Caerfyrddin, 1779), advertisement at the end.

62. J Bunyan, *Dull Priodas Ysprydol* (Caerfyrddin, 1723–4), Sig A4^{v}.

63. *Acct. of Silver Plate, Books, China, Pewter...late the Property of Jno Adams of Peterwell Esqr. Sold by auction at Carmarthen...1781*, NLW Gogerddan papers.

64. I Jones, *A History of Printing...in Wales*, p 194.

65. *The Literary Remains of the Rev Thomas Price, Carnhuanawc...With a Memoir...by Jane Williams...* vol 2 (Llandovery, 1855), p 41.

66. E Davies, *Theophilus Jones*, p 27.

67. *The Literary Remains of the Rev Thomas Price*, pp 18–19.

68. G M Roberts, *Bywyd a Gwaith Peter Williams* (Caerdydd, 1943), p 69.

69. Quoted in I Jones, *A History of Printing...in Wales*, p 36.

70. E Rees, 'The Sales-book of Samuel Williams, Aberystwyth printer', *Ceredigion*, vol 10 (1986–7).

71. NLW Add MS 14916A, f 75.

72. NLW Wp1995.

73. NLW Add MS 1807E, f 1031A.

74. NLW Add MS 2844E.

75. *North Wales Gazette*, 25 February and 3 March 1808.

76. *The Rules, Orders and Premiums, of the Society for the Encouragement of Agriculture...in the County of Cardigan* (Carmathen, 1787).

77. *The Cambrian*, 8 December 1810.

78. *The Cambrian*, 24 August 1816.

79. *Appointment and Charge for the Surveyors of the Highways* (Welsh-Pool, 1820).

80. *Articles of a Friendly Society at Coleford* (Monmouth, 1808), p 16.

81. *The Cambrian*, 15 and 22 September 1810.

82. E Rees, *The Welsh Book-trade before 1820*, p XXXIX.

83. *Universal British Directory*, vol 3 (1791–5), p 386.

84. *Gwaith y Parch. Walter Davies...* vol 3 (Carmarthen, 1868), p 394.

85. R Davies, *Sermons* (Brecon, 1815).

86. *Society for Promoting Christian Knowledge and Church Union in the Diocese of St David's* (Carmarthen: Printed for the Society by Jonathan Harris, 1810), Sig A2.

87. NLW Iolo Morganwg Letters, f 197.

88. *The Minutes and Proceedings of an old Tract Society of Bangor Diocese (1804–12). Annotated...by...A O Evans* (Bangor, 1918), p 24.

89. A Shadrach, *A Looking-glass* (Carmarthen, 1807). 'Whoever prints Drych Gwrthgiliwr without the author's permission will surely receive pain and punishment for daring to steal his work'.

90. Painter had printed Philip Yorke's *The Royal Tribes of Wales* in 1799.

91. *The Cambrian*, 26 February 1814; *Seren Gomer*, 5 March 1814; *North Wales Gazette*, 14 April 1814.

92. E Rees and G Morgan, 'Welsh Almanacks: problems of piracy', *The Library*, 6 ser, vol 1 (1979), pp 144–63.

Patrick Neill and the Origins of Belfast Printing

WESLEY McCANN

'Belfast', wrote E M Forster in 1919, 'as all men of affairs know, stands no nonsense and lies at the head of Belfast Lough'.[1] In drawing attention both to the city's geographical location and, by allusion, to the character of its citizens (many of whom are of Scots Presbyterian origin) Forster provides us with a convenient starting point for an examination of the beginnings of printing and the book trade in Belfast.

There has been a settlement where the confluence of the rivers Lagan, Farset and Blackstaff enters Belfast Lough since early Christian times.[2] The name Belfast means 'the mouth of, or approach to, the sand bank' and it was the presence of the sandbank which made possible at low tide the crossing from Upper to Lower Clandeboye (modern Antrim to Down). The ford remained the only crossing until the contruction of the first bridge in the 1680s. The Normans under John de Courcy occupied much of eastern Ulster in the years after 1177 and they built a series of motte-castles around the head of the Lough including one at Belfast. Their major stronghold was Carrickfergus, eleven miles to the north, with its formidable stone-built castle and harbour.

It was not until the early decades of the seventeenth century that Belfast began to grow as a centre of manufacture and commerce and eventually replace Carrickfergus as the principal town in the north. Following the defeat in 1603 of Hugh O'Neill, earl of Tyrone, who had risen in rebellion against the English Crown in 1595, Belfast and the surrounding lands were granted to Sir Arthur Chichester, a veteran of the defeat of the Armada and one of Elizabeth's most ruthless generals in Ireland. The plantation of Antrim and Down by lowland Scots Presbyterians under Hugh Montgomery and James Hamilton and the flight of the last of the Irish Earls in 1607 prompted Chichester to begin the development of the town and the rebuilding of the castle.

In 1613 Chichester was created baron of Belfast, and in the same year the town was one of forty in Ireland granted a charter by James I. This allowed Belfast to return two members to the Irish Parliament, but of more lasting importance was the establishment thereby of a system of civic government which was to serve the town for over two hundred years. The charter created the offices of Sovereign and twelve burgesses who had the power (subject to the veto of the Chichesters) to order the commercial life of the town by making by-laws and enrolling

125

freemen. The freemen were admitted on payment of a fine (although this was sometimes waived), and those who had served an apprenticeship in the town were admitted gratis. The freemen had no part in the municipal government but enjoyed the right to carry on their trade free of the tolls or customs imposed on strangers.

A roll of the freemen survives from 1635, although no doubt a record was kept from 1613 which has since been lost, and it is this roll which provides the first evidence of a member of the book trade at work in the town.[3] Some time between 19 January and 7 March 1661 James Anderson, stationer, was sworn free on payment of a fine of five shillings.[4] Where Anderson came from or how long he remained in business is not recorded, although the later undated addition of the word 'mort' in the margin of the roll beside his name suggests he probably died in Belfast. The name Anderson is well known in the Scottish book trade in the seventeenth century and it may well be that James Anderson was a member of the dynasty founded by George Anderson, who began printing in Edinburgh in 1637, and which lasted till the death in 1716 of the Agnes Anderson, widow of George's son Andrew.[5]

Twenty years later, on 8 September 1681, the roll of the freemen records the admission of 'ffrancis KinCaid, stationer', and only seven days later of 'James Callwell, bookebinder'.[6] The close proximity of the two names might be no more than a coincidence, although it would not be unusual to find a stationer and binder in business together. Like Anderson before them nothing is recorded of their origins or later careers, and no reference to either has been found in records of the English or Scottish trade, but again it should be noted that neither surname is uncommon in Scotland.[7]

The population of Belfast in the middle years of the century has been estimated at about one hundred and twenty households suggesting a total population of about 600.[8] By the century's close this had risen to about 1000, although at times the population was swollen further by large numbers of troops garrisoned in the town. It was not until the eighteenth century that the town could support a book trade of any size, but that there was a market for books from an earlier date is illustrated by the cargo of the 'William' from Holywood in County Down which arrived from Glasgow in January 1682. In addition to a large quantity of linen the ship carried a selection of printed items with a total value of £6.2s.6d. including Bibles, Testaments, Psalm books, other unnamed books both bound and un-bound, and 'one gross of Ballets'.[9]

It is clear that it is to Scotland rather than to Dublin or London that we must look for the origins of the Belfast book trade, and this holds true also for the town's first printer, Patrick Neill.[10]

The events of 1690 have reverberated through Irish history for three hundred years and Belfast was caught up in them from the very beginning. The Sovereign and burgesses of Belfast were among the first to pledge their loyalty to William of Orange on his arrival in Ireland, and the King lodged in the town on his way to the decisive battle at the Boyne.[11] William is known to have brought his printer, Edward Jones, with him, but it is unlikely that he did any printing before reaching Dublin. A letter from Belfast dated 25 June 1690 makes clear the difficulties encountered by an itinerant press: 'one day's sudden motion will more disturb and disorder their utensils than in three days can be rectified...the printers cannot work but in a House'.[12]

It was not until the ravages of war were ended, and those of the population who had fled to Scotland had returned that Belfast was to welcome its first printer. The date of his arrival cannot be fixed with any certainty as the roll of the freemen breaks off in 1682 and does not resume until 1723,[13] but a letter published in the *Belfast News-Letter* on 12 September 1806 supplies much of the evidence.

Written by Daniel Blow, who as we shall see was a direct successor to the first printer, it begins by describing the relationship between the Blows and the Griersons, a famous Dublin printing family.[14] The letter continues

> It may be worthy of remark, that the late James Blow, abovementioned, with his brother-in-law Patrick Niel [sic], came from Glasgow about the year 1696, by invitation from Mr Crawford, then Sovereign of Belfast, who entered into partnership with them in the art of printing, being the first in the North of Ireland, which continued till the death of Patrick Neil, who leaving no male issue, the business was continued by the said James Blow, who, about the year 1704, printed the first edition of the Holy Bible in Ireland, and many succeeding editions.

Daniel Blow was an old man when he wrote the letter – he died four years later at the age of 92 – and this probably explains the vagueness of some of his statements, but he is unequivocal in giving Glasgow as Patrick Neill's place of origin. However, when we turn to the records of the Scottish book trade in search of Neill no certain identification can be made. The earliest appearance of the surname is a certain John Neill who is recorded as a bookseller in the years 1642 to 1645,[15] and he is probably to be identified with the binder and stationer of the same name recorded in 1649[16] and 1657.[17] A stationer of the name of David Neill is known from 1667,[18] and he is probably the same as the binder recorded two years later.[19] The dates noted suggest the strong possibility of a father and son relationship.

The first known reference to someone called Patrick Neill comes from 1691 when a binder of that name was admitted burgess and guild brother (ie freeman) in Glasgow.[20] Another occurrence of the name has been noted by W J Couper in his study of the Glasgow printer Robert Sanders.[21] Couper describes how three months before his death in July 1694 Sanders granted a discharge that he had 'sold and delivered and received payment therefor from John Wilson, Patrick Neill and James Handshaw a certain parcel of books to the value of 583 lib Scots money'.[22] The original of this discharge quoted by Couper cannot now be traced, but the transaction it describes seems to have been part of the asset-stripping which Sanders indulged in following his son's marriage in 1691. The full account of this unhappy affair is given by Couper,[23] and from it it appears that Sanders, having settled all his printing materials and unbound books on his son at the time of the latter's marriage decided subsequently 'to defraud and frustrate' his son by selling off entire impressions in sheets and by employing additional binders to bind up what remained, as bound books did not form part of the original settlement. Wilson, Neill and Handshaw seem to have taken advantage of this bargain sale to acquire some stock for their own use. Wilson is probably to be identified with the bookbinder and stationer of that name who became a burgess and guild brother in Glasgow on 29 September 1692[24] and who was still in business in 1726.[25] Of Handshaw nothing further is recorded unless he is the same as John Hindshaw, a Glasgow binder of 1715.[26] Possibly all three were the extra hands taken on by Sanders.

The possibility we are faced with is that the binder Patrick Neill who became a guild brother in 1691 is the same as the Patrick Neill who bought the books from Sanders, and that he, with a basic stock conveniently to hand, moved to Belfast to set up on his own account there. However, two other occurrences of the name undermine this rather neat hypothesis. Gillespie has noted a reference to the burial in Glasgow in January 1717 of an unnamed son of a binder called Patrick Neill,[27] and further, the death is recorded on the 9 July 1724 of 'Patrick Neil, sometime stationer at Culross, late bookbinder in Glasgow'.[28] If either or both is (are) the same as the 1691 Glasgow guild brother and the purchaser of Sanders books, then we must look elsewhere for Belfast's first printer, for the impression given in Blow's letter, reinforced by Neill's will (see below), is that he died in Belfast in about 1705. Perhaps all that can be said with any certainty is that the name is a common one in the Glasgow trade of the late seventeenth century and that some relationship between Belfast's first printer and the several Neills at work in Scotland is more likely than not.[29]

To the obvious objection that all the bearers of the name so far identified in Scotland were binders and/or stationers while what is sought is a printer, it can of course be argued that the transition from one trade to another is not uncommon, especially in a small provincial centre far from the control of a strictly regulated system of apprenticeship. Robert Sanders was himself described as a binder in 1655, six years before he became a printer, and it was one of the charges later brought against him in his dispute with the Anderson that 'he never served an apprenticeship or was freeman as a printer'.[30]

Daniel Blow continues his account by asserting that Neill came from Glasgow 'about the year 1696 by invitation from Mr Crawford,[31] then Sovereign of Belfast'. William Craford was first elected Sovereign for the year ending Michaelmas 1693, and served for a second term in the following year.[32] He was no longer Sovereign in 1696. If the statement of the Archbishop of Dublin, William King, is correct that an edition of the *Solemn League and Covenant* was printed in Belfast in 1694 (an edition which so far has not been identified) then we may with some confidence push the date of Neill's arrival back to that year, the second and last of Craford's period as Sovereign.[33]

If it was in his capacity as Sovereign that Craford invited Neill to Belfast, it raises the possibility that he came to occupy an official post, a possibility first noted by Benn who quotes the example of Glasgow where Robert Sanders was appointed printer to the town in 1661.[34] In fact the office existed at an even earlier date. In 1638 George Anderson, Glasgow's first printer, came from Edinburgh at the expense of the Glasgow Town Council who granted him 'an hundrethe pundis in satisfactioun to him of the superplus he debursit in transporting of his geir to this burghe'.[35] This initial grant was followed by a series of annual payments of £16.8s.4d. until his death in 1647,[36] and again to his widow for 1648 until her return to Edinburgh in the same year.[37] The office of town printer must have proved useful to the Council, for eight years later in 1656 (during which period Glasgow had been without a printer) the City Magistrates approached Andrew Anderson, George's son, in Edinburgh 'in the tounis name' to invite him to come to Glasgow. He was offered a salary of 'ane hundreth merkis Scottis money, that the[y] wont of old to pay his deceist father'.[38] Andrew accepted the invitation and the 'maister of wark' was instructed to prepare suitable premises for him. When he arrived, by July 1659, he was compensated for his removal expenses, and he was duly paid his salary for 1659 and 1660.[39] In May 1661, however, he decided to return to Edinburgh, and the Town Council again assisted him with the cost of removal.[40] On his departure the Council lost no time in inviting Robert Sanders (whom they had already commissioned to publish a sermon on their behalf) to take Anderson's place, offering him 'the sowme of fourtie pundis at twa termes in the year…so long as he keeps wp his prenting press within the burgh'.[41]

It is clear therefore that by this date the post of town printer was well established and of benefit to the commercial and administrative life of Glasgow.

Andrew Anderson's first task had been 'to prent the table of the bridge cus-tomes',[42] and Sanders was required 'to print gratis any thing the toune shall imploy him to print'.[43] No doubt it was precisely these short official items (scales of charges, regulations etc) which the Council found it useful to have printed in multiple copies and in an authoritative form. The trouble and expense to which the Council went to employ a printer suggests there must have been a steady demand for work of this type. The Corporation of Belfast might well have followed the example of Glasgow when its Sovereign invited Neill to come to the town, but the few records of the town's administration which survive from that period afford no direct proof of this.

Daniel Blow continues his letter by claiming that Craford entered into partner-ship with Neill, a statement which might detract from the theory that Neill came at the town's behest. Possibly, however, Craford provided additional capital to allow Neill to print 'non-official' items, and in this connection it is significant that all of Neill's surviving imprints are in the form 'printed by Patrick Neill and Company'.[44]

William Craford was a man of some wealth and standing. In addition to his two years as Sovereign he represented Belfast as member of Parliament in 1703 and again in 1707,[45] despite having been removed from his office as Burgess in 1705 for 'not being qualified according to statute'.[46] He is described as a merchant and had premises in High Street, the main thoroughfare of the town.[47] In 1691 together with John Craford (possibly his brother) he was owed the considerable sum of £494.9s.3d. by William Montgomery of the Ards.[48] Craford died in 1716 leaving his real estate in County Down to his son and heir David, and consider-able sums of money to other relations.[49]

Benn has suggested that another leading merchant of Belfast, Brice Blair, was also a member of Neill's company.[50] A leading Presbyterian, Blair was one of the ruling elders of Belfast and in 1708 he was chosen as treasurer of the *regium donum*, the annual grant to Presbyterian ministers first made by Charles II and confirmed by William III. Blair was required to give a surety of £1200 on taking up this post.[51] He also seems to have had a part to play in the provision of books to the Presbyterian community; this much we know from the difficulty he had in obtaining payment for them.[52] Moreover, he is several times named in the Dublin newspapers as taking subscriptions for books published there.[53] He died in 1722, and in his will he is described as a haberdasher and bookseller, and English and Latin books are included among his estate.[54] Whether or not Craford and Blair were members of Neill's company it is nevertheless clear that Belfast was not lacking in men who had the means to underwrite a printing venture and who were familiar with the peculiar ways of the book trade.

Daniel Blow's comments about Neill's successor will be examined shortly, but his final statement about the printing of the first edition of the Bible in Ireland 'in about the year 1704' cannot be proved.[55]

At this point it will be helpful to examine the evidence contained in Patrick Neill's will. The original has unfortunately been destroyed and we have only the extract from it quoted by Benn.[56] The will is dated 21 December 1704, and Benn's account of it is as follows.

> after directing that he [Neill] shall be interred in Belfast 'as to my brother-in-law James Blow, and Brice Blair shall seem meet,' he appoints John Crawford and Charles Anderson of Glasgow his executors, desiring that they shall pay all the debts he owes to any person, 'and first to relieve my brother James Blow of all the debt he stands engaged for me, and next to pay Mr Anderson of Edinburgh, who for the good of my children will take books for the debt; and my real and clear estate I order to be equally divided among my children, John, James, and Sarah, and I recommend my son John to the care of my brother Blow to teach him the trade I taught him, and if he keep the printing house in Belfast, to instruct him in that calling.

Scant and ambiguous though this summary and extract are they add considerably to our knowledge. The familial relationship between Neill and James Blow (referred to by Daniel) is confirmed, and according to Alexander Gordon, James Blow married Neill's sister Abigail.[57] The choice of executors is an interesting one, although it is not clear whether both were from Glasgow or simply Charles Anderson alone, but it points to a continuing link between the printer and his city of origin. It is perhaps noteworthy that neither of the supposed partners, William Craford or Brice Blair, is named as an executor, although Blair is charged with helping to arrange Neill's funeral. (John Crawford may be a relation of William.) The Mr Anderson of Edinburgh to whom Neill was in debt may have belonged to the same printing family which has already been noted. When Andrew Anderson left the employ of the Glasgow town Council to return to Edinburgh he remained in business there until his death in 1676.[58] Thereafter the business was in the hands of his widow, Agnes, and their son James.[59] Neill's confident assertion that Mr Anderson 'would take books for the debt' suggests that Anderson was himself in the book trade. Neill was possibly in debt to the Andersons for paper and type, as supplies of neither would have been available in Belfast. The several references to debts suggests that Neill's printing venture was still not in a financially secure position some ten years after his move to Belfast.

Neill's bequest of 'his real and clear estate' to his three children contradicts Daniel's statement in his letter that Neill left no male issue. However, nothing further is known of these three children. Neill's instructions concerning his eldest son are not altogether clear and are open to a number of interpretations.

He recommends John to the care of James Blow 'to teach him the trade I taught him'. This can mean 'to teach him [John] the trade I taught him [John]', which would imply that John had already begun his apprenticeship under his father and that this was to continue under Blow. Alternatively it can be read 'to teach him [John] the trade I taught him [Blow]', that is, that Blow had himself been Neill's apprentice and is now charged with instructing his former master's son. The following clause is similarly ambiguous. Neill possibly meant 'and if he [John] keep the printing house in Belfast, to instruct him [John] in that calling.' This would mean that John was to inherit the business (as part of the 'real and clear estate'), and that Neill hoped that Blow would stay on and assist his son. A second possible reading is 'and if he [Blow] keep the printing house...to instruct him [John]...'

The resolution of this depends in part on the nature of the relationship between James Blow and Patrick Neill. It has already been noted that Blow had married Neill's sister, and if he was also Neill's partner then no doubt he would have inherited the business on his death and have kept on John Neill as an apprentice. However, if Blow was only Neill's employee then John, though not yet out of his time, would have inherited and his father would have been keen for Blow to stay on and assist him. It is perhaps significant that Blow's son Daniel, writing a century later, should explain his father's takeover of the business on the grounds that Neill left no male heir, and although wrong in this belief, it does perhaps lend weight to the theory that Blow took over not as of right (as a full partner would surely have done) but because John Neill had no wish to continue the business or soon died. Furthermore, had Neill and Blow been partners might we not expect to find the latter's name in imprints, unless of course Blow was a member of the Company? Blow's date of birth is given as 1676[60] which made him seventeen or eighteen in 1694, too young perhaps to be a full partner in a printing firm, but consistent with the possibility that he was at the time Neill's apprentice.[61] Neill is presumed to have died in 1704 or 1705; the earliest imprint bearing Blow's name is from 1706.[62] Blow died in 1759 when he was succeeded by Daniel who, as we have seen, lived on until 1810.

Fourteen editions survive bearing Neill's imprint, and advertisements in some of the books point to another seven titles no copies of which appear to be extant.[63] All are dated between 1699 and 1702, and seven come from 1700. Only one is unique to Neill's press (the latest, Robert Craghead's *Advice for the Assurance of Salvation*); the others are reprints of popular religious works. In addition, a fragment of a ballad sheet is found in the binding of one of them.[64] At first sight they appear to be an undistinguished group, but on closer examination there are two editions which are of considerable literary interest, and others pose an interesting bibliographical problem.

In the earliest of two editions of the *Psalms of David in Meeter* (1699), Wing B2620A, Neill advertised three titles the second of which is 'The Bible the best New-Years-Gift. Recommended as useful for Children to learn by heart, being in Verse. Price 3*d*.'. The work was unknown until an incomplete copy in the John Rylands Library was brought to the attention of E R McC Dix in 1906.[65] Dix, however, failed to recognise that it is in fact a hitherto unrecorded edition of the *Verbum Sempiternum* and *Salvator Mundi* by the 'water poet' John Taylor.[66] Neill's is the first edition of this work to have been printed outside London.[67] Of greater literary interest is the edition from the following year of Alexander Montgomerie's long allegorical poem *The Cherrie and the Slae*, Wing M2503. Montgomerie's work has been the subject of good deal of literary and bibliographical interest in recent years,[68] and again it is noteworthy that this Belfast edition was the first to have been printed outside Scotland. The work enjoyed considerable popularity in Ulster and it was one of the last works published by James Blow in 1759.[69]

All of Neill's editions are in small formats, printed on poorish paper and with undistinguished type. They are wholly typical of provincial printing of their time and might seem to hold no mysteries for the bibliographer. Four of them, however, pose a dilemma to which there is no obvious solution, namely the presence of what appear to be press figures. In Joseph Allaine's *A Most Familiar Explanation of the Assemblies Shorter Catechism* (1700), Wing A975A, there is a small five-pointed star on the direction line on $C1^a$, and in John Fox's *Time and the End of Time* (1700), Wing F2028, a triangular arrangement of three asterisks (two below and one above) on sig $A11^b$, and in an inverted form on $A12^b$. The same grouping of asterisks is found in Benjamin Keach *War with the Devil* (1700), Wing K107, where the former arrangement is found in $B11^b$, $B12^b$ and $D12^b$ and in the inverted form in $A12^b$, $C11^b$, $C12^b$, $E1^a$ and $G12^b$ (signatures F and H have none). Edward Pearse, *The Great Concern* (1700), Wing P986, similarly shows the first form in $D11^b$, $E11^b$, $F11^b$, $G12^b$, $H12^b$, and $I12^b$ and the inverted form in $F12^b$, $G11^b$, $H11^b$ and $I11^b$ (signatures A, B, C, and K have none). Gaskell states that press figures in this form were used by individual pressmen to distinguish their work for the purposes of payment and that their use dates from the 1680s.[70] Are we then to assume that Neill had two pressmen working for him who were so determined to protect their earnings that they used this new-fangled system of identification? The idea seems improbable, and the reason why these figures were used in a few of the books from a fledgling press in an out-of-the-way place must, like much of the early history of the Belfast book trade, remain a subject for further investigation.

NOTES

1. 'Forrest Reid', reprinted in *Abinger Harvest* (Harmondsworth, 1967), p 89.

2. This summary is based on the first three chapters of *Belfast: the Origins and Growth of an Industrial City*, edited by J C Beckett and R E Glasscock (London, 1967). The standard work, and the first to include the history of printing in Belfast is George Benn, *A History of the Town of Belfast* (London, 1877).

3. The roll of the freemen and a translation of the charter are published in *The Town Book of the Corporation of Belfast*, edited by R M Young (Belfast, 1892).

4. *Town Book*, p 259.

5. H G Aldis, *A List of Books Printed in Scotland before 1700*, photographically reprinted with additions (Edinburgh, 1970), pp 107–8.

6. *Town Book*, p 285.

7. W S Mitchell, *A History of Scottish Bookbinding 1432 to 1650* (Edinburgh, 1955), pp 21–2 lists an Edinburgh binder called Patrick Kincaid at work in the early sixteenth century.

8. *Belfast: the Origins and Growth*, pp 33–4.

9. Benn, *Belfast*, p 316.

10. The west coast of Scotland was only a short sea crossing away from Ulster and was more accessible than Dublin one hundred miles of indifferent roads to the south. On the history of this crossing and its influence on trade see Fraser G MacHaffie, *The Short Sea Route* (Prescot, 1975), pp 1–12.

11. *Belfast: the Origins and Growth*, p 39. It should be said that five years earlier they had enthusiastically welcomed the accession of James ii who amended the charter in favour of the Presbyterians.

12. Quoted in Benn, *Belfast*, pp 424–5. The author of the letter .was Christopher Carleton, Collector of Belfast, but it is not known to whom he was writing.

13. A roll was probably kept in another place as the practice of enrolling freemen continued during at least part of this period; see *Historical Notices of old Belfast and its Vicinity*, edited by R M Young (Belfast, 1896), p 82.

14. Daniel Blow's sister Jane was the second wife of George Grierson (d 1753). A child of this marriage was Hugh Boulter Grierson who, like his father and his half-brother George Abraham Grierson (whom he succeeded) and his own son George, held the patent as the King's Printer in Ireland. See J R H Greeves, 'Two Irish printing families', *Belfast Natural History and Philosophical Society Proceedings and Reports*, 2 ser, vol 4 (1950–5), pp 38–44.

15. Aldis, *List*, p 118.

16. *The Burgesses & Guild Brethern of Glasgow, 1573-1750*, edited by J R Anderson (Edinburgh, 1925), p 130.

17. *The Commissariot Record of Glasgow: Register of Testaments 1547-1800*, edited by Francis J Grant (Edinburgh, 1901), p 375.

18. *Register of Testaments*, p 374.

19. *Burgesses & Guild Brethern*, p 186.

20. *Burgesses & Guild Brethern*, p 226.

21. W J Couper, *Robert Sanders the elder: Printer in Glasgow 1661-1694* (Glasgow, 1915).

22. Couper, *Sanders*, pp 5-6.

23. Couper, *Sanders*, pp 25-8.

24. *Burgesses & Guild Brethern*, p 227.

25. H R Plomer, G H Bushnell, E R McC Dix, *A Dictionary of the Printers and Booksellers who were at work in England Scotland and Ireland from 1726 to 1775* (London, 1932), p 368.

26. Ian Maxted, *The British Book Trades: 1710-1777* (Exeter, 1983), p 48, no 0774. John Hyndschaw, stationer, who was made a burgess of Stirling on 27 February 1724 may be the same man; see R H Carnie 'Scottish printers and booksellers, 1668-1775: a study of source material', *The Bibliotheck*, vol 4 (1963-6), pp 213-27.

27. R A Gillespie, 'A list of books printed in Glasgow 1701-1775 with notes on the printers and booksellers' (FLA thesis, 1967), pt II, p 100, quoting the manuscript Glasgow Parochial Register.

28. *The Commissariot Record of Edinburgh: Register of Testaments, part III, 1701-1800*, edited by Francis J Grant (Edinburgh, 1899), p 205.

29. None of the Patrick Neills noted is the same as the Patrick Neill who was a partner in the famous Edinburgh firm of Hamilton, Neill and Balfour. He was a son of Robert Neill of Haddington and was born in about 1725. See *The House of Neill 1749-1949*, edited by Moray McLaren (Edinburgh, 1949).

30. Couper, *Sanders*, p 5.

31. Blow uses the modern form. In contemporary records he always appears as Craford or Crafford.

32. *Town Book*, p 243.

33. Trinity College Dublin MS 750/5, p 171. A transcript of a letter dated 2 June 1719 from King to the Archbishop of Canterbury (William Wake): 'I send your Grace...four Editions [of the Solemn League], one in Glasgow 1690 3 in Ireland, which I am assured were printed at Belfast, the first 1694 the 2^d 1700 & the last 1717'.

34. Benn, *Belfast*, p 425, n 1, where the date is wrongly given as 1660; see also Couper, *Sanders*, p 1.

35. James Maclehose, *The Glasgow University Press, 1638-1931, with Some Notes on Printing in the last Three Hundred Years* (Glasgow, 1931), p 23. The quotations are taken from the manuscript Glasgow Town Council Records.

36. Maclehose, *Glasgow University Press*, pp 24-5.

37. The same, pp 30-1.

38. The same, p 42.

39. The same, pp 42-4.

40. The same, pp 44-5. Couper, *Sanders*, pp 7-8, suggests that Anderson possibly left following complaints about defective printing and that Sanders might have had a hand in his removal. This would help to explain the bitter rivalry between the Sanders and Anderson families which lasted for nearly a quarter of a century.

41. Maclehose, *Glasgow University Press*, pp 56-7.

42. The same, p 43.

43. The same, p 57.

44. Apart from the obvious exception of the Stationers' Company imprints this appears to be an usually early example of this form of imprint.

45. *Town Book*, pp 231, 235.

46. This was the oath of abjuration of the Pretender, required of all holders of public office in Ireland after 1703. Many dissenters refused to take it believing it obliged them to recognise and defend the established church and to imply the illegitimacy of the Pretender; see J C Beckett, *Protestant Dissent in Ireland 1687-1780* (London, 1948), pp 64-5.

47. Benn, *Belfast*, p 425, n 2.

48. *The Montgomery Manuscripts: (1603-1706)*, edited by George Hill (Belfast, 1869), p 383.

49. Public Record Office of Northern Ireland T 732/22.

50. Benn, *Belfast*, p 427.

51. *Records of the General Synod of Ulster from 1691 to 1820* (Belfast, 1890), vol 1, pp 156-7: 1 June 1708.

52. Prebyterian Historical Society Belfast, Minutes of the Sub-Synod of Derry 1706-1736, which record attempts by Blair in April 1706 and again in the following year to obtain payment for books supplied. (I am grateful to my colleague John Erskine for bringing this to my attention.)

53. *Dublin Intelligence* [Dickson], 24 June 1710, 21 October 1712, 14 November 1719, and 14 November 1720.

54. Benn, *Belfast*, p 427.

55. No Irish printed edition of the English Bible earlier than 1714 is known; see A S Herbert, *Historical Catalogue of Printed Editions of the English Bible 1525-1961* (London, 1968), no 928. John S Crone, 'An interesting find', *Irish Book Lover*, vol 6 (1915), pp 159-60 reproduces a fragment of St Mark used as binder's waste in one of Neill's books and cites no less an authority than A W Pollard suggesting that this too was printed by Neill. The fragment can no longer be traced.

56. Benn, *Belfast*, pp 427-8. Many of Benn's working papers are in the Public Record Office of Northern Ireland, D3113, but no transcript of or notes on Neill's will are included. In his manuscript draft of this chapter (D3113/4/13) at the point where he quotes from the will he has written 'copy will here'.

57. Alexander Gordon, 'Patrick Neill', *Dictionary of National Biography*, vol 14, p 178.

58. Aldis, *List*, p 107.

59. The same, p 108.

60. Alexander Gordon, 'James Blow', *Dictionary of National Biography*, vol 2, pp 722-3.

61. Couper, *Sanders*, p 25, describes how Sanders when he was disposing of his stock in order to frustrate his son also released from his service an unnamed apprentice who had not completed his time. Was this Blow who, suddenly finding himself without a job, decided to to join Neill in the printing venture in Belfast?

62. James Kirkpatrick, *The Saint's Life and Death. In a sermon preach'd on occasion of the...lamented death of...Arthur Upton Esq; who dy'd Novemb. 13th 1706* (Belfast, printed by James Blow, 1706). Copy in the National Library of Ireland.

63. John Anderson, *Catalogue of Early Belfast Printed Books, 1694 to 1830*, new edition (Belfast, 1890); supplements 1894 and 1902. A first edition of this pioneer bibliography was issued in 1886 and an updated manuscript copy is maintained by the Linen Hall Library, Belfast. Both Anderson and E R McC Dix, 'List of books and tracts printed in Belfast in the seventeenth century', *Proceedings of the Royal Irish Academy*, sect C, vol 33 (1916), pp 73-80 include a number of items published without imprint which have traditionally been ascribed to Neill's press, but the evidence for these attributions is inconclusive.

64. *Mr John Flavell's Remains* (Belfast, Patrick Neill and Company, 1700), Wing F1182. In the copy in the Ulster Museum, Belfast, the lower flyleaf and pastedown are part of a ballad sheet of which only the last verse is complete. The colophon reads '[BELFA]ST, Printed and Sold by Patrick Neill. 1700'; see R M Young,'An account of some notable books printed in Belfast', *The Library*, vol 7 (1895), pp 135-44.

65. E R McC Dix, 'Early Belfast printing', *Ulster Journal of Archaeology*, 2 ser, vol 12 (1906), pp 44-5.

66. First printed in London by John Beale for John Hamman, 1614; see W M Stone, 'The Verbum sempiternum of John Taylor', *The American Collector*, vol 5 (1928), pp 46-59.

67. The John Rylands copy is the only one known and it lacks the title-page of the Old Testament. The New Testament has its own title-page with the imprint 'Belfast, Printed by Patrick Neill and Company, and sold at his Shop. 1699.' Dix, 'Early Belfast printing', supplies what looks like a facsimile of the title-page, but although textually correct it does not accurately reproduce the layout of the original. For a fuller account of this edition see my article 'An unrecorded Belfast edition of John Taylor's *Verbum sempiternum*', *Linen Hall Review*, vol 6, pt 2 (1989), pp 14-15. (I am grateful to Mr D W Riley of the John Rylands University Library of Manchester for providing me with photographs of the copy and for answering queries regarding it.)

68. For a recent study of this complex work see R D S Jack, *Alexander Montgomerie* (Edinburgh, 1985), pp 106-34.

69. Andrew Craig (1754-1833), a Presbyterian minister in Lisburn, recalled learning the poem by rote from his mother; see *Ulster Journal of Archaeology*, 2 ser, vol 14 (1908), pp 10-15. The National Union Catalog pre-1956 imprints apparently lists two copies of Neill's 1700 edition, but that at Maine Historical Society Library, Portland, is in

fact a copy of Blow's 1759 edition. The copy of the Neill's edition in the Library of Congress is (so far as is known) unique.

70. Philip Gaskell, *A New Introduction to Bibliography* (London, 1972), pp 133–4.

Some Late 18th- and Early 19th-Century Dublin Printers' Account Books: the Graisberry Ledgers

1. Daniel Graisberry's ledger 1777–1785

VINCENT KINANE

Historians of the eighteenth-century London printing trade have a range of primary account books to draw on – Ackers, Bowyer, Strahan – while his counterpart in the United States has a veritable embarrassment of riches. In Ireland by comparison, despite the burgeoning trade in that period, hitherto no comparable records have come to light. A perspective on the Irish, and especially the Dublin, printing trade was to be had by piecing together all the scattered fragments of information, often from secondary sources, and by making inferences from the known practices of the overshadowing London trade. The resulting theoretical picture has always begged proofs. The discovery of the Graisberry account books, the first such Irish printers' records known to exist, should now provide the means to test the theories and give new insights.

The Graisberry accounts were unearthed in this way. In January 1988, in connection with my researches on the Dublin University Press, I approached Michael Gill of the Dublin publishing company of Gill and Macmillan, and whose great-great-grandfather Michael Henry Gill was manager of the Press from 1842 to 1874, to see if any DUP records had survived in the company's archives. He discovered some, but in the search also discovered the Graisberry accounts. M H Gill had served his apprenticeship under the partnership of Graisberry and Campbell, so that provides the provenance of the volumes.[1] Michael Gill has generously presented all this material to Trinity College Library, Dublin.

The volumes consist of a ledger of Daniel Graisberry senior covering the period 1777 to 1785, and two account books of the Graisberry and Campbell partnership, a ledger for the period 1797 to 1806 and a cash book for 1799.[2] The ledger for the earlier period, the subject of this paper, is a small folio volume covered in green vellum. It consisted of 360 numbered pages, preceded by four unnumbered pages of preliminaries. The pagination in a few places is erratic, but I have calculated that the volume contained 370 pages, of which 140 are blank, and a further four are missing, although the index would indicate that no accounts have been lost.

It documents accounts with fifty customers, a few private individuals, but in the main belonging to the trade.

From other sources[3] we know that Daniel Graisberry was son of William Graisberry, printer of Drumcondra, then a village about two miles north of the centre of Dublin. He was probably born in 1740 and served his apprenticeship to Boulter Grierson, the King's Printer. In 1765 he married Mary Kennedy – 'an agreeable young Lady, with a handsome Fortune' to quote the contemporary newspaper reports – and had at least a dozen children by her. Although Daniel is noted as a 'printer' in his marriage announcement, it is not until the middle years of the 1770s that his name is recorded in the books of the stationers' guild, the Guild of St Luke. By this time he had established his own business and his name begins to appear in imprints. It was at a meeting of the Guild on 6 February 1782 that he was 'very much bruised' when the floor collapsed, and these injuries may have been responsible, as will be seen, for the recurrent problems he appears to have had with his health. He died less that four years later, on 26 December 1785, at the age of 45, the newspapers lamenting the passing of 'one of the most eminent printers in this kingdom'. At his death he was among the top half dozen printers of the twenty-eight listed in *Wilson's Dublin Directory* for that year.

The ledger provides a glimpse of Graisberry on a domestic level, as when in 1785 he supplies the bookseller Patrick Wogan with some stockings and in turn bought an 'umberrella' from Wogan; or again when he bought four hundred-weight of potatoes from James Williams, presumably to feed all those hungry children.[4] From the ledger it is evident that Graisberry was in partnership with Williams from early 1778 to late March 1781, a fact not recorded elsewhere. The partnership account is styled the 'Printing House' and both Williams and Graisberry did business with it as individuals, although on vastly different scales. For example in the period April 1779 to April 1780 Williams had over £740-worth of work done by the 'Printing House' while Graisberry commissioned less than £15-worth.[5] This underlines the fact that Graisberry was essentially a printer, and did not combine the dual role of printer/bookseller that often occurred in the Dublin book trade of the period. Final settlement of the partnership took place in September 1781[6] but there appears to have been nothing acrimonious about it, and Williams continued to do business with Graisberry right up to the latter's death.

The relationship with Williams ran deeper than partnership for it is evident that he owned the premises at 10 Back Lane that Graisberry occupied. On 25 March 1782 Graisberry is recorded as paying him £45 for one year's rent, while Williams is repeatedly charged for maintenance on the premises. For example on 11 August 1781 Williams's account is debited for two-thirds of the cost of painting the 'Dwelling House & Printing house' and on 5 January 1784 he is charged for 'three Pains of Glass broke by a car taking old Timber out of the Back Yard'.[7]

The ledger allows us to chart the ups and downs of Graisberry's health. A usually firm hand becomes enfeebled in the first half of 1782, probably the consequence of the injuries he received at the Guild's meeting in February. The same shaky hand is again evident in the period September to October 1784, and early in 1785,[8] leading one to wonder if it was a recurrence of problems caused by his injuries. He was dead within ten months.

It is of course for insights into the Dublin book-trade practices of the time that the ledger is of most interest. The volume manifests the complex relationships that existed between printers. Graisberry composed matter for others, printed off their formes, and even imposed matter set by them.[9] There are several instances of shared printing. For example in March 1782 the printer Thomas Henshall had Graisberry print six sheets of David Baker's two-volume *Biographica Dramatica* for him, while in the same month Henshall is credited with printing one sheet of the *Annual Register* for Graisberry.[10] Again in the same month Henshall composed one sheet of an ordinal in the Irish language for Graisberry, who in turn printed off an edition of 500 of it for the bookseller Patrick Wogan.[11] Graisberry probably had no fount of Irish type and presumably Henshall was one of the few Dublin printers who had cases of Moxon's Irish face, the only suitable character available to Irish printers at this date.

The close examination of multiple copies of eighteenth-century books occasionally turns up mysterious examples of variant states where a few gatherings have been reset although without any variation in text. The ledger supplies at least one explanation for these: 'Re Printing first 8 Sheets of [Johnson's *Lives of the Poets*] for being Short in Number - charged to Mr Beatty, Paper Mercht'.[12] Does this indicate that Beatty sent in deficient reams that were not spotted by the warehouse-keeper when preparing the tokens for the pressmen (an unlikely interpretation); or does it mean that Beatty acted as warehouse-keeper and supplied paper in ready-made tokens, in this case some sheets short? The relatively small scale of the Dublin trade may suggest the latter interpretation.

Full analysis of the ledger will in time provide new insights into such matters as patterns of production, ratio of jobbing to bookwork, average edition sizes, hierarchy of various formats, costs of printing. However as an interim measure I took two samples and analysed them. I selected 1782 to see how Graisberry's business varied over a year, and I also analysed the month of April in each year to see how his business progressed.

I was somewhat surprised to find how little the results conformed to expected patterns and indeed how little pattern there was. For example, the number of jobbing transactions in April over the nine-year period was four times that for books, while charges for bookwork were ten times that for jobbing. However the ratios in each year fluctuated wildly; the comparable figures for 1782 were: jobbing to bookwork transactions, nine times; bookwork to jobbing charges, two times.[13] Only when the ledger has been fully tabulated will it be possible to tell the relative importance of jobbing and bookwork in Graisberry's business. Again in the analysis of 1782 the expected pattern of bookwork rising to a peak towards the end of the year did not emerge. Charges were highest in March, October and May; the slackest months were June and December.[14]

From an analysis of the physical nature of his bookwork it will be found that there is little close correlation between the figures for the months of April in the period 1777 to 1785 and those for 1782. For the sample in the former period we find that Graisberry printed books in formats from quarto down to 32mo, the most popular being duodecimo (used in 53% of cases). In 1782 his range was folio to 18mo, with octavo and duodecimo winning a dead heat at 30% each.[15] The smallest format used by Graisberry was 64mo employed in the *Path to Paradise*, printed for Patrick Wogan in 1783.[16] The edition size was 10 000, making it one of the largest in the ledger. Needless to say the dominant edition sizes were much less. The most popular in 1782 was 500 (36% of cases), while in the extended period 1000 wins out (33%).[17] As would be expected, with 100 excepted, edition sizes were all multiples of 250, the 'token' employed as the unit of work by the pressmen.

From an analysis of the type employed it is possible to say that Graisberry had a stock of bookwork faces ranging in size from great primer (approx 18pt) down to brevier (approx 8pt). Given the dominance of octavo and duodecimo formats it is not suprising to find that small pica (approx 11pt) and long primer (approx 10pt) were the most favoured.[18] There is only one indication in the ledger of a supplier of type, and that happens to be a local typefounder. On 25 October 1783 Graisberry bought 3lb 8oz of pica from Stephen Parker for 3s.6d.[19] However we know from a newspaper advertisement that Graisberry also bought type from the Caslon and Wilson foundries.[20]

Accounts were settled at varying intervals and in a variety of ways. Among Graisberry's customers Luke White made half-yearly settlements in cash and promissory notes redeemable in twelve months;[21] Richard Moncrieffe made yearly settlements in kind, cash and notes at three months;[22] while Mary Hay made partial payments in cash and exchequer bills over a period of three years.[23] From the bookseller Richard Cross Graisberry accepted six promissory notes, payable at three-monthly intervals over a period from three to eighteen months, in settlement of his account for 1783.[24] Today, when 'cash flow' is the watchword of all businesses, such extended credit is difficult to comprehend. But in the eighteenth century it was the norm in trade, and prices were adjusted to allow for it. When customers did default on their bills the solutions were equally flexible: in 1784 L Cawton could only pay cash for a portion of his notes and 'left as a Security for Remainder of Debt, 1 Silver Cream Ewer & 1 Pinch back Watch.[25]

Daniel Graisberry's ledger then is a rich source of information on the book trade of late eighteenth-century Dublin, but it should be used with caution. Analysis of it makes one aware of what is missing: where did he record his purchases of printing equipment, of paper, of wages to employees? The unfinished state of some of the accounts makes one wonder if there were other ledgers. Greed makes me ask what other account books of Daniel Graisberry's we are missing.

2. Graisberry and Campbell's account books

CHARLES BENSON

Daniel Graisberry and Richard Campbell were in partnership running a printing firm in Dublin from 1790 to 1820. Two ledgers survive which document part of their activity: the first, a ledger of customers' accounts with the printing office at 10 Back Lane; the second, the first sales book for the shop which Daniel Graisberry established in 1799 at 33 Capel Street, a quarter of a mile across the River Liffey from the printing office[26]. The printing-house ledger runs from 8 February 1797 to 25 October 1806. It is a small folio volume containing 230 leaves in which there are 153 numbered openings. The ledger covers the time of that watershed of Irish history, the Act of Union of 1800, and the apocalyptic event for the Irish book trade, the Copyright Act which came into force on 2 July 1801.[27] This act placed the Irish book trade under the same regulation of literary property as that prevailing in the rest of the United Kingdom and undermined the foundation of the prosperity of much of the Dublin trade, namely, the production of cheap reprints, some authorized and some unauthorized, of works published elsewhere, principally in London.[28]

The printing-house ledger contains the accounts of sixty-four people and associations; eighteen of these are connected with the book trade. The scarcity of business records for the eighteenth-century book trade in Dublin makes this ledger an essential document for the interpretation of its structure and economics, the size of editions in the bookwork executed, and the range and balance of the jobbing work. The firm appears to have been 'unionized' since a copy of *Prices of Printing Work, Agreed upon by the Employers and Journeymen of the City of Dublin, Commencing January 1, 1800* [Dublin, 1799] is pasted inside the front cover of the ledger. This is the earliest known document for Dublin regulating piece-work for compositors and pressmen and formally signed by representatives of both parties. No names of workmen or wages paid are apparent in the ledger.

The firm has the expected range of typefaces, pica, small pica, long primer and brevier, which are all entirely standard. Greek type was also available, as obviously was a competent compositor. There are extra charges made for some work such as setting tables in brevier, for proof-reading and correction, and cancellations. Graisberry and Campbell were jobbing and book printers, as willing to print 50 summonses for the first company of the local militia, the Liberty Rangers, on 28 May 1798 for 3s.3d., as to print 500 copies of volume 3 of Agnes Bennett's *The Beggar Girl*, containing 15^1_2 sheets in 12mo, at a cost of £22.1s.3d. for Patrick Wogan on 4 April 1798.

The majority of the big accounts belong to members of the book trade: men like Patrick Wogan who commissioned work throughout the period covered by the ledger, John Milliken, William Jones and John Stewart. The most substantial account of all was for work printed for Abraham Bradley King, the King's Stationer, and prior to 1800 Printer to the House of Commons, later Baronet, and ultimately public disgrace. Work done for King in 1803 was entered in the ledger at a total of £515.13s.7^1_2d.[29] The firm had a useful regular account as printers to the [Royal] Dublin Society producing the various substantial volumes of the county surveys published by the Society. They also printed for the Royal Irish Academy.

The smaller accounts include several of individuals who were organizing the publication of their own works by subscription, such as Samuel Burdy for whom *Proposals* were printed in June 1799. The work itself, a poem entitled *Ardglass*, was printed in 625 copies for the subscribers in May 1802. Burdy took long credit, for the account was not discharged until April 1803 with a bill at 61 days' notice.[30] The account for the Liberty Rangers is an extreme example of a jobbing account, as between 1 May 1797 and 20 October 1799 a total of 306 transactions were entered in the ledger yet the total invoiced value of the work came to only £86.7s.4^1_2d.[31] There are entries of one or more tiny jobs almost every week; 126 of the 306 transactions were valued at 3s.3d. or less. Summonses were ordered with great frequency in small quantities of 50 to 70 at a time, often twice a week. When the Liberty Rangers planned to take part in a sham battle in July 1797 only 50 plans were required, and even on what should have been a full-dress occasion

the ledger for 15 May 1799 records only 286 copies being printed of a summons
to attend a charity sermon at a cost of 6s.6d.[32]

Some of the most illuminating information in the ledger comes in the accounts
of booksellers dealing with current political and legal affairs, men such as John
Milliken, William Jones, John Exshaw and Matthew Neary Mahon. The years
immediately preceding the Act of Union were ones of intense political ferment.
A threatened French invasion was averted in 1796. An uprising organized by the
United Irishmen and a French invasion took place in 1798. The Act of Union was
passed in 1800, coming into force on 1 January 1801. In 1803 Robert Emmet tried
to organize a rebellion, which petered out as an affray in the streets of Dublin.
The public debate and interest in these issues are reflected in entries in the ledger.
Between 20 April and 17 May 1798 a total of 13 000 copies of a small pamphlet
called *French Fraternity* were printed for John Milliken. By contrast with the fear
of the French, the various arguments for and against the Act of Union were not
presented in huge numbers. This is surprising as, due to the repression and
'management' of the periodical press, much of the public discussion on the union
was conducted through the medium of pamphlets.[33] Recent calculations suggest
that about 120 pamphlets were published on this issue. Graisberry and Campbell
printed seventeen of these for John Milliken, William Jones and John Archer.
Analysis of the size of the editions hardly bears out any suggestions of widely
informed public debate. Eleven of the seventeen pamphlets were first printed in
editions of 500 or fewer copies, eight being in 500 copies and three in 250 copies.
Of the rest there were editions of one pamphlet in 1000 copies, two in 1500 copies,
one at 1600 copies, and two at 2000 copies.[34] These are not enormous figures for
works dealing with a measure which was universally perceived to be of crucial
importance to the country. Only four of the pamphlets were reprinted, three of
which started with 500 copies: Joshua Spencer's *Thoughts on an Union* which was
reprinted three times to bring a total of 2000 copies; Richard Jebb's *A Reply
to...Arguments for and against the Union*, reprinted twice at 250 copies a time for a
total of 1000 copies; Archibald Redfoord's *Union Necessary to Security*, which had
a second edition of 750 copies printed for a total of 1250 copies; and William Pitt's
Speech...January 31, 1799, on... an Union which after a first edition of 1500 copies,
had a second edition of 500 copies.

To judge by the entries in the ledger the public interest in trials, especially in
spicy ones, was at least as lively as its interest in politics. Following the failure
of the 1798 rebellion, several of the leading United Irishmen were tried and found
guilty of high treason. Milliken had accounts of the trials of three of them printed,
details of the printing suggesting that the text of some was being corrected (or
doctored?) during the course of printing.[35] The first trial, printed on 16 July 1798,

was of the Sheares brothers, which was published in an edition of 500 copies, and advertised by means of 1000 handbills. The entry in the ledger records an additional charge for the cancellation of one forme, and a charge for 'sundry amendments from copy'. It was a successful venture as Milliken required a second edition of 250 copies in September 1798. The printing of the second trial, of Michael Byrne, was completed without incident in an edition of 500 copies by 25 July 1798. The third trial, of Oliver Bond, was printed late in August that year. Again, 500 copies were required, but this time things went less smoothly: there was an additional charge for the cancellation of one sheet and 2 pages printed in 250 copies, as well as a charge for amendments from copy. The fact that only 250 copies of the cancels were produced suggests a bibliographical leveret, but also points to the essentially ephemeral appeal of these accounts. Separate reports of the trials of three of Robert Emmet's associates, John Begg, Henry Howley, and Dennis Lambert Redmond, following the politically much less serious rising in 1803, were judged by the publisher John Exshaw to have a greater public interest for he had each printed in an edition of 750 copies.[36]

These figures are insignificant compared with those in the case of the Marquess of Headfort. On 27 July 1804, the Marquess was sued in Ennis Crown Court by the Reverend Charles Massy for damages for the heinous crime of criminal conversation with Mrs Massy. The charge was amply proved and the injured husband was awarded the large sum of £10 000, though in fact he had put a value of £40 000 on his loss. The bookseller Matthew Neary Mahon anticipated a good public interest in the trial. The account in $6^1{}_2$ sheets 8vo was printed in an edition of 1000 copies by 20 August 1804 at a cost of £11.4s.3d., proof-reading being charged at $7s.0^1{}_2$.[37] Very quickly, for the entry in the ledger is dated 1 September, a second edition of 1000 was printed. There was a lesser charge £9.10s.4d. because of '3 sh[eets] standing', but proof-reading and alterations amounted to 10s.6d., and an indication of the urgency of the business is the entry on the same day 'To cash pd: 6 Men for Expedi[t]ion by Candle Light', a sum of £2.15s.$1^1{}_2$d. Within five days there was a third edition of 1000 copies though on this occasion only two sheets were in standing type. Once again 10s.6d. was charged for proof-reading and alterations.

Quite apart from this sensationalism, entries in the ledger confirm our beliefs about other aspects of the market for books. There are clear signs of an extensive trade in plays for reading. That perennial favourite by R B Sheridan *The Rivals* was printed in an edition of 1500 copies in July 1802 for Patrick Wogan.[38] Between December 1798 and February 1799 John Archer had editions printed of three of F von Schiller's plays, *The Minister* in 750 copies 12mo, *The Robbers* in 500 copies 12mo, and *Don Carlos* 500 copies in 12mo. Much more in demand was the adaptation by R B Sheridan of a play by another German, August von Kotzebue's *Die Spanier in Peru*. Sheridan's version entitled *Pizarro* was a runaway success from its first performance at Drury Lane on 24 May 1799. Coming too late to be rehearsed and produced in Dublin in the after-season, it was, however, quickly reprinted here. *The Hibernian Journal* for 5 July 1799 announces the publication of three editions, one that day, and two to appear on the morning of 6 July. The printing ledger shows evidence of haste: a debit to Daniel Graisberry for printing 3000 copies of a half sheet of *Pizarro* occurs on 26 June.[39] Clearly the work was shared out among different printing houses, for Graisberry was only one of twenty-one booksellers associated with one edition. Evidence of continuing popularity follows: an entry for 3 August records the printing of a further 1000 copies. Reference to Daniel Graisberry's sales ledger confirms the public interest for he sold twenty-two copies on the day of publication, and by the time the last entry was made in the sales ledger on 6 November 1799 he had sold a total of 98 copies.[40] As the play was not performed in Dublin until 28 April 1800, these were entirely for reading.

Though some of these plays and pamphlets caught the public interest the really large editions of works were in the old reliable staples, education and religion. This is particularly borne out in the account of Patrick Wogan, who was one of Graisberry and Campbell's most longstanding customers.[41] Wogan's business with the firm has no bookwork of contemporary political interest, but has a large educational and devotional content. Twenty-five out of sixty-three entries for bookwork done for him deal with broadly educational works, a further sixteen with religion. Edition sizes for educational books range between 1500 for Euclid to 5000 for the ancient stalwart, Lily's *Grammar*. Wogan's connexions with education are emphasized by occasional entries of jobbing work for particular schools, such as '200 Large Cards for Crumlin School' on 28 May 1800 or '100 Large Cards for Mr Lee's School' on 4 September 1803. The religious printing has a wider range of edition size and is split between simple catechisms and solid works like Bishop Challoner's *Works* and the Douai version of the New Testament. Many of these were closely overseen by clerical authority. The entry to Wogan's account on 2 April 1802 for the printing of 8000 copies of an 18mo two-sheet *General Catechism* is immediately succeeded by an entry of a charge 'to overrunning one sheet to add new matter to order Dr Troy [R C Archbishop of Dublin] & sundry clean proofs'. Catechisms are printed in editions of 6 to 10 000. A total of 30 000 of various catechisms was ordered by Wogan. A simple devotional work like to *Key to Paradise* was printed in a total of 5500 copies.

A number of entries show evidence of marketing tactics. A case in point is the edition printed for John Milliken of Patrick Duigenan's diatribe *Answer to the*

Address of the Right Honourable Henry Grattan, Ex-representative of the City of Dublin in Parliament, to his Fellow Citizens of Dublin. The ledger entry for 16 June 1798 records an edition of 500 copies on ordinary paper and 12 fine-paper copies. The last leaf of the preliminaries, A4^v, has an extensive list of errata. The entry is accompanied by further charges for '500 title and contents for posting' and 6 broadsides. Four days later there is an entry for '100 contents and title for the second edition', and a further entry for 500 titles and contents used as handbills. Examination of the work shows that the so-called 'second edition' is merely sheets of the first edition, with preliminaries altered by the addition of the words 'second edition' to the title and the removal of the list of errata. Readers of the 'second edition' were getting the defective text without the improving guidance of the errata list. There are numerous other instances of 'hyping' by passing rapidly through the numbering of 'editions'.

This ledger throws new light on edition sizes of work done in Dublin. It illuminates for the first time the huge volume of jobbing printing which accompanied the bookwork in most printing offices in the city. Its future publication will make possible fresh assessment of the scale of political argument, educational and religious works circulating in Dublin at the turn into the nineteenth century. Providing as it does bibliographical detail for over 300 works it allows, along with the other evidence available from newspapers and catalogues of private libraries, an assessment of the reading habits of the educated classes in Dublin, and an invaluable insight into the conduct of an important Irish industry.

NOTES

1. J J O'Kelly, *The House of Gill*, unpublished typescript c 1955, p 3–4; Trinity College Library, Dublin MS 10310.

2. Trinity College Dublin (hereafter TCD) MSS 10314, 10315, 10316.

3. For many of these references I am grateful to Mary Pollard, who allowed me access to her notes for her forthcoming *Dictionary of the Dublin Booktrade to 1800.*

4. TCD MS 10314, pp 170–1 (July, Aug 1785), p 45 (Nov 1783).

5. The same, pp 23, 206.

6. The same, p 209.

7. The same, pp 39, 43, 46.

8. For example see TCD MS 10314 pp 40, 48, 214.

9. V Kinane, 'Some eighteenth century Dublin printer's account books', *Printing Historical Society Bulletin*, no 26 (Summer 1989), pp 4–5.

10. TCD MS 10314 pp 176 (17 March) and 217 (4 March).

11. The same, pp 177 (4 March 1782) and 106 (30 March 1782).

12. The same, p 18 (28 Sept. 1779); for a similar example see p 158 (1 Nov. 1785): 'Re Printing 2 Sheets of Woodfall's Debates Defficent in Count of Paper'.

13. Months of April, 1777–85

    Jobbing: 99 transactions cost £38.5s.3d.

    Bookwork: 26 transactions cost £408.13s.10d.

    1782

    Jobbing: 381 transactions cost £225.19s.1d.

    Bookwork: 42 transactions cost £436.16s.10d.

14. 1782: March £97.7s.0^1_2d.; October £69.16s.0d.; May £60.13s.9d. December £2.10s.0d.; June £1.11s.3d.

15. Months of April, 1777–85

Format	Instances	%		1782 Instances	%
fo	—	—		1	4.3
4to	1	6.6		6	26.1
8vo	5	33.3		7	30.4
12mo	8	53.3		7	30.4
18mo	—	—		2	8.7
32mo	1	6.6			

16. TCD MS 10314, p 190 (21 June).

17. *Edition sizes*

Months of April, 1777–85

Number	Instances	%		1782 Instances	%
100	3	14.3		3	7.7
250	1	4.7		8	20.5
500	2	9.5		14	35.9
750	3	14.1		4	10.3
1000	7	33.3		1	2.6
1500	—	—		1	2.6
2000	2	9.5		4	10.3
2500	2	9.5		—	—
3000	—	—		1	2.6
4000	—	—		1	2.6
5000	—	—		1	2.6
6000	—	—		1	2.6
10000	1	4.7		—	—

18. *Type occurrences*

Months of April, 1777–85

Size	Instances	%
Great primer	1	5
Pica	4	20
Small pica	6	30
Long primer	6	30
Bourgeois	1	5
Brevier	2	10

19. TCD MS 10314, p 144.

20. *Dublin Evening Post*, 13 Feb 1783.

21. TCD MS 10314, pp 272–3.

22. The same, pp 286–7.

23. The same, pp 276–84, 288–91.

24. The same, p 199.

25. The same, p 190.

26. TCD MSS 10315, 10316.

27. 41 Geo iii c 107.

28. For the standard treatment of the eighteenth-century trade see M Pollard, *Dublin's Trade in Books 1550–1800* (Oxford, 1990).

29. TCD MS 10315, openings 65–6, 76–7, 80–3, 87, 89–90, 103.

30. The same, opening 44.

31. The same, openings 1–2, 7–10, 16, 28–30.

32. The same, openings 1, 29.

33. For the treatment of the press see B Inglis, *The Freedom of the Press in Ireland 1784–1841* (London, 1954).

34. TCD MS 10315, openings 13, 19–22, 24, 35–6.

35. The same, openings 13, 17, 18.

36. The same, opening 101.

37. The same, opening 111.

38. The same, opening 70.

39. The same, opening 50.

40. TCD MS 10316, entry for 6 July 1799.

41. TCD MS 10135, openings 10, 41, 57, 70–1, 93, 114, 130–1.

Hampshire Notices of Printing Presses, 1799–1867

MICHAEL PERKIN

The collecting of 'firsts' of all kinds and in all fields is a time-honoured sport and seems to fulfil a basic collecting instinct within us, as books like the *Guinness Book of Records* seem to suggest. Establishing the first dates of printing in provincial towns has obviously a useful function in correcting the historical record both for that town and for its place in the printing map of the region. Many new records will appear in the new edition of the Eighteenth-Century Short-Title Catalogue (ESTC) and the projected Nineteenth-Century Short-Title Catalogue (NSTC). But it is clear that some will also emerge from as yet unexamined ephemera collections and uncatalogued materials in Public Libraries and other uncharted local history collections, and, especially, in Record Offices. To take a small example. In a bundle of documents related to Winchester in the Hampshire Record Office I recently discovered a broadsheet printed by J Lucas in Basingstoke in 1786.[1] The authorities have not credited Basingstoke with a press before the end of the 18th century, and it does not occur in the ESTC place-name fiche (but I hasten to say that it may well be in the revised edition!)[2] Very gradually such small discoveries may cumulatively add to our knowledge of the beginnings and extent of the provincial book trade, but it is perhaps unlikely that they will substantially change generally held opinions about the workings of the trade or the pattern of distribution.

Hampshire was a late starter in the history of provincial printing. Various attempts to establish as 17th-century certain examples in Winchester and Gosport have been generally discredited as misinterpretations. At the time of writing records suggest that printing began in Gosport probably in 1710, in Winchester in 1732, in Portsmouth in 1745, in Southampton in 1768, and in a handful of other places before 1800. Evidence of the book trade in the widest sense exists of course from a much earlier period, as in many other provincial centres. The Winchester bookseller William Taylor appears in an imprint of 1663, and William Clarke in imprints and other records from the 1680s into the 18th century.[3] But printing generally developed in a direct ratio with the growth of the provincial towns. Winchester expanded only towards the end of the 18th century; Southampton developed as a spa town rivalling Bath in the 1780s, and Portsmouth became increasingly important as a naval base throughout the century.

Documentation about any aspect of the provincial printing trade is sparse indeed and the existence of the Hampshire printing notices, small though the collection is, does give us some picture, tantalisingly imperfect, of the persons in the trade mainly at the end of the century.

The immediate background to the Seditious Societies Act, of 1799, has often been described before but it might be helpful to give a brief account here.[4] The war with France had not gone well and by 1798 a French invasion was a distinct possibility. The government had for some years shown itself to be extremely sensitive to any comment seeming to show sympathy to the French and to any criticism of its conduct of the War. There were several prosecutions for sedition, notably that of Gilbert Wakefield for his *A Reply to Some Parts of the Bishop of Llandaff's Address*, which attacked the corruption in the ministry of the time. In addition there were prosecutions for seditious libel in Ireland in 1797, and the move for increasing legislation for stricter control of the press began in earnest. The Stamp Duty steadily rising was twopence in 1789 and then in 1797 was almost doubled to threepence-halfpenny a sheet. But even this was not enough since, although it was illegal to hire out newspapers, reading rooms were springing up everywhere. To deal with a potentially dangerous situation an Act was passed 12 July 1799 'for the more effectual suppression of Societies established for seditious and treasonable practices', commonly known as the Seditious Societies Act. It became illegal to run a circulating library or reading room unless an annual licence was granted by two magistrates. In the Southampton City Record Office there is an example of just such a licence granted by two Justices of the Peace on 20 August 1799 to Thomas Skelton, stationer and bookseller in Southampton, provided that 'no treasonable or seditious books or pamphlets...be read therein'.[5]

But of course, although distribution was important, the main thrust of the act was directed at the means of production, the printers, typefounders and printing-press manufacturers, who were required to give notice of their trades to the Clerk of the Peace, stating that they had a press and types for printing and giving their business address. Moreover they were required to keep a file copy of every book or pamphlet printed, with a note of for whom it was printed and an address, and also the name and address of the printer was to appear in every publication. Accidental omission of this last resulted in very heavy penalties for printers until a maximum fine was introduced in 1811.

It is difficult to assess either how efficiently the Act was enforced (registrations were common in 1799 but steadily less so afterwards) or how effectively it succeeded in controlling the press. Paul Morgan has shown in his tables published in *The Library* in 1966-7 that the number of surviving certificates ranges widely from two in Huntingdonshire to 1307 in Middlesex. In the south the Hampshire total of 52 certificates is higher than some of its neighbours but below Sussex with 97 and well below Surrey with 414. Some 13 counties have no surviving records. But few deductions can be made from these figures and it would be certainly unwise for me to attempt one here. But one thing is clear: imperfect though the coverage may be the surviving notices are a valuable source of information on the provincial book trade not yet fully exploited.

Schedule IV in the 1799 Act lays down the formula for the printers and as an example I quote the first completed Hampshire notice.

> To the Deputy Clerk of Peace for the County of Southampton.
>
> I, Joseph Samuel Hollis of Romsey do hereby declare, that I have a printing press and types, which I propose to use for printing, within Romsey, and which I require to be entered for that purpose, in pursuance of an Act, passed in the thirty-ninth reign of His Majesty King George the Third intilled [sic] 'An Act for the more effectual suppression of Societies established for seditious and treasonable purposes, and for better preventing treasonable and seditious practices'.
>
> Witness my hand this ninth day of August 1799. Signed in the presence of J Woodham.

This printed form, filled in by the printer, is the pattern for ten of the Hampshire notices; there are a further 41 in manuscript, with various alterations from the schedule, and one printed form and one manuscript draft of schedule five, the form of certificate that the Clerk of the Peace gave on receipt of a notice of a printing press.

The act required one witness; two of the Hampshire notices have two witnesses. Notaries, predictably, form the largest class of witnesses, but a company clerk, a naval officer and a Postmaster also occur, as do four other printers submitting notices, suggesting trade relationships of one kind or another. The 46 Hampshire Record-Office notices (with a few additional fair copies) are in chronological order (with one slight discrepancy) and are numbered in pencil, perhaps by an archivist rather than a Clerk of Peace. The six Southampton City Record-Office notices are also in order. There are three pairs of duplicates. Robert Edward Howe of Gosport wrote to Peter Kirby, Deputy Clerk of Peace at Winchester, on 13 May 1801 requesting a certificate for a printing press and other materials, but was then evidently sent the printed form which he duly completed on 21 August. Similarly there are two manuscript applications from William Wheaton of Ringwood, the first dated 31 December 1813 was evidently mis-addressed to Mr Jacob printer, Winchester; the second, dated 5 January 1814, is signed by the Clerk of Peace, T Woodham. The third pair is more puzzling: George Brannon, of Arreton, Isle of Wight, applied for a certificate on 1 January 1831 and again on 18 February 1835, in both cases to Thomas Woodham. Perhaps there was an irregularity in the first certificate since it was not witnessed. There are also two schedule-five certificates given out by the Clerk of Peace on receipt of a notice of a printing press. Therefore although there are 53 notices in all only 48 names are given.

There are 18 place-names in the Hampshire notices and four on the Isle of Wight. Southampton with eight has the highest number followed by Lymington with six, Winchester with five, Gosport with three, and most other places with one or two, but again the Isle of Wight with nine notices. By far the greatest number of notices was submitted in 1799 – some 14; thereafter there were never more than one or two a year every other year or so up to the early 1840s. Inexplicably there were three in 1845, three in 1853 and even one in 1867, though the Act of 1839 made section 27, requiring all printed papers to bear the name of the printer, virtually the only registration requirement left under the 1799 Act.

This tally of 48 printers is by no means the total number of printers at work in Hampshire in the period of 1799 to c 1840. From admittedly only a sample checking of directories and imprints it would seem to represent rather less than 50% of the total number. But this is a cautious estimate since it is clear that many of those who did not submit notices were not printers as a first trade, and equally, many were related to, or the heirs of, printing dynasties which did obtain certificates. Portsmouth and Portsea together account for nearly half of the non-registrations. I have not as yet formed any view as to why this should be so.

Few of the registered persons were printers alone; most were also booksellers, stationers, bookbinders, proprietors of circulating libraries, and so on, in conjunction with other trades. As one would expect most businesses were very small. But as Paul Morgan pointed out, in his masterly analysis of the Warwickshire notices, the schedule only required acknowledgement of 'a printing press and types for printing' and the notice is thus no indication of the size of a business.[6] But very few indicate more than one press. Benjamin Long of Winchester had two in 1799, as did James Robbins also of Winchester, and Thomas Skelton of Southampton, in the same year. William Roe of Alton admitted to three in 1799; John Nelson of Harmony, East Tytherley, had two presses in 1845. This last notice is the only record of the existence of this printer that I have been able to trace; even the place-name was difficult – a small parish on the Salisbury plain. There is little additional information given on the purposes for which a press is required. Some were evidently for private use: Lt J L Bourgeois, of Lymington, requests a certificate in 1806 for a 'small printing press and types which I use for my amusement', and Edward Vernon Utterson of Ryde in the Isle of Wight applies for a certificate in 1840 for a press 'within my dwelling house called Baldornie Tower'. James Hollingsworth and Samuel Mills of Portsmouth register their press on 18 May 1816 'which we propose for printing a newspaper to be entitled the Hampshire Courier'. George Brannon registered as a printer and engraver both in 1831 and 1835 from his house at Wootton Common in the parish of Arreton, Isle of Wight, implying that he ran a rolling press, but I have not traced any imprints.[7]

The elusive nature of many of these persons is brought out by the fact that of the 48 names occurring in the documents some 18 do not appear in the trade directories I have been able to consult, and for 22 names no imprints at all are recorded in the Cope-Collection indexes. It would seem to be further evidence, if any such is needed, that the provincial book trade in the first half of the 19th century was still primarily a concern of bookselling, distribution networks, and, increasingly, shared publication ventures, and that printers were largely anonymous figures except where they happened also to be prominent booksellers and/or publishers. I have selected three Hampshire printers who did emerge from anonymity in one way or another, for a brief examination of the record of their business activities.

According to Plomer's *Dictionary* Thomas Baker's name occurs in the imprint of an anonymous *Manual of Religious Liberty* published in 1767.[8] In a Poll Book of 1774 he still appears as a bookseller only, but in an advertisement in the following year he emerges fully-fledged as printer, bookseller, stationer and seller of patent medicines, in the High Street, Southampton, and shortly afterwards he began what was to be a successful circulating library 'two doors above Butcher Row'. He submitted a printer's notice on 20 August 1799. From about 1802 he was in partnership with his son, also Thomas, and from about 1805 with Isaac Fletcher, another Southampton bookseller and printer. The business presumably passed to the son as he appears alone in an imprint of 1831. The last book I have a record for is dated 1841. This bald summary completely disguises Baker's parallel careers in Southampton as a successful trader in Baltic timber, iron and hemp, and as a radical politician who, by 1803, had become one of the leaders of the opposition in the town.[9] But what were the publications issued by this family business lasting close on 80 years? The first I have seen is a 13-page address relating to the Southampton elections of 1774, and election addresses, poll books and local administrative printing were regularly produced by Baker and his two rival contemporaries, James Linden and Alexander Cunningham. Sermons, single and collected, local and occasional, occur often; they were printed frequently for the author or by request. Baker also printed two issues of the *Hampshire Chronicle* in 1778 but, unlike many provincial printers of the time, he was not otherwise involved in the newspaper business. He had, however, an unusually wide range of publications, including Latin primers, local verses, anthologies of printing and religious lives. But without doubt the main staple of his business was local topography, and his success in this field eventually gained his business a place in the London publishing empire.

In 1774, the same year as his first election pamphlet, Thomas Baker published *The Southampton Guide; or an Account of the Antient and Present State of that Town* which was to pass through at least 12 editions by 1841 in keen competition with Andrew Cunningham's *Guide*, published over much the same period and often confused with it by bibliographers. There were other successful topographical works most of which were written by Baker's close friend, John Bullar. Born in 1778, John Bullar became a prominent deacon and preacher at Above Bar Chapel in Southampton over a period of 43 years and was also a highly esteemed philanthropist and reformer. He left his substantial library to the Hartley Institute at his death in 1864, and it subsequently became the foundation collection of Southampton University Library.[10] The first of Bullar's topographical books was *A Companion in a Tour Round Southampton*, printed and sold by T Baker; sold also by the neighbouring country booksellers, and G Wilkie, London, 1799, a 260-page book. This too was reprinted in 1801 and 1809. Another popular work from the Baker firm was Bullar's *An Historical and Picturesque Guide to the Isle of Wight*, which first appeared in 1806. This is an attractive book which by its eighth edition in 1832 consisted of 162 pages and included a folded map and 'two elegant engravings'. An anonymous work which appeared in 1800 under the title *A Companion on a Visit to Netley Abbey* proved also to be mainly the work of John Bullar, with an accompanying elegy by George Keate. Perhaps it should not surprise us that a guide to a romantic ruined Cistercian abbey, some three miles from Southampton, should have been popular at this time when Southampton was attempting to rival Bath as a fashionable resort. At all events this work, too, appeared in an eight edition by 1837. Alongside Bullar's works there were topographical works by other hands, for example, Sir Henry Englefield's *A Walk Through Southampton*, published in 1801, and much enlarged in 1805, and there were others. In 1824 Baker issued a two-page advertisement of his topographical books. From the earliest period his books were regularly sold and distributed in London – by more than 30 different firms up to 1820, and in the provinces by a dozen or so, in Oxford, Salisbury (by Benjamin Collins of course), Bath, Lymington, Stratford and Devizes.

But in 1820 there is a change in the style of imprint indicating that Baker was attempting to obtain a publishing foothold in London for his successful topographical titles. Bullar's *Historical Particulars Relating to Southampton* of 1820 has the imprint 'Southampton, printed by and for T Baker. And published by him, Finsbury Place London', and this imprint occurs in five further reprints up to

1824. In 1827 the Finsbury Place address is only given as a place of sale for Baker and Son, and this disappears in 1828 to be replaced by Simpkin and Marshall, continuing to 1832. However on the eighth edition of Bullar's *Netley Abbey* of 1837 Southampton is finally dropped for 'London, printed for T Baker, New North Street, Bloomsbury', with London and Southampton booksellers. This is reinforced in 1841 with the imprint for a new edition of the Southampton *Guide* 'London publisher [*sic*]: T Baker, New North Street, Bloomsbury'. From records of later imprints it would seem that the London operation of Thomas Baker continued at least until 1844.[11]

The topographical theme continues with the second printer I have chosen to look at, James Robbins of Winchester, who, unlike Baker, was firmly connected with a newspaper business. He was born in 1760 and in business by 1785, perhaps earlier. In that year he appears in a brief partnership with one of the Gilmours, a family connection, in a pamphlet by James Chelsum. He described himself as 'printer and stationer to the County of Southampton' from as early as 1786.[12] He was operating two presses according to his notice of 1799. In 1805 he purchased the property of the *Hampshire Chronicle* from B Long, and in the following year succeeded to the bookselling business of John Burdon.[13] The newspaper printing office transferred from the High Street to his house in College Street in 1807, which is today the premises of Wells Bookshop. From 1824 he was in partnership with Charles Henry Wheeler in College Street, as printers and booksellers to the College. James Robbins died in 1844 and the business of Robbins and Wheeler was taken over some time in 1845 by the London bookseller David Nutt. The published output of this firm was much as one would expect of a fairly small provincial business of this date: local sermons, concert programmes, school texts (some naturally for Winchester College), political and election material, local poetry and prose miscellanies, and so forth. But the performance of this firm was transformed, and thereafter sustained, by one author and one book.

That most useful reference book, the *Oxford Dictionary of the Christian Church*, does not mention the Winchester interlude in the career of the Roman Catholic apologist John Milner, but it was of great significance for the printer James Robbins. After attending the English College at Douai, and a brief period in London, John Milner came to Winchester in 1779 where he was in pastoral charge of the Catholic congregation for some 24 years, until his appointment in 1803 as titular Bishop of Castabala and Vicar Apostolic of the Midland District caused him to leave. He was an enthusiastic amateur antiquarian, writing articles for learned journals including *Archaeologia*, and in 1790 was elected a Fellow of the Society of Antiquaries of London. James Robbins asked him to write 'a faithful account and description of Winchester'. He was tempted at first merely to offer

a survey and revision of previous accounts but in the end decided on a wholly
new work. This eventually appeared in two volumes published from 1799 to 1801
as *The History, Civil and Ecclesiastical, and Survey of Antiquities of Winchester*, printed
and sold by James Robbins, and sold in London by Cadell and Davies. It is a
lavish quarto, well printed on good paper, with drawings by James Cave of
Winchester, 'a young artist of great ingenuity and unwearied application', engraved by Mr John Pass of Pentonville (with one by Basire after John Carter in
volume two). The first volume caused a considerable stir when it was published
and prompted John Sturges, Prebendary and Chancellor of Winchester Cathedral, to publish *Reflections on the Principles and Institutions of Popery Occasioned by
Milner's History of Winchester*, also printed by Robbins in 1799. Sturges was a
disciple of Bishop Hoadly and strongly objected to Milner's criticisms of Hoadly
as 'undermining the church of which he was a prelate'. This provoked in the
following year a 300-page response by Milner, *Letters to a Prebendary: Being an
Answer to Reflections on Popery*, which of course was also printed and sold by
Robbins, and caused nothing less than a sensation with even the suggestion that
Milner had received offers of a pension if he would suppress it.[14] As is well
known, there is nothing like publicity, good or bad, to sell a book, and there is
no doubt that Milner's *History* was the staple of Robbin's business, in one form
or another, for the next 40 years or so. He wasted no time in exploiting the work.
The first popular version appeared in the same year that volume one of the
History was published. *A Short View of the History and Antiquities of Winchester...Chiefly Extracted from the Rev Mr Milner's History* was published in 1779 for
the lucrative guidebook market where it at once became very competitive. A
seventh edition appeared by 1829, and an eleventh in 1864, finally printed in
London 20 years after Robbin's death. The next offspring was *An Historical and
Critical Account of Winchester Cathedral*, which first appeared in 1801, again extracted from Milner, and intended for visitors to the Cathedral, with the note that
'a few lines in the original which have given offence to some respectable individuals, with the author's permission, have here been omitted'. By the 1830s this
too had reached a 10th edition. In the meantime the parent work went into a
second edition in 1809, corrected and enlarged by the author, and a third,
appearing in 1839 after his death, included Husenbath's biographical memoir
and was printed by D E Gilmour for Robbins. Yet another marketing of the
original was published first in 1822. This was *A Short Description of the History and
Antiquities of St Cross near Winchester. Extracted from...Milner's History*. By 1850 this
illustrated booklet was in its 22nd edition. Nor was it only the text which was
marketed in various ways; the engraved plates for the first and subsequent
editions of the *History* were each separately published, and were also used in

other publications by Robbins, for example Robert Mudie's *Hampshire*, appearing in 1838.

Finally to turn from one printing/publishing business largely sustained by one author to another, but on a much smaller scale. For the space of some three years the output of Joshua Blake Rutter, a printer at Lymington (his notice is dated 10 August 1799) consisted entirely of works by William Gilpin, Vicar of Boldre, in the New Forest. At Winchester James Robbins actively sought out his author; at Lymington the patronage was that of the author himself. William Gilpin dedicated his sermon *The Lord's Cup*, in 1797, the first work which can definitely be assigned to Rutter's press, 'To the inhabitants of Lymington, this discourse, preached formerly at their church, and now printed to encourage a deserving young townsman of theirs, who has just set up press, is inscribed by their affectionate and humble servant Will: Gilpin'.[15] By 1797 Gilpin was a well-established and successful author following the publication in London of his religious biographies, and, especially, his long series of sketching tours illustrated with aquatint drawings, beginning with *Observations on the River Wye* in 1782. After some thirty years as a master at a school in Cheam in Surrey, where he had introduced a number of important educational reforms, he unexpectedly accepted in 1777 the vicarage of Boldre, in the New Forest, where he devoted himself to the life and wellbeing of his parish until his death in 1804. Following *The Lord's Cup* in 1797, Rutter printed Gilpin's *Account of a New Poor-house, Erected in the Parish of Boldre* in 1798, his *An Explanation of the Duties of Religion for the Use of Boldre School* and a religious work, *Moral Contrasts* in the same year, and a series of *Sermons Preached to a Country Congregation*, published in two volumes in 1799 and 1800. Two later volumes of sermons were taken over by London publishers in 1803 and 1805 and frequently printed. As, at present, no other work from Rutter's press appears to be extant, it seems likely that it was Gilpin's patronage which caused it to be set up in 1799 and his death in 1804 which brought about its closure.

NOTES

1. In Hampshire Record Office 44M69/K1/22.

2. F A Edwards, 'Early Hampshire printers', *Papers and Proceedings of the Hampshire Field Club*, vol 2 (1891). John Morris, in his *Provincial Printing and Publishing in Great Britain* catalogue (K Books, 1978) suggests that Lucas's press was established in Basingstoke in about 1804 but offers no evidence.

3. A C Piper, 'The early printers and booksellers of Winchester', *The Library*, 4 ser, vol 1 (1921).

160   SIX CENTURIES OF THE PROVINCIAL BOOK TRADE

4. For example in Donald Thomas, *A Long Time Burning: the History of Literary Censorship in England* (1969), pp 140-3.

5. Southampton City Record Office D/PM5/3/10/1.

6. Paul Morgan [ed], *Warwickshire Printer's Notices, 1799-1866*, (Dugdale Society, vol 28, 1970).

7. Since writing this paper I have been informed that Brannon had a large business as a printseller and guide-book publisher: see P T Armitage, *A Bibliography of George Brannon's 'Vectis Scenery', 1820-1857* (Newport, I O W: County Press, 1974). I am indebted to Mr B C Bloomfield for this reference.

8. H R Plomer and others, *A Dictionary of the Printers and Booksellers who were at Work in England, Scotland and Ireland from 1726 to 1775* (1932).

9. A Temple Patterson, *A History of Southampton*, vol 1 (1966), p 73.

10. Alexander Anderson, *Hartleyana, Being Some Account of the Life and Opinions of Henry Robinson Hartley...Founder of the University of Southampton*, (1987), p 44.

11. Philip A H Brown, *London Publishers and Printers, 1800-1870* (London, 1982).

12. In the imprint to a broadside *A Temporary Plan for the Better Maintenance and Regulation of the Parochial Poor of the Kingdom of England* (in HRO 44M69/K1/22). I am grateful to Mrs Claire Bolton for this and, other references to Robbins's business.

13. *Hampshire Chronicle*, 11 March 1805; and later references for further details of his career.

14. From F C Husenbeth's Memoir in Milner's *History*, 3rd edition (1839).

15. Quoted in William D Templeton, *The Life and Work of William Gilpin (1724-1804)* (1939), p 137.

APPENDIX

Hampshire Notices of Printing Presses, 1799-1867

Abbreviations
W = witness
Form A = printed form (schedule four) completed in manuscript
Form B = printed form (schedule five) completed in manuscript
MS = manuscript notice
CP = Clerk of the Peace
DCP = Deputy Clerk of the Peace

1. 9 Aug 1799; Joseph Samuel Hollis; Romsey; one press; W: J Woodham. Form A. To: DCP of Southampton.*

2. 13 Aug 1799; Benjamin Long; Winchester; two presses (altered in MS); W: J Woodham. Form A. To: DCP of Southampton.

3. 10 Aug 1799; Joshua Blake Rutter; Lymington; one press; W: J Philip, R.N. MS. To: the CP of Southampton or his Deputy.

4. 15 Aug 1799; James Robbins; Winchester; two presses (altered in MS); W: J Woodham. Form A. To: DCP of Southampton.

5. 19 Aug 1799; William Donaldson; Portsmouth; one press; W: A Cunningham. Form A. To: DCP of Southampton.

6. 20 Aug 1799; Jacob Legg; Gosport; one press, 'for printing within my printing office situate behind my dwellinghouse in the High Street in Gosport'; W: Edwd J Cant jr clerk to Messrs Hollis & Bayton, Gosport. MS. To: the CP of Southampton or his Deputy.

7. 23 Aug 1799; William Roe; Alton; three presses (altered in MS); W: J Woodham. Form A. To: DCP of Southampton.

8. 27 Aug 1799; Moss Dimmock; Winchester; one press; W: J Woodham. Form A. To: DCP of Southampton. See also no 20.

9. 28 Aug 1799; Joseph Watts; Gosport, in the parish of Alverstoke; one press; W: John Carter, Thomas Cox. Form A. To: DCP of Southampton.

10. 19 Dec 1799; William Thompson; Portsea, 68 Havant Street; one press; W: Jacob Legg; docket: Mr Kirby, Town Clerk, Winchester. MS. To: the CP of Southampton or his Deputy.

11. 3 Mar 1800; Thomas Willmer; Petersfield, within my dwelling house in High Street; one press; W: Thos Patrick; docket: James Ralfe (?), attorney, Winchester. MS. To: the CP of Hants.

12. 27 June 1801; Robert Serle; Winchester, 'my dwelling house in Southgate Street in the parish of St Michael'; one press; W: Geo Edsall. Form A. To: the DCP of Hants.

13. 13 Aug 1801; Robt Edward Howe; Gosport; one press 'and other materials'; W: Wm Thompson, printer. MS. To: Peter Kirby, DCP, Winchester.

14. 21 Aug 1801; Robert Edward Howe; Gosport; one press; W: Wm Thompson, printer. Form A. To: the DCP of Hants.

15. 9 Nov 1801; William Jacob; Winchester; one press; W: J Woodham. Form A. To: the DCP of Southampton.

16. 3 Nov 1802; Jane Jones; Lymington; one press; W: M Brown, notary public, Lymington; docket: registered 6 Nov 1802. MS. To: the CP of Southampton or his Deputy.

17. 3 Nov 1802; Charles John Coleman; Lymington; one press; W: M Brown, notary public, Lymington; docket: registered 6 Nov 1802. MS. To: the CP of Southampton.

18. 24 June 1806; Richard Galpine; Lymington; one press; W: A Brown, notary public, Lymington. MS. To: the CP of Southampton.

19. 2 Dec 1806; J L Bourgeois, Lieut; Lymington; 'a small printing press and types which I use for my amusement...I beg you to send me a certificate'. MS. To: T Kirby, CP, Winchester.

20. 7 Jan 1809; Moss Dimmock; Alresford; attestor: John Arlott; letter-founder or maker or seller of types for printing; W: T Woodham. Form B. To: Thomas Woodham, DCP of Southampton. See also no 8.

21. 31 Dec 1813; William Wheaton; Ringwood; one press; W: John Jennings Westcott; docket: Mr Jacob, printer, Winchester. MS. To: The CP of Southampton.

22. 5 Jan 1814; William Wheaton; Ringwood; one press; W: T Woodham. MS. Another version of no 21.

23. 3 June 1813; William Minchin; Petersfield; one press; W: Js Seward. MS. To: Thomas Woodham, DCP of Southampton.

24. 10 Oct 1814; Henry Shelton; Havant; one press; W: Orestes Silverlock; covering letter to Thomas Woodham, same date, 'enclosing a shilling...bearer will call again; if certificate is not ready you can send it by him if not by the post'. MS. To: DCP of Southampton.

25. 18 May 1816; James Hollingsworth and Samuel Mills; Portsmouth; one press 'which we propose for printing a newspaper to be entitled the Hampshire Courier'; W: Wm Pottle (?); docket: Certificate of printing a newspaper called 'The Hampshire Courier'. MS. To: the CP of Southampton.

26. 3 Nov 1817; Augustus Nicholson; Fareham; one press; W: W Nicholson; docket: received 7 Nov 1817. MS. To: the DCP of Southampton.

27. 27 Sept 1820; John Perkins King; Andover; 'I am about to commence the printing business...enter a printing press for me'. MS. To: Woodham, solicitor, Winchester.

28. 28 Oct 1822; Thomas Henry Toll; Christchurch; one press; W: Wm Dibsdall Toll (?). MS. To: DCP of Southampton.

29. 2 Aug 1824; Isaac Skelton; Havant; one press; W: J Skelton; docket: Mr Woodhouse, CP, Winchester. MS. To: DCP of Southampton.

30. 1 Jan 1831; George Brannon, printer and engraver; Wootton Common in the parish of Arreton, Isle of Wight, at my house; one press. MS. To: Thomas Woodhouse, DCP, Winchester. See also no 32.

31. 1 Aug 1833; James Shayler; Wonston; one press; W: Tho Mann; docket: rec'd 5 Aug 1833. MS. To: DCP of Southampton.

32. 18 Feb 1835; George Brannon; Wootton Common in the parish of Arreton, Isle of Wight, at my house; one press; W: W Burnett (?). MS. To: Thomas Woodham, DCP, Winchester. See also no 30.

33. 1 June 1836; Robert Budd, in conjunction with my sons; Fordingbridge, within my dwelling house; one press; W: William Reeves, Fordingbridge; docket: rec'd 3 June 1836. MS. To: the DCP of Southampton.

34. 28 July 1837; George Alexander Hillier; Ryde, Isle of Wight, Morpeth House, Union Street; one press; W: William H Coleman, George Street, Ryde. MS. To: Thos Woodham, DCP, Winchester.

35. 13 July 1840; Edward Vernon Utterson; Ryde, Isle of Wight, within my dwelling house called Baldornie Tower; one press; W: Henry Hearne, of Ryde. MS. To: the DCP of Southampton.

36. 25 July 1842; Frederick Stephen Knight; West Cowes, Isle of Wight; one press; W: Thomas Mercer; letter headed: Thomas Woodham, DCP, West Cowes of same date; docket: rec'd 26 July 1812. MS. To: Thos Woodham, DCP.

37. 10 Jan 1844; John Richard Smith; West Cowes, Isle of Wight; one press; W: John Smith, Cowes; Rob Bryant, Newport. MS. To: the DCP, Hants.

38. 4 Feb 1845; John Nelson; Harmony, East Tytherley; two presses; W: George Simpson. MS. To: the DCP, Southampton.

39. 20 Mar 1845; John Clarke; Clanville, in the parish of Penton Grafton; one press; W: James Hedderly. MS. To: the DCP, Southampton.

40. 7 May 1845; William Lejeune Galpine; Lymington; one press; W: J D Robins, Lymington. MS. To: the DCP, Southampton.

41. 11 Sept 1846; Frean Frederick Le Maître; Portsea, 19 Hanover Street; one press in College Street, Portsea; W: Edwin Kent. MS. To: the DCP, Southampton.

42. 13 Aug 1852; James Briddon; Ryde, in the parish of Newchurch, Isle of Wight; one press; W: W Whittington, Ryde. MS. To: the DCP, Southampton.

43. 4 May 1853; William Geball; Ryde, Church (Towne?) in the parish of New-church, Isle of Wight; one press; W: George Hopgood. MS. To: Francis Woodham, CP for Hants.

44. 14 May 1853; William Richard Yelf; Newport, Isle of Wight; one press; W: James [ ]. MS. To: CP, Borough of Newport, Isle of Wight.

45. 24 May 1853; Thomas Kentfield, Newport, Isle of Wight; one press; W: James [ ]. MS. To: the DCP of Southampton.

46. 29 May 1867; Frampton James Ames; Crondall, Southampton; one press; W: James Barnard. MS. To: the DCP, Southampton.

Hampshire Record Office Q16/6/1–46, reproduced by permission of the County Archivist.

* Note: Until 1959 the formal name of Hampshire was 'County of Southampton'

1. 12 Aug 1799; Thomas Skelton, bookseller and stationer; Southampton, house and premises situate in the parish of St Lawrence; two presses; W: John Carpenter. MS. To: Thomas Ridding, CP, Southampton.

2. 3 Aug 1799; Thomas Skelton; Southampton; two presses (altered in MS); W: Thomas Ridding; endorsed 'Draft certificate of entry of types and printing presses under 39th Geo 3, c 79 passed 12 July 1799. Copd.' MS. To: Thomas Ridding, CP, Southampton.

3. 19 Aug 1799; Alexander Cunningham; Southampton, parish of Holy Rhood; one press. MS. To: the CP, Southampton.

4. 20 Aug 1799; Thomas Baker, bookseller and stationer; Southampton; one press; W: Edwd Baker. MS. To: the CP, Southampton.

5. 10 Sept 1832; Thomas Henry Skelton and Matthew James Preston; Southampton, parish of All Saints; one press; W: A Wood, Southampton. MS. (With two fair copies) To: the CP, Southampton.

6. 8 Sept 1832; Charles Bell; Southampton, parish of All Saints; one press; W: A Wood, Southampton; endorsed 'printing licence'. MS. To: the CP, Southampton.

(6.) 22 Sept 1826; John Coupland; Southampton, parish of Holy Rhood; one press; W: Wm Hesketh. MS. To: the CP, Southampton.

Southampton City Record Office D/PM/5/3/9/1–6 and D/PM/5/2/7/6, reproduced by permission of the City Archivist.

A Century of Saltmarket Literature, 1790-1890

ADAM McNAUGHTAN

Glasgow in 1790 was a town of some 66 000 inhabitants. When the Shop Tax had been repealed the previous year there had been 1030 shops, with a total annual rental of £8782.15s. The Trades Directory of 1790, by no means an exhaustive list, showed that there were 16 booksellers and 8 printing houses – and there was a pocketbook-maker, Francis Orr.

The centre of the town was still Glasgow Cross, at the intersection of the four main streets: Gallowgate, running east to the burghs of Calton and Barrowfield; Trongate, running west to the areas where the capital from the town's American trade was now being invested; High Street, which housed the University with its splendid Gardens; amd Saltmarket, leading to the River Clyde, too shallow for seagoing vessels and still liable to flooding at this point. Biographers of the early 19th century frequently recall boats among the tenements at the bottom of the Saltmarket. This was no longer the solid street of merchants that Scott's Bailie Nicol Jarvie had known; the old mansions remained, but they were now densely populated tenements. Of the twenty-four people engaged in the book trade eleven had their premises in the Saltmarket.

By 1890 Glasgow was a city of over 800 000 inhabitants. The deepening and channelling of the Clyde had made it a world centre of shipping and shipbuilding. The town centre had shifted, with the Municipal Buildings and the Central Post Office both in George Square, and the University even further west at Gilmorehill. The Corporation with its involvement in health, housing, markets, water supply and tramways, had become a model for municipal development throughout Europe. Among its enterprises had been the clearing of the slums of the Saltmarket, and their replacement with dignified three-storey tenements of honey-coloured sandstone. The Post Office Directory for 1890 lists around 300 letterpress printers, 119 publishers, 132 booksellers and 111 bookbinders. None of them had their premises in Saltmarket.

To return to the list of 1790. The newest booksellers were the firm of Brash and Reid who had started that year in the Trongate premises formerly occupied by Dunlop and Wilson, of whom Robert Reid (Senex) wrote[1]

These gentlemen were the fashionable *west-end* booksellers, and they were the only booksellers who dealt in new publications...– the old Saltmarket biblio-polists confining themselves mostly to religious works, and to the interesting pamphlets and histories of Jack the Giant-Killer, Valentine and Orson, Leper the Tailor, and the Seven Wise Men of Gotham and such like. Dunlop and Wilson had one of their shop windows fronting the Trongate, and another fronting the Candleriggs. In the inside of these were displayed stucco busts of Adam Smith, David Hume and other celebrated literati; also, a goodly set-out of handsomely bound and gilt new publications of the times: while the unfortunate Saltmarket Street booksellers were prevented from making any display at their shop windows, in consequence of their premises being situated in the dark recesses under the pillars; they therefore rested satisfied with decking out their establishments by exhibiting splendid assortments of half-penny prints, and gold-feuilled children's books, such as 'Goody Two-Shoes', 'Babes in the Wood', 'Puss in Boots', 'Robinson Crusoe', etc. The most striking article of their display, however, was the celebrated penny print of Paul Jones shooting a sailor who attempted to strike his colours; and the miserable countenance of poor Jack when the pistol was being presented to his head, never failed to attract a fair assemblage of window gazers.

Brash and Reid inherited the west-end trade of their predecessors, but the most famous production from their firm was a set of niney-nine penny books of poems, printed for them by Robert Chapman or by Chapman and Lang, which rapidly became collectors' items in a four-volume issue, described as 'exceedingly rare' in the sale catalogue of Chapman's library in 1822. Nor were Brash and Reid adverse to using the broadside form in the right circumstances, issuing in 1802 a version of Burns's *Does Haughty Gaul Invasion Threat*, with Ayrshire place-names altered to landmarks more familiar to a Glasgow readership, and the tune given as the well-known, but hardly warlike, *Merrily Danc'd the Quaker's Wife*.[2] Willie Reid himself was presumably responsible for this adaptation, as he was for the additions to a number of other Burns pieces published in the penny series. The firm dissolved in 1817, with both partners continuing in the bookselling trade, but apparently not as publishers.

The penny productions of Brash and Reid, with pretensions beyond the usual run of chapbooks, undoubtedly widened the readership for the real 'Saltmarket literature' in Glasgow. The recognised kings of that production in the 1790 list were James and Matthew Robertson, then at 95 Saltmarket, who are frequently remembered in memoirs and autobiographies of the nineteenth century. Among the many volumes of chapbooks now in the Murray collection in Glasgow University Library, there are some 150 eight-page song garlands printed by J and M Robertson between 1802 and 1809. In addition, there are twenty prose or verse chapbooks, dated from 1792–1805 including the classics like *John Cheap the Chapman*, *Jack and the Giants* and Forbes's *Dominie Depos'd*. This might lead one to speculate that the Robertsons changed over to songbook production in 1802, were it not for the existence in the Wylie collection in the same library of 41 Robertson garlands from 1799–1802, reminding us how much we owe our knowledge to the chance survival of these little books in personal collections. A catalogue from 1798 of books sold in their shop advertises historical and religious chapbooks, stitched pamphlets and catechisms, 'with a great variety of Sheet Pamphlets, Ballads etc'. The list of 'Books for the Instruction and Amusement of Children, bound in Gilt Paper, and adorned with Cuts', which were printed by the Robertsons, shows a considerable correspondence with the later Lumsden juvenile repertoire. One religious pamphlet in the Lauriston Castle Collection in the National Library of Scotland, *Faith's Plea upon God's Covenant* gives an indication of the firm's history, existing in three editions: 1772, printed by J Robertson; 1777, J and J Robertson; 1787, J and M Robertson.[3] In fact, John Robertson began printing around 1753, taking his son James into partnership in 1774; when John died, James was joined by his brother Matthew.[4] J and M Robertson remained in the business until 1810, although James died in 1805. While the bulk of their publication, aside from the chapbooks, was religious, they also issued several editions of Graham's metrical history of the Rebellion, of Dean's *Hocus Pocus*, Defoe's *Robinson Crusoe*, McIlquham's *English Grammar* and, in 1790, *The Vicar of Wakefield*.

The songs in the garlands were typical of street literature at the end of the eighteenth century. About 70% were songs of the day, recently composed songs by such as Dibdin, fit for any drawing room. The second largest group, 20–25%, was the Scottish songs, including the songs of Burns, in the original versions rather than the Reid adaptations, and a number of traditional songs like *The Rigs o'Rye* and *Lord Thomas o'Winesberry*. The proportion of Scottish songs was perhaps the only thing to distinguish Robertson's production from the London printers like Catnach and Pitts. Local songs, such as *The Beauties of Glasgow City* or *John Highlandman's Remarks on the City of Glasgow*, were very rare. Among the approximately six hundred surviving songs there are eighteen Irish pieces, including stagey items like *Murphy Delaney* and *The Wedding of Ballyporeen*, political pieces like *Boyne Water* or *Old Ireland Free (The Croppy Boy)*, and folk songs and broadside ballads such as *Gragal Machree* and *Reilly's Courtship*. Most of the imprints include the year of issue, and it seems, though I would repeat my reservations about the imcomplete nature of the collections, that the Robertsons probably began by copying the practice of English garland publishers, but increased the Scottish content slightly through the years.

The third name I would extract from the directory of 1790 is that of Thomas Duncan, Gibson's Land, 159 Saltmarket. He is presumed to be both the partner from the firm of Robert and Thomas Duncan which was dissolved before 1785, and the Thomas Duncan who published broadsides and song garlands from 1800 to 1826, but if so, he was strangely inactive as a publisher between 1785 and 1800. The *Athenaeum* journalist saw him as a rival to the Robertsons, but in the dates of his surviving production, and in the items he issued, he appears more a rival to two other firms: John Muir and William Carse.

Duncan twice had to change his address, as a result of his premises collapsing, in 1814 and in 1823. These premises were in the garret above the fifth floor of the tenement known as Gibson's Land in Saltmarket. The 1814 incident saw a remarkable escape[5]

> As soon as the dust which arose from the ruins subsided, several individuals were seen mounting the wreck, regardless of the danger which the hanging remains threatened them with, searching for the persons who were buried in the rubbish. The first persons observed were Neil McViccar, pressman, and a young son of his employer, Mr Duncan, who had been precipitated from the garrets, six stories high, and escaped without any great hurt. The pressman chiefly regretted the loss of his jacket, containing five shillings and a certificate for his soldier's pension...Mr T Duncan and his son, William, were brought by the ladder from the garrets, an alarming height and perilous situation as part of the roof every moment threatened to hurl them down...The loss in furniture and working materials was considerable.

The loss of materials presumably forced Duncan to re-equip, because in the 1823 collapse of the building, a Ruthven press was seen to be precariously balanced on the edge of what remained of the sixth floor. This was not the worn-out machine usually associated with street literature, but a modern press of Scottish design, which had been perfected precisely in 1814.

Duncan, William Carse and John Muir appear as rivals if only because all three printed broadside lists of the persons to be tried at the Circuit Court in the years round about 1820. They also competed in dying declarations and lamentations from the scaffold, often ranging furth of Glasgow to avoid duplication. For example, Duncan's *An Account of the Death and Dissection of that Extraordinary Impostor, Joanna Southcott* or Muir's *The Last Speech, Confession and Dying Words of Mary Smith, Who was Executed at Durham, for a Horrid Murder Committed on the Bodies of her Father and Sister, by Poisoning them with Arsenic.*[6] But while all three printed broadside songs and verses, a mere handful of their chapbooks have survived. Muir, or rather his widow, who continued the business until 1844, later printed large-format song books of four or eight sides, such as *The New British Melodist for 1843*, which could easily have come from a London press, the Scottish items being widely acceptable songs such as *Annie Laurie* and *The Scottish Blue Bells*. Writing in 1902, Muir's grandson recalled how his grandfather, made redundant from the pressroom of the *Glasgow Herald*, was given an old wooden printing press and type to set him up in business. He also recalled 'Granny' Muir's hospitable round table, which attracted some of Glasgow's leading literati, such as the radical poet, Alexander Rodger, and William Motherwell, editor of the *Glasgow Courier.*[7]

When any news article reached the composing room that was exciting enough for Grandmother to publish – such as an execution, a dying speech on the scaffold, a dreadful murder, curious scenes in the police courts, shipwrecks and loss of life, a trial for murder and a sentence of death, etc – as soon as it was in type and proof taken, there were always volunteers ready to go to Granny Muir's to set it up. Granny's news-slips might be said to be the pioneer of the evening newspaper of today. The speech-sellers were usually gathered from the loafing class of the city – great ungainly fellows some of them were, and made the streets hideous by the way they yelled the headlines of the news-slips.

Speech-selling was not without its hazards. The best-known of Glasgow's flying stationers, William Cameron (Hawkie), claims in his autobiography that fifty of his colleagues were arrested by the Glasgow police for crying the execution of William Robertson in 1819. Hawkie frequented both Muir's and Duncan's, though he preferred to have his own compositions printed by someone who would observe his sole right to distribution. Duncan refused to be bound by restrictions such as an author's copyright.

The other Saltmarket garland publisher of the first three decades of the 19th century, was Robert Hutchison, bookseller, 1801–31. Some thirty of his songbooks survive in various collections and show a distinct predilection for Scottish material. His garlands appear from the middle of the second decade on, with a particularly productive year in 1823, not only because of the songs about the royal visit to Scotland. The songs for that occasion, however, do show a willingness to include local and topical material in the garlands.

The pocketbook-maker of the 1790 directory, Francis Orr, was one year old when his father, the bookseller John Orr, died in 1766.[8] His mother Anna took over the printing and bookselling business in Saltmarket, passing it on to her elder son Andrew. Presumably to avoid competition, Francis set up as a pocket-book-maker round the corner in Gibson's Wynd (later called Princess Street). That was his directory description until 1824, when he moved to Brunswick Street and became a 'Wholesale stationer'. By 1831 his three sons, James, Andrew and William were working with him, though it was not until 1834 that the directory entry changed to 'Francis Orr and Sons'.

Their stationery activities included the supply in reams to the trade of

> Ballads both 8 pages and slips, a large assortment embracing all the Old and most Popular of the New Songs. IRISH BURTONS. An immense variety of Glasgow and London Royals, both coloured and plain. A great variety of Religious Tracts, One Penny Each.

In addition, they published 150 twenty-four page history books, recognisable by the numbering and by the imprint 'Glasgow, Printed for the Booksellers'. Numbered among the 'histories' were fourteen song books, including *Watts' Divine*

Songs and *Prince Charlie's Songbook*. These were printed by stereotype, and it seems probable that the plates were made by the Paisley firm of Neilson. John Urie, an apprentice with Neilson in the 1830s, writes[9]

> ...after three or four year's service I was in practical charge of the stereotyping department, the journeymen having all left one after another. I was then receiving four shillings a week, but on my representing that I was underpaid for having the responsibility of this department on my shoulders, Mr Neilson raised my wages at a bound to what I then considered the princely salary of twelve shillings a week. After three months of this, Mr Neilson received a big order from Francis Orr & Sons. Mr Neilson intimated that he would have to get in a journeyman from Glasgow, and that I would have to go back to my old wages. This arrangement did not suit my views, and accordingly I left.

Francis Orr & Sons remained one of Glasgow's leading stationery concerns into the twentieth century, styling themselves 'Queen's Printers' from 1861, and providing in Sir Andrew Orr another book-trade Lord Provost of the city to add to the Lumsdens and Sir William Collins.

The Scottish element in their song repertoire forms about 45% of the output, with a similar amount drawn from the standard British garland reportoire. Burns songs are given in the street-literature editions, with the extra verses by Willie Reid and others. The few local songs are those already established, like *John Highlandman's Remarks*. As one might expect with a reliance on stereotypes, there are no topical pieces. There are a few additions to the Irish songs from the Thomas Moore canon, *Oft in the Stilly Night* and *The Minstrel Boy*. A number of the books carry the date 1828 or 1829. A ninety-page songbook in two volumes, *The Vocal Repository*, published in 1842, indicates that the songs were published in series over the previous sixteen years.

In 1851, Francis Orr & Sons moved from Brunswick Street. Though one or two chapbooks carry the imprint 'Francis Orr and Sons, Union Corner', it appears that he did not take the 'Glasgow: printed for the Booksellers' stereotypes with him. They passed to an erstwhile rag merchant, James Lindsay, Junior, who had become a stationer in the suburban village of Anderston in 1848, and who now appears in King Street, City, one street west from the Saltmarket, as the publisher of the garlands and twenty-four page histories with the imprint 'Glasgow, Printed for the Booksellers'. A catalogue,[10] issued in about 1856, lists 152 titles as opposed to the 150 of the Orr catalogue. Lindsay also offered 'New and Improved Series' numbered 1–61. Also in the catalogue are listed 200 slips each with two songs, many of which survive in the Murray collection.[11] Having come late to bookselling (he was 31 in 1850) Lindsay remained in the trade for a remarkable sixty years, all but the last four in King Street, if we except temporary displacements when a new street linking King Street with Saltmarket was being built. Since the sheets are undated it is impossible to say how long he continued to publish, but the surviving topical sheets all come from the fities and sixties. They include, for example, songs about Glasgow's three famous murder cases: Dr Pritchard, Madeleine Smith and Jessie MacLachlan. We cannot, however, judge from what survives. All the sheets in these volumes, whether from Lindsay or Harkness of Preston or from other Glasgow printers, date from the same decades, though we know that some of the others printed later.

The 24-page histories, inherited from Orr, reflect the taste of the 1830s, or indeed of the eighteenth century. It is to the slip-songs selected by Lindsay himself that we must look for changing tastes. The most obvious trend is the increase in Irish material. Scots and Irish songs in equal amounts make up half the repertoire. Given the vast numbers of Irish who came to Glasgow in the 1840s it is hardly surprising. The songs cover a wide range of folk song, stage Paddy and drawing-room ballad. The Irish political/religious songs are relatively few. Topical and local songs are also more frequent in the garlands. As well as the murders, the Crimean War and the Australian Gold Rush feature in the verses. There are around twenty-five songs on the list which have specific Glasgow place-references. Some of these are of the music-hall type where a comedian took a comic song and set it locally; others are songs about actual local events. *Sunday Sailing* is one such, dealing with the altercations over steamer trips to Gareloc-head on the Sabbath. There is, as earlier, an overlap with English broadsheet publication. More striking, however, is the overlap with the other Glasgow printers, and particularly two who came fresh to the trade about the same time as Lindsay.

Robert MacIntosh makes his apearance in 1849 in King Street, Calton, about quarter of a mile east of Lindsay in King Street, City. In 1860 he moved round the corner to 203 Gallowgate, and in 1874 round another corner to Kent Street. There are sheets surviving from all of these addresses, though again the sheets in the Murray Collection are all from the 50s and 60s. The English and drawing-room element is less in McIntosh's repertoire, and the Scots/Irish songs seem closer to the oral tradition than those of other printers. Deep in the East End there would be little demand for drawing-room songs. The topical song, however, would always take a trick, no matter how distant its subject. Thus he issued several songs about the Roger Tichborne case, including the Lament of Roger Tichborne, which detailed the claimant's responses to the 1874 verdict. The sheet also carried the announcement of McIntosh's impending change of address to 25 Kent Street, at Whitsunday that year. More than any of the others I have mentioned, McIntosh conformed to the accepted picture of the broadside printer, with poor quality paper and type, hurriedly set up, with frequent spelling errors and the usual shifts to cover for shortage of type. For example, the Tichborne sheet has to employ italic *I* throughout its last verse. Where the chapbook and broadside had in the case of Duncan and the Robertsons been at the bottom end of a book-printer's range, in the case of McIntosh and Lindsay it is at the top end of the jobbing stationery printer's range, though Lindsay's on-sheet advertising puts him perhaps in a class above McIntosh.

> Sold by James Lindsay, Printer and Wholesale Stationer &c, 9 King Street, (Off Trongate) Glasgow. Upwards of 5000 sorts always on hand; also a great variety of Picture-Books, Song- Books, Histories &c. Shops and Hawkers supplied on Liberal Terms. Handbills, Circulars, Invoices, Business and Fancy Cards, Large Posting Bills, Society Articles, Pamphlets and Letter-Press Printing of every description, neatly and expeditiously executed on moderate terms. Printing office, 28 Nelson Street and 58 Trongate.

> Robert McIntosh, Printer, 203 Gallowgate, Glasgow. A good variety of Slip-Songs always on hand, Shops and Travellers supplied. Children's Toy-Books. House:Lets and Window Labels. Paper, Envelops, Pens, Pencils, Inks, &c. McINTOSH'S LIQUID BLUE IS UNSURPASSED.

As advertisers, however, they were both surpassed by the third slip-song publisher to start up in mid-century.

> Say, who attracts the countless crowd?
> Who makes for care her neatest shroud?
> Who tells the truth and speaks it loud?
>> The Poet!

> Who writes PETITIONS, SONGS, and PUNS?
> Who prizes all Apollo's sons?
> Who puts the pen 'fore swords and guns?
>> The Poet!

> Who sells nick-nacks of every kind?
> Who loves the handiwork of mind?
> Who is to bigot-logic blind?
>> The Poet!

> Who loves the songs of every land?
> Who keeps the largest Stock on hand?
> With nothing foul, or contraband?
>> The Poet!

> Who keeps a stock befitting all?
> From Petersburg to old Pall Mall?
> From Lomond's Hill to Donegall?
>> The Poet!

> Who thinks not of one's clime or creed?
> Who is a bard, and that indeed?
> Who gives you every song you need?
>> The Poet?

At Number Six Saint Andrew's Lane,
You'll find him there - you'll go again
To see this prodigy of Brain,
                    The Poet!

This was one of several poetical puffs given to himself by Matthew Leitch, proprietor of the Poet's Box, Glasgow, from 1849 till 1859, when he was succeeded by his son, William Munsie Leitch, who continued in the business, then known as the Minerva Printing Company, until his death in 1910. By that time, indeed by 1880, the song-printing had become spasmodic, though the title, 'The Poet's Box' was to be kept alive until 1961 by the firm who took it over in the 1920s.[12] The heyday, then, of the Glasgow Poet's Box was 1849-75. Geographically half-way between King Street City and King Street Calton, Matthew Leitch was in direct competition with Lindsay and McIntosh. (Of 395 titles in Lindsay's catalogue of slip-songs, 212 were also published as Poet's Box slips.) Judging from the surviving evidence in the form of catalogues, he outstripped them.

In 1849 Matthew Leitch moved his draper's business from 200 Gallowgate to 130 Gallowgate. The earliest songsheets from his press, and presumably the last items of drapery, appeared in that year. He was not permitted to keep the address long; in what he saw as a piece of sharp practice, the shop was sold from under him and he moved round the corner to a 'more commodious Box', which was to be described in his imprint as

Glasgow, printed by the Poet's Royal Yankee Press, at the Poet's Box, the Grand Temple of the Muse! the boast and pride of millions! the attraction of the cities! the glory of the Nations! and the luminary of the World! no.6 St.Andrews Lane, off Gallowgate Street, and first street from the Cross, right hand side.

What distinguished the Poet's Box from the other printers was the offer to produce poems and other pieces of writing on request. David Murray, the Glasgow bibliographer, recalled making use of the Poet's services when he was a student at the College in the 1850s, both for the composition and printing of Rectorial election ballads, and for setting out petitions.[13]

The 'Royal' part of his imprint came into use as a result of one of Leitch's rare excursions into 'book' printing, like the other example in the Mitchell Library, a spin-off from one of the regular contributors to the sheets. In 1851 Leitch published *The Queen's Visit to Scotland or The Days of Victoria the Beloved* by Daniel Norris. Among the preliminaries to this slim drama, he included a letter addressed to the author from Buckingham Palace, September 28, 1849

Sir, I am directed by Mr Anson to return the enclosed papers, and to inform you that you may exercise your own discretion with regard to publishing their contents. I am, Sir, Your obedient Servt. Wilbraham Taylor

On the doubtful strength of that letter, the Poet's press is ever afterwards 'Royal'.

We know of Daniel Norris also from the songs which he contributed, because Matthew Leitch did not simply print the title, text, and imprint. He frequently added an idiosyncratic little introduction puffing the song and its author or performer. From the Poet's Box sheets we know of fifty-six songwriters, past and contemporary, and seventy-seven singers. The performers' names clearly indicate that though the printer had moved one street to the east, what he printed was still Saltmarket literature. In 1848 there were about twenty-five spirit dealers in the Saltmarket, eight of them running singing saloons, with names like 'The Shakespeare', 'The Jupiter' or 'The Sir Walter Scott'. Anyone who heard a song he liked at one of the entertainments could apply for a copy at St Andrew's Lane. If Leitch did not have it in stock, he promised he would quickly acquire it. A typical Poet's Box introduction is the following from 5th July 1851

> The author of this version of 'Johnny Cope' is a Mr McGregor Simpson, well-known among the singers of Glasgow. He has been regularly singing for the last few months in the *Shakespeare Saloon*, Saltmarket, Glasgow, and few, if any, have sung with more taste in that place of amusement since it opened. His talents as a singer are too well-known to require any comment in this flying ballad. Along with this song of Mr McGregor Simpson you will find in this Box those beautiful other songs which he sings with so much spirit.

In fact, the version differs little from the well-known set of words to *Johnny Cope*, but the musical taste of McGregor Simpson figures in an anecdote of the Poet's Box recalled in a local paper in 1888.[14]

> One day a lot of the professionals who were engaged at the *Shakespeare* were standing at the bar, when the conversation turned to a song entitled 'Jeanett and Jeannott', which had become very popular. While they were discussing its merits a hurdy-gurdy came into the close and began to play it. At the same time a street arab came up to the bar and offered to sing the song for a halfpenny. This so put up McGregor Simpson's choler that he proposed to send for a copy of the song and bury it to show their disgust at it. No sooner said than done. The writer was sent off for a copy which he procured at the Poet's Box, at that time situated in St Andrew's Lane. Back I came with it, and by this time the word had spread to the other adjacent halls that a funeral was about to take place. So a goodly company gathered and with McGregor Simpson and his bagpipes at our head, off we marched to Nelson's monument to the stirring sound of the pipes. Here a clod was cut and the obnoxious song, 'Jeanett and Jeannott', consigned to its last resting place; while McGregor Simpson and W G Ross made all those present promise that they would never sing the song again.

The pieces printed ranged then from *Johnnie Cope* to *Jeannett*. They also ranged as far as speeches from Shakespeare's *Hamlet* or Addison's *Cato*. There were several local songs and songs written by local authors. The over 450 Irish songs embraced the worst of the stage-Paddy ditties, such as *Kate Mooney*, in which the singer's wife absconds with her thirty-second cousin and the pig; Moore's concert songs like *The Young May Moon*, genuine local effusions like *Innishowen*; and folk songs like *The Irish Girl*. The political and religious songs, on both sides, are presented, sometimes with an introduction deploring the excesses of sectarianism. There is a similar wide range in the 800 Scottish songs. The romanticised bens, glens, thistle and tartan tradition is well established, but there are also genuine folk ballads such as *The Beggar Man* and *Still Growing*. Songs by the older songwriters, Burns, Lady Nairne, Tannahill, Hector MacNeill, Sandy Rodger, are well represented. Many of the temperance songs have a Scottish setting, so the comic Scottish drunk was a familiar figure. The stranger in the city, particularly the highlander, was another stock figure of fun. There is as yet little sign of the stingy Scot beloved of some later comics. The remainder of the repertoire was mainly that held in common with the forty-six English printing houses represented in the Kidson collection. The overlap with Lindsay and McIntosh has already been mentioned. A possible closer relationship is perceptible with the other 'Poet's Boxes' in Edinburgh and Dundee, catalogues for both of which survive. It is intriguing that in the collections in the National Library of Scotland and Dundee Central Library, there are a number of Leitch sheets with the Glasgow address cancelled and 'Dundee Poet's Box' substituted.

Possibly of more importance than the chatty introductions to the songs is the fact that almost every sheet from the Glasgow Poet's Box is dated not simply to the year, but to the Saturday of publication. Indeed, on many of them a date of previous issue is given. Thus we can see that it was Matthew Leitch's practice to issue between four and ten titles each week, including re-issues. Nor does there seem any reason to doubt the statement that a song is the second issue of 10 000 since an earlier date. One can see when a song is truly topical, like *The Death of Wellington*, on sale in the month of the event. One can also see that the name of Daniel O'Connell was still powerful in Glasgow twenty years after his death, since songs about him were regarded as saleable in 1865 and 1870. The dating of the sheets, which was kept up by Leitch's successors into the twentieth century, makes the collection of great value both to local historians and to song historians.

This is by no means an exhaustive survey of the Glasgow chapbook and broadside printers of the nineteenth century. I have said nothing of the Lumsdens, of William and Robert Inglis, of Bristo, of James Barr, not to mention the many names which crop up on one or two sheets either as printer or publisher. However, the figure who rounds off the history of the chapbooks in Glasgow is again a bookseller. Robert Lindsay was so described at the age of twenty in the Census of 1861, and so he remained in the directories until 1916. A 'W R', writing in a west-end magazine called *The Milden Miscellany* in 1948, recalled 'Lindsay's bookshop in Argyle Street, with old Lindsay in tall hat and shirtsleeves'. He appears to have been unrelated to James Lindsay, though his father, also Robert, had his wright's workship in Main Street, Anderston, just around the corner from James Lindsay's original premises in Washington Street. In 1887–88 Lindsay became the third publisher to use the imprint 'Glasgow, Printed for the Booksellers', when he issued 'John Cheap, the Chapman's Library: The Scottish Chap Literature of Last Century, Classified. With a Life of Dougal Graham'. It was issued first in one-shilling parts sewn in yellow paper covers with the imprint 'Ingram Street', and then in three bound volumes with 'Queen Street'. The paper is heavier than the original chapbooks and the series number is replaced by a section signature on the title page of each new story. The page numbering is separate for each chapbook, but is consistently present even where it was lacking in the original.

With this publication, chapbooks were stamped as an antiquarian interest, though they were to remain inexpensive for some time. Because of the large numbers issued, several booksellers were able to offer cheap bound sets of remainders with chapbooks dating from throughout the first half of the century. The text-only songsheet lasted longer, especially for topical songs. Older Glaswegians recall, for example, a ballad about Edith Cavell being cried in the streets. A guaranteed mass readership, like a Glasgow football crowd, can still make it worthwhile rushing out a song, though the latest example, verses on the signing by Glasgow Rangers of a Catholic player, is available not through the book trade, but printed on a T-shirt and sold in stalls at the local markets.

NOTES

1. 'Senex', *Glasgow Past and Present, Embracing Loose Memoranda on Glasgow Subjects, and Desultory Sketches by J B* (Glasgow, 1856), pp 420f.

2. Glasgow University Library Mu54-a.6(26).

3. National Library of Scotland LC 2832 & LC 2850.A.

4. R A Gillespie, *A List of Books Printed in Glasgow 1701-1775 with Notes on the Printers and Booksellers* (Mitchell Library RBf015.41443 GIL)

5. *Glasgow Chronicle,* 5 March 1814.

6. Glasgow University Library Mu1-x.11.

7. *Glasgow Weekly Herald,* 1 March 1902.

8. *Glasgow Past and Present,* pp 543f.

9. John Urie, *Reminiscences of Eighty Years* (Paisley: Alexander Gardner, 1908), p 42.

10. Catalogue in present writer's possession, in volume of garlands compiled by David Murray: *Wholesale Catalogue of Slip Songs, Histories and Songbooks, Large Sheet*

Songs, Hymns, Dialogues and Miscellaneous Articles Printed and Sold by James Lindsay, 9 King Street, (off Trongate,) Glasgow.

11. Glasgow University Library Mu22-x.11–13.

12. J & D Burnside, Stockwell Street, Glasgow.

13. Letter from David Murray to Dr Maclehose, 22 February 1918 (Glasgow University Library Mu23-y.1).

14. *Glasgow Weekly Mail*, November 1888

APPENDIX 1

.Books for the Instruction and Amusement of Children, bound in Gilt Paper, and adorned with Cuts (from the Catalogue of J & M Robertson, 1798)

Tom Thumb's Playbook

London Cries

Entertaining Fables for Children

Nurse True Love's Christmas Box

Tom Thumb's Folio

The Puzzling Cap

Jack Dandy's Delight

Death and Burial of Cock Robin

The Father's Gift

Polly Cherry

History of Mr Jackey and Miss Harriet

Abridgement of the History of the Bible

House That Jack Built

Lilliputian Auction

Child's Guide to his Letters, or Horn Book Improved

New England Primer

Gulliver's Voyage to Lilliput

Lilliputian Masquerade

History of Little King Pippin

Tommy Thumb's Song Book Fairy Tales

A Little Lottery-Book

Tom Thumb's Exhibition

Food for the Mind

The Young Scholar's Pocket Companion; being an early Introduction to the Art of Reading

The Fairing, or Golden Toy

A Bag of Nuts Ready Cracked

The Royal Primer

The Sugar Plumb, or Sweet Amusement

The Picture Exhibition

The History of the Bible

The History of England

A New History of Scotland

History of Four-Footed Beasts

Christmas Tales

Mother Bunch's Fairy Tales

Goody Two Shoes

A Compendious English Grammar

History of the Heathen Gods

APPENDIX 2

Twenty-four-page Penny History Books

(from the Catalogue of Francis Orr & Sons, *c* 1840)

1 Battles of Drumclog and Bothwell
2 Life of Rob Roy
3 Ali Baba, or the Forty Thieves
4 Toast-Master's Companion
5 Aladdin, or the Wonderful Lamp
6 Comical Tricks of Lothian Tom
7 Prince Lupin, Yellow Dwarf, &c
8 Jane Shore, Allan Barclay, &c
9 Cinderella, and Babes in the Wood
10 Duncan Campbell
11 The Seraphim
12 The New Minstrel
13 The Comic Minstrel
14 Wild Huntsman, Conscience, &c
15 The Reciter
16 Thrummy Cap and the Ghaist, &c
17 The Golden Dreamer
18 George Buchanan
19 The Bitter Wedding
20 Blue Beard
21 Paddy from Cork
22 Saunders Watson, Bill Jones, &c
23 Life of Robin Hood
24 The Long Pack
25 The Ghost of My Uncle, &c
26 Historical Catechism
27 Cookery Book, and Butler's Guide
28 Bewitched Fiddler, &c
29 Young Robber, and Puss in Boots
30 The Little White Mouse
31 Three Beggars, Soldier's Wife, &c

32 The New Valentine Writer
33 The New Scrap Book
34 Leper the Tailor
35 Prayer Book
36 Will and Jean
37 The Scotch Haggis
38 The Two Drovers
39 Vermin Killer
40 Pictorial Bible
41 Joseph and his Brethren
42 Abraham, Isaac and Jacob
43 Pilgrim's Progress
44 Life of David Haggart
45 Charles Jones the Footman
46 Robinson Crusoe
47 Vocalist Song Book
48 Laird of Cool's Ghost
49 Wife of Beith
50 Wise Willie and Witty Eppie
51 Daniel O'Rourke
52 Sleeping Beauty
53 Simple John's Twelve Misfortunes
54 Scots Proverbs
55 The Complete Letter Writer
56 King and the Cobbler
57 The Village Curate
58 John Cheap the Chapman
59 John Falkirk's Carritches
60 Life of Robert Burns
61 Life of John Knox
62 Jack the Giant-Killer

63 A Wedding-Ring Fit for the Finger
64 Life of the Rev John Welch
65 History of Hero and Leander
66 Madrid Shaver
67 British Humourist
68 Art of Money-Catching
69 Blind Allan
70 Elocutionist
71 History of Jane Arnold
72 George Barnwell
73 Robin Hood (in verse)
74 Grinning Made Easy
75 Thomas Hickathrift
76 Spaewife
77 Irish Assassin
78 Fortune-Teller
79 Mansie Wauch
80 Story-Teller
81 Art of Swimming Rendered Easy
82 Select Miscellany
83 Life of Peter Williamson
84 Hocus Pocus
85 World of Spirits
86 Song Book, No 1
87 Song Book, No 2
88 Song Book, No 3
89 Song Book, No 4
90 Song Book, No 5
91 Prince Charlie's Song Book
92 History of Fair Rosamond
93 Adventures of Redmond O'Hanlon
94 Mother Bunch's Fortune-Teller
95 Jemmy and Nancy of Yarmouth
96 Honey from the Rock of Christ
97 Shepherdess of the Alps
98 Four Interesting Tales

99 Sins and Sorrows Spread before God
100 Watt's Divine Songs
101 History of Paul Jones the Pirate
102 Sir Robert Bewick and Graham
103 Adventures of 16 British Seamen
104 Napoleon's Book of Fate
105 Spouter's Companion
106 A Groat's Worth of Wit
107 Life of Sir William Wallace
108 Life of King Robert Bruce
109 The Pleasures of Matrimony
110 Wise Men of Gotham
111 Adam Bell, Clym of the Clough, &c
112 A Token for Mourners
113 Jocky and Maggy's Courtship
114 Thomas the Rhymer
115 Peden's Life and Prophecies
116 Satan's Invisible World discovered
117 Life of Richard Turpin
118 A Tale of the Rebellion in 1745
119 History of Dr Faustus
120 History of Prince Charles
121 History of the Negro Robber
122 Lithgow's Travels in Europe
123 Life of Donald Cargill
124 Female Policy Detected
125 Adventures of Moore Carew
126 Life of Mahomet
127 Allan the Northumberland Piper
128 History of Valentine and Orson
129 Life and Death of Judas Iscariot
130 Watty and Meg, &c
131 Coalman's Courtship
132 Conjuror's Guide
133 Kings of England
134 Kings of Scotland

135 Plant of Renown, a Sermon

136 Economical Housekeeper's Guide

13 Aesop's Fables

138 Burns' Songs

139 Sea Songster

140 Black Bird Songster

141 The Dominie Deposed

142 Laird of Lag's Elegy

143 Way to Wealth

144 Jachin and Boaz

145 Barrie's Assistant, 18mo

146 Mother's Catechism, do

147 Shorter Catechism, do

148 Small Preceptor, do

149 Iron Shroud, or Italian Revenge

150 The Sentimental Songster

Working Towards a History of Scottish Book Collecting

BRIAN HILLYARD

When Peter Isaac suggested to me that I should present this Progress Report, I readily accepted because I welcome the opportunity to tell you about some of the work that is being done on the history of the book in Scotland apart from the contribution to the British Book Trade Index itself. Reflecting on this occasion as being also the Silver Jubilee of the History of the Book Trade in the North, I wondered whether the North was the North of Britain, once a standard way of referring to Scotland, as when John Spottiswood, one of the Keepers of the Advocates' Library in Edinburgh, wrote in 1711 that the Library was 'already the best in North-Britain, & in process of time, may come to be the best in the Isle'.[1] Whether or not this is what North signifies, Scotland does in any case have a role to play in the History of the Book Trade in the North if only because its National Library counts Berwick upon Tweed as its territory and assiduously acquires and analyses Berwick printing. Actually I have nothing today to say about Berwick, but rest assured that if I come across a Berwick book collector, I shall include him as one of ours.

I suppose that the eventual outcome of what I am going to describe will be a history of the collecting of books in Scotland, but a shorter-term objective is a working list of Scottish book collectors, with names, dates, brief descriptions, and references. Perhaps the need is obvious and always has been to everybody, but it became obvious to me only a few years ago when I was preparing a talk on the Edinburgh collector David Steuart, who does not figure in Seymour de Ricci's *English Collectors of Books & Manuscripts (1530–1930)* (London, 1930), though his ownership of a copy of the Gutenberg Bible, not to mention other choice incunabula, would have qualified him to do so; that is assuming that de Ricci did not intend 'English' to be interpreted in the narrow sense.[2] The auctioneer Cornelius Eliot, in an advertisement mentioning his Edinburgh 1801 sale of Steuart's library, described it as 'the most uncommon and certainly the most valuable private library ever brought to the hammer on this side the Tweed', and I felt that I should comment on this judgement, especially as Eliot was not an impartial judge.[3] Looking for comparative material, in the limited time then available I found it difficult to draw up much of a list of earlier Scottish private libraries. So ever since then I have noted any relevant details that have come my way, and more recently I have begun to work on my list more systematically. I have not yet formulated any very precise criteria for inclusion. Certainly those on my list are not all bibliophiles like Steuart, but include scholars and professional men and anybody else who acquired enough books to form a 'library'. I see little point in stating a minimum number of books for a 'library'. After all, what might seem a smallish number for 1800 might seem a largish number for 1550.

While, in these days of a diminishing number of public servants with an increasing amount of work to do, this has to be mostly private research, the National Library of Scotland provides an obvious centre for it. One sub-project is to compile a list of book sales – some of which will be of named individuals' libraries but some not, but a useful list all the same – that took place in Scotland, and this from two sources: extant catalogues, and advertisements or other reports in the press. The evidence of newspapers was very carefully sifted for the Aberdeen area by W R MacDonald;[4] similar work needs to be done for other areas. At the National Library some Edinburgh newspapers were recently read by a library fieldwork student (from Aberdeen curiously enough), and perhaps there may be similar opportunities in the future to have such work done. I might also mention that absolutely complete files of the relevant newspapers do not exist in any one library, and therefore the creation of microfilm files so important for preservation reasons is also to be welcomed by the book-trade historian. As for extant sale catalogues, the relevant items can of course be extracted from Munby and Coral's *British Book Sale Catalogues 1676–1800* (London, 1977) and, for after 1800, from the earlier *List of Catalogues of English Book Sales 1676–1900 now in the British Museum* (London, 1915). But when many are unique – as far as I know, David Steuart' s 1801 catalogue, for example, survives in a single copy in New York Public Library – one wonders how many more might turn up. Not all libraries have separate lists of their holdings of catalogues, and I hope that my list of names of collectors might lead to some profitable searching in library catalogues. I also look forward to the retrospective conversion of old library card catalogues which should make my task much easier. When the ESTC file becomes available in CD-ROM format, I will certainly be exploiting that. In the meantime, you may find it interesting to know that a search on 'catalogue' and 'books' with Edinburgh as place of publication gave 73 hits, of which I was pleasantly sur-prised to find some 18 to be for items qualifying for, but missing from, Munby & Coral.

Having identified catalogues in wide-flung libraries, we need to build up a research collection of microfilms: at least within one country, Scotland, if not within one library. Inasmuch as the National Library of Scotland's collection development policies include the acquisition of microforms of books of Scottish relevance not available in the original, such microfilms have been acquired from time to time over the years, mainly when the items have been encountered in the course of routine work or in response to individual researchers' needs. One hopes that in the context of a History of the Book in Britain – for which, as Alan Bell said in a recent *Book Collector* editorial, Edinburgh should be an important centre[5] – the Library will be able to continue, and perhaps even hasten, this accumulation.

So much for a list of book sales. But of course this is only one kind of evidence, and it has limitations. Most obviously, it allows us to detect libraries only when they are being dispersed, and also with the odd exception – such as the private auction of Humphry Galbraith's books in 1684, documented in a manuscript[6] – it will not take us back beyond 1686, the date of the earliest extant printed Seottish book-sale catalogue; and even then sales were few and far between for the remainder of the century.

It is difficult to split up the history of libraries by chronological periods, but if we consider the years before (say) 1700, published work tempts us to view it in two periods, dividing about 1560. The pre-Reformation period is the subject of work done by John Durkan and Anthony Ross and originally published in the *Innes Review* before being expanded in book form as *Early Scottish Libraries* (Glasgow, 1961). It is characteristic of this period that much of the evidence has had to be painfully collected – and goes on being collected, as witness the various supplements appearing over the years in *The Bibiotheck*[7] – from individual books with their inscriptions or binding stamps. Few if any libraries within this period are known from contemporary inventories or catalogues; the 1594 inventory of Adam Bothwell's books – over 400 volumes – is the major exception, and that was mainly a post-Reformation collection.[8] I hope that this work will be continued, and that it will before too long be consolidated in a new edition, and that perhaps information other than that of extant volumes (for example, the texts of any relevant inventories) will be incorporated in it. A new edition should also be provided with an index of the later provenances – of which there are many hundreds – included in the descriptions.

The period from about 1560 to about 1700 is the one I have been most concerned with of late, and, until recently anyway, this was probably the least well do-cumented period. My late colleague Ian Rae, who died just over a year ago, before his essay 'The origins of the Advocates' Library' was published in the National Library's book of essays *For the Encouragement of Learning* (Edinburgh, 1989), had to rely almost entirely on original sources to provide a sketch of Scottish private libraries as a background to the first reference, in 1680, to the founding of an Advocates' Library.

Some of the book owners in this period are relatively easy to deal with. For example, Walter Dalgleish, who was factor to the Earl of Dunfermline, listed on a flyleaf, in 1652, his library of 157 books, and in 1661 William Ker, 3rd Earl of Lothian, compiled the earliest existing catalogue – some 1350 books – of what has been variously known as the Lothian or Newbattle Library.[9] In this last case we are fortunate to have the 1661 catalogue, because otherwise the different strata of the library, collected over many generations, would be difficult to disentangle. One such family library, intact until recently, for which there are no early catalogues, is that of the Earls of Haddington at Tyninghame House, which was dispersed, and in large part sold, in 1987. But staff of the National Library of Scotland were given the opportunity to examine the books prior to the dispersal. Fortunately, as had in fact been pointed out by Hugh Trevor Roper (now Lord Dacre) in a small pamphlet, *Tyninghame Library* (privately printed, 1977), Thomas Hamilton, who became Sir Thomas Hamilton, then Lord Binning, then Earl of Melrose, and finally first Earl of Haddington, had a great predilection for signing his various names in his books, and the National Library was able to purchase all 345 volumes seen that were so inscribed, though subsequent investigation suggests that some of those signed 'M[agister] T Hamilton' had actually belonged to the first Earl's father, another Thomas, who, like his son, had been a student in Paris. There were also other books, a few of which were purchased, inscribed by the second or third Earls, not to mention later members of the family.[10]

By being transferred, in part, to institutional ownership, the Tyninghame Library takes me to another category of evidence: that of collections donated or bequeathed or acquired in other ways, in part or whole, by libraries. The Rare Books Group's publication *A Directory of Rare Book and Special Collections in the United Kingdom and the Republic of Ireland* (London, 1985) is a valuable tool here. Scottish libraries will probably provide most evidence, but English libraries should not be overlooked. For example, York Minster Library holds the French and Italian books from the library of James Fall, ex-Principal of Glasgow University who became Precentor of York, now probably best known as Robert Leighton's executor.[11] But we also need to look overseas. For example, the libraries of the Scottish physicians Robert Erskine (1677–1718), who actually lived and died in Russia as Chief Physician to the Tsar, and Archibald Pitcairne (1652–1713) were both acquired by the Russians in 1719–20 and are now in the Library of the Academy of Sciences in Leningrad, where they were affected by the disastrous fire of 14 February 1988, though their specific losses are not yet known.[12] Therefore directories of special collections compiled in other countries will also need to be scrutinized. One could add that not only the present content of institutional libraries but their history has a contribution to make, for sometimes we learn details about collections not acquired. In February 1691 the Curators of the Advocates' Library were recommended to consider the books of the physician and antiquary Christopher Irvine which were 'lying in the bibliothecque' (Faculty Minutes, 27 February 1691), and a catalogue of them, dated 1693, the year of Irvine's death, is mentioned in the Advocates' Library 1742 catalogue. To judge from the description given there, the 1693 catalogue was a printed catalogue. It has not been traced, and nothing is now known about Irvine's books.

Pitcairne, by the way, also demonstrates the usefulness of correspondence, for the recently published selection of his letters entitled *The Best of our Owne: Letters of Archibald Pitcairne, 1652–1713* (Edinburgh, 1979) includes references to catalogues, desiderata lists, and commissions, passing between, on the one hand, Pitcairne and others in Edinburgh and, on the other hand, their friends such as Hans Sloane and Dr Robert Gray in London. Jumping forward a century, at present one stray letter is our only evidence for what was obviously a close working relationship between the Edinburgh collector David Steuart and the important London bookseller James Edwards.

Finally, I come to the provenances of individual volumes. I have tended not to work from these because I am wary about creating a long list of persons many of whom owned a mere handful of books. But just as intact collections can provide the only evidence for a collector, so likewise can a dispersed collection which has been recreated from individual provenances. For example, Patrick Moray (Murray), of Livingstone, would not be on my list if it were not for the provenance index of D T Bird' s *A Catalogue of Sixteenth-Century Medical Books in Edinburgh Libraries* (Edinburgh, 1982). Bird records some eighty items with Moray's signature, and very interesting they are too, for the majority of them are inscribed as acquired in Paris in 1669 or 1670 and others in Toulouse in 1670 or Montpelier in 1671. More catalogues with provenance indexes would help here; David Pearson's *Provenance Indexes for Early Printed Books and manuscripts: A Guide to Present Resources* (Huntingdon, 1987) underlines, I think, the scarcity of such indexes. Also useful are the extensive files John Morris is compiling towards his *Armorial of British Bookbindings*. But – to end with a plea – what we really want is the inclusion of indexed provenance details in automated catalogue records that can be brought together one day in vast national and then international networks.

NOTES

1. J Spottiswood, *The Form of Process* (Edinburgh, 1711), p xlv.

2. B Hillyard, 'History of the National Library of Scotland's 42-line Bible', *The Bibliotheck*, vol 12 (1984–5), pp 102–25.

3 The advertisement is found at the end of *Catalogue of the Entire Bound Stock of Ross & Blackwood, Booksellers in Edinburgh* (Edinburgh, 1803).

4. W R MacDonald, 'Book-auctions and book-sales in the Aberdeen Area, 1749–1800', *Aberdeen University Review*, vol 42 (1967), pp 114–32.

5. A S Bell, 'The Edinburgh Tercentennial', *The Book Collector*, vol 38 (1989), pp 445–63 (p 463).

6. T I Rae, 'The origins of the Advocates' Library', in *For the Encouragement of Learning*, edited by P Cadell and A Matheson (Edinburgh, 1989), pp 1–22 (p 10).

7. J Durkan and J Russell, 'Further additions (including manuscripts) to J Durkan and A Ross, *Early Scottish Libraries*, at the National Library of Scotland', *The Bibliotheck*, vol 12 (1984–5), pp 85–90, with references to earlier supplements.

8. Durkan and Ross, *Early Scottish Libraries*, p 12.

9. Rae, 'Origins', pp 10–11.

10. B Hillyard, 'Books for the National Library from Tyninghame House', *Scottish Book Collector*, vol 6 (June/July 1988), pp 26–7.

11. C B L Barr, 'The Minster Library', in *A History of York Minster*, edited by G E Aylmer and R Cant (Oxford, 1977), pp 487–539 (p 509). An article on Fall, by M C T Simpson, is forthcoming in *Edinburgh Bibliographical Society Transactions*.

12. J H Appleby and A Cunningham, 'Robert Erskine and Archibald Pitcairne – two Scottish physicians' outstanding libraries', *The Bibliotheck*, vol 11 (1982–3), pp 3–16; J H Appleby, 'Archibald Pitcairne re-encountered – a note on his manuscript poems and printed library catalogue', *The Bibliotheck*, vol 12 (1984–5), pp 137–9. For the recent fire see L I Kiseleva, *The Library Association Rare Books Group Newsletter*, no 33 (May 1989), pp 19–20.

History of the Book Trade in the North
The first twenty-five years

J C DAY & W M WATSON

That the History of the Book Trade in the North Group has not only survived its first twenty-five years, but flourished as well, comes as no surprise to its members, for it is centred on a region with a long and proud tradition of local studies. Newcastle can boast the oldest provincial Society of Antiquaries founded in 1813, and Northumberland a multi-volumed county history which was so accurate and detailed that a Victoria County History series was felt to be unnecessary. The region also fostered the first provincial natural history society – the Berwickshire Naturalists Field Club[1] – and one of the earliest bibliographical societies in the form of the Typographical Society of Newcastle upon Tyne in 1817.[2] More specifically to the book trade the region can claim association with a number of practitioners of national significance foremost amongst whom were Thomas Bewick and his pupils Luke Clennell and William Harvey, with both William Bulmer and William Ged having substantial links with the area. The North also saw the proliferation of a number of good-quality provincial printers like John White, William Davison, Solomon Hodgson and Eneas Mackenzie. Their printing would compare favourably with that of any of their contemporaries elsewhere in the provinces.

The study of book-trade history in the region has been greatly stimulated – and sometimes frustrated – by the work of a number of nineteenth- and early twentieth-century local antiquarian collectors and commentators. Preeminent amongst the collectors were John and Thomas Bell, whose vast collections are now unfortunately to be located on both sides of the Atlantic. Of particular significance, however, are their collections of regional book-trade ephemera which are still preserved in Newcastle. Later collections and outline histories were made by James Clephan (1887), R A Peddie (1901) and Richard Welford whose notes eventually formed the basis for his 'Early Newcastle typography', published in 1907.[3] Nor was Newcastle treated in isolation; short book-trade histories had also appeared for Alnwick (1896), North Shields (1902), Sunderland (1905) and Berwick upon Tweed (1919).[4]

The formation of the History of the Book Trade in the North Group in October 1965, therefore, had much on which to build. As Peddie himself had stated as early as 1904,[5] perhaps bearing in mind his own manuscript notes on Newcastle printers, and later to be reiterated by Paul Morgan,[6] the study of provincial book-trade history and development should not be undertaken lightly, but if carried out diligently might throw light on economic and social facets of human activity not previously explored. It was with these facets in mind that a number of enthusiastic bibliophiles and historians in the North-East and North-West embarked on the compilation of what they rightly deduced would be an essential reference tool for anyone undertaking serious research in the book-trade history of the area.

The outcome of their combined efforts saw the publication of Chris Hunt's now oft-quoted biographical dictionary *The Book Trade in Northumberland and Durham to 1860.*[7] The work took over ten years to bring to fruition, the details of the methodology having been described at length elsewhere.[8] The content of the dictionary provided an overall picture of the breadth and depth of book-trade activities in the two counties for the first time, and gave the North-East region a sound framework on which more in-depth sociological and economic studies could be based. The reviews were highly favourable,[9] and James Moran, the President of the Printing Historical Society, in his foreword to the dictionary, expressed a hope that many other areas would produce similar retrospective book-trade guides.[10] In total Hunt's work covered over eleven hundred tradesmen and craftsmen involved in varying aspects of the book trade, giving for each person their occupation(s), working dates, address(es) and a short biography with, where known, details of examples of their work. (Fig 1 shows a typical page.) A very full picture of a lively free press in both a rapidly developing industrial and rural environment emerges for the two counties.

Hunt and his collaborators made extensive use of provincial newspapers, directories, local histories and collections of manuscripts and printed ephemera. If any fault is to be levelled at the compilation it is that papermakers were excluded, and it is to the credit of the Group that even as the dictionary was being printed work commenced on collecting new data and evidence. The outcome was *A Supplement to C J Hunt's Biographical Dictionary*, edited by P J Wallis, in 1981.[11]

It had taken the Group fifteen years to complete an authoritative biographical reference work, which was to become a model for many other provincial printing-history societies. Wallis's *Supplement* made great use of poll books, original imprints and the subscription lists compiled by the Project for Historical Biobibliography, of which he is the director. Between them the two volumes provide

Fig 1 (*opposite*) Typical page from Hunt's *Dictionary*
(reduced from 225 x 152 mm)

GRAHAM, James 1739–1819. Pr, Bslr, St, Bbr, Drst.
Sunderland: –1767–1816. High St, 1767–97. Maude's Lane, 1797–1816.
Graham came originally from Alnwick; he was possibly son of Alexander Graham of Alnwick with whose name he is frequently linked in imprints. He issued a printed list of his stock in 1776. In 1797 he purchased T. Wetherald's premises in Maude's Lane. He printed slip songs. Retired 1816, and was succeeded by T. Rae.
Plomer 1932. Bain 1905. Purchased book-binders' tools from Beilby & Bewick, Apr 27, 1780, and 'fable cuts' Mar 16, 1782.

GRAHAM, Joseph I d. Feb 6, 1792. Bslr, St, CircLib.
Alnwick: 1789–1792.
Son of Alexander Graham. Succeeded by sisters, Mary Graham and Ann Smith.
Surtees Society, Vol 118.

GRAHAM, Joseph II 1778–Mar 29, 1870. Pr, Bslr, St, Bbr, CircLib.
Alnwick: 22 Fenkle St, –1802–1838–
Son(?) of Joseph Graham I. In partnership with Mary Graham in 1802, when they were together granted a licence to print, and alone by 1807. Printed a number of tracts and many broadsides and slip songs. His books included a 12-volume Boswell's *Johnson* in 1816. Granted another licence on July 3, 1828.
Burman 1896. D1823: 1834. Cannon. Isaac 1973, 71.

GRAHAM, Mary Pr, Bslr, St, CircLib, Drst.
Alnwick: 1792–1802–
Sister of Joseph Graham I. From 1792 until at least 1797 she was in partnership with her sister, Ann Smith. In 1802 the partner-ship was between Mary Graham and (nephew?) Joseph Graham (d. 1870).
Surtees Society Vol 118. *N. & Q.*, 1906. Burman 1896. *Nc Courant*, Feb 18, 1792.

GRANT, James Bslr, St.
Newcastle: 38 Westgate St, –1839–1841–
In 1839 he was also a tea dealer at a different address. Succeeded by Miss Jane Grant.
D1839: 1841.

GRANT, Jane *Miss* Bslr, St, CircLib.
Newcastle: 38 Westgate St, –1844–1847–
D1844: 1847.

GRANT, Mary Ann CircLib.
Newcastle: 83 Pilgrim St, –1847–
D1847.

GRAY, Eleanor Bslr, St.
Chester-le-Street: –1847–
D1847.

GRAY, Gilbert 1699?–Feb 12, 1794. Bbr.
Newcastle: –1778–1794. Manor Chare, 1778. Stock Bridge, 1792. Pandon Chare, 1787–1790.
Born in Scotland and worked as journeyman bookbinder for Alan Ramsay in Edinburgh. Gray came to Newcastle about 1750 and was employed by Martin Bryson, William Charnley, Thomas Slack and Solomon Hodgson as warehouseman and bookbinder, as well as being in trade on his own account. Bewick, in his *Memoir*, called him 'the most invaluable acquaintance and friend I ever met with'.
Welford 1895. Mitchell 1955.

GRAYDON, Robert Pr, Bslr, St.
Sunderland: –1817–1858– Monkwearmouth Shore, 1817–31. Wear St M, 1834–56. 16 Barclay St M., 1858.
The first Monkwearmouth printer. 'Evidently in a small way' (Cannon 1831).
Bain 1905. D1820/23: 1858.

GREEN, George Pr, St.
Newcastle: 1837–1861– 19 Dean St, 1839–1841. 99 Side, 1844–56. 1 Side, 1858–61.
In partnership with Thomas Brown, 1837–1839 or 1840. Traded as George Green & Son' from 1858 onwards.
Bell Coll. D1841: 1861/62.

GREEN, Joseph Bslr, St, Pslr, CircLib, Drst.
Newcastle: –1785–1789. Amen Corner, 1785. Mosley St, 1787. Quay Side, 1788.
Took over the shop and business of Martin Barber in 1784 but became bankrupt in 1785. His 'Stock in Trade and Circulating Library' was sold by auction, Oct 1785. Green was in business again primarily as a

evidence for over seventeen hundred persons involved in the book trade and ancilliary occupations from 1626 to 1860. The scale of activity in Northumberland and Durham, particularly between 1750 and 1860, was further attested by the fact that nearly seventy towns and villages had some involvement at one time or another with the trade. The rapid industrial and commercial expansion of the area during the nineteenth century was, therefore, very much mirrored in the work and activities of the region's printers, papermakers, engravers and newspaper proprietors.

Whilst Hunt and Wallis had been editing their compilations other members of the Group were already engaged in examining more specific topics. A series of *Working Papers* and the distribution of a number of offprints by members and friends of the Group on a very wide range of topics commenced from 1965. To date this constitutes fifty-six *Working Papers* and sixteen *Miscellaneous Papers* (the Appendix gives details), which have appeared at regular intervals. Not surprisingly ten of the first fifteen papers were produced as part of the preliminary stages for Hunt's dictionary and consisted of the names and dates of tradesmen from directories and archival sources. So too, prior to Wallis's work, many of the Group's papers were bibliographical in nature dealing with previously untapped sources relating to papermaking and newspaper printing. More in-depth studies nevertheless did begin to appear in the formative years with the issue of papers on the book trade in the North-East, the role of the Victorian printer, and the part played by provincial stationers' companies.

Many later papers have examined the contribution to the development of printing and the book trade by individuals during the nineteenth century. They include studies of Ralph Beilby and Thomas Bewick, the Mackay family of Morpeth, Andrew Reid and William Davison. More general papers have attempted to analyse and evaluate the printed output from specific centres such as Hexham, Wallsend and Sunderland, and on a regional basis the late C F Maid-. well's extensive notes on papermaking in the North of England are currently being issued.

Nor has the social impact of the printed word been neglected by the Group. The importance of reading rooms and libraries in both Northumberland and Newcastle has been the subject of five papers, and the survival of early locally printed materials has formed the basis of two *Miscellaneous Papers*. The development of the provincial newspaper press in Sunderland, North Shields, Cumbria and Newcastle has also merited a number of detailed articles. As the histogram clearly shows (Fig 2), the subject range covered by the Group's publication programme is steadily encompassing a broad spectrum of technical, social and economic aspects.

Membership of the History of the Book Trade in the North Group has slowly expanded over the years. Individuals from the contemporary printing and bookselling fraternities, academics from Newcastle and Durham Universities and Newcastle Polytechnic, together with local librarians and archivists formed the nucleus of the Group in 1965. They are still the driving force although the numbers have grown from the initial twelve to over fifty, and include many institutional members. An interesting development has been the relationship with the Department of Information and Library Management at Newcastle Polytechnic, where some undergraduate and postgraduate students have undertaken local-history topics dealing with the book trade for their dissertations or projects – a number having later appeared in an edited form in the Group's publication programme. Indeed the *Working Papers* are now taken by many individuals and institutions outside the region and have provided encourage-

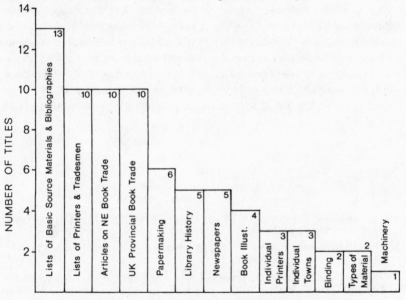

SUBJECT CONTENT OF PUBLICATIONS

Fig 2 Scope of the Papers issued by the Group

ment for a number of similar book-trade groups currently engaged in producing biographical dictionaries of their areas based on the seminal work produced by Chris Hunt for this Group.

The first twenty-five years have succeeded in establishing a sound academic base on which future studies of the book trade in our region can be built. Provided that the income from subscriptions, sales and occasional grants and donations are forthcoming there are many facets left to investigate. Not only can the work of individual printing houses, newspaper offices etc be examined, but a thematic approach is a possibility like the studies of local chapbooks and ephemera already undertaken.[12] Much of the Group's work is now incorporated in the British Book Trade Index (BBTI), a computerized index based on the Robinson Library of the University of Newcastle upon Tyne, which commenced operations in 1985, with the aim of establishing a national index of historical book-trade data.

The link between the History of the Book Trade in the North Group and the BBTI is Professor Peter Isaac. It would be remiss of the authors not to mention his name as he is a founder member and the inspiration behind both projects. Without his enthusiasm, subject knowledge, tenacity, and sometimes bullying, neither would have gained the success or acclaim which has so far been achieved. The first twenty-five years of the History of the Book Trade in the North Group are a tribute to Professor Isaac's dedication, and as such can be compared to the monumental collections of printed material amassed by those equally dedicated historians John and Thomas Bell during the nineteenth century. Both have been crucial in advancing our understanding of provincial book-trade history and activity in the region.

NOTES

1. D E Allen, *The Naturalist in Britain* (Allen Lane, 1976), pp 161–2.

2. L A Leake, 'The Typographical Society of Newcastle upon Tyne', *Private Library*, 2 ser, vol 1–3 (1986–9), pp 86–99.

3. R Welford, 'Early Newcastle typography', *Archaeologia Aeliana*, 3 ser, vol 3 (1907), pp 1–142.

4. G W Bain, 'The early printing presses of Sunderland, *Antiquities of Sunderland*, vol 7 (1908), pp 1–12; C C Burman, 'An account of the art of typography as practised at Alnwick', *History of the Berwickshire Naturalists' Club*, vol 23 (1919), pp 305–59; J L Hilson, 'Berwick upon Tweed typography', *History of the Berwickshire Naturalists' Club*, vol 23 (1919), pp 433–555; C J Spence, 'A list of books…printed at North Shields', *Tynemouth Public Libraries Report* (1902), pp 19–26, and (1903), pp 9–15.

5. R A Peddie, 'Notes on provincial printers and booksellers', *Library World*, vol 7 (1904), pp 57–60.

6. P Morgan, *English Provincial Printing*. Lecture delivered at School of Librarianship, Birmingham, 1958. [Privately printed, 1958?].

7. C J Hunt, *The Book Trade in Northumberland and Durham to 1860* (Newcastle upon Tyne: Thorne's, 1975).

8. P C G Isaac, 'The History of the book trade in the North: a preliminary report', *The Library*, 5 ser, vol 23 (1968), pp 248–52; P C G Isaac, and W M Watson, 'The History of the Book Trade in the North', *Journal of the Printing Historical Society*, vol 4 (1968), pp 87–98.

9. For examples see *Papers of the Bibliographical Society of America*, vol 70(4) (1976), pp 547–50, and *Times Literary Supplement* (30 January 1976), p 119.

10. Hunt, *Book Trade*, p ix.

11. P J Wallis, *The Book Trade in Northumberland and Durham to 1860. A Supplement to C J Hunt's Biographical Dictionary* (Newcastle upon Tyne: Thorne's, 1981).

12. F M Thomson, *Newcastle Chapbooks in Newcastle upon Tyne University Library* (Newcastle upon Tyne: Oriel Press, 1969).

APPENDIX

Publications of the Group

Dictionaries

Christopher J Hunt, *The Book Trade in Northumberland and Durham to 1860* (Newcastle upon Tyne, Thorne's Bookshops Ltd, 1975), 116 pp, illustrated

Peter J Wallis, *The Book Trade in Northumberland and Durham to 1860. A supplement to C J Hunt's Biographical Dictionary.* (Newcastle upon Tyne, Thorne's Bookshops Ltd, 1981), 60 pp, illustrated

Hunt's Dictionary is still available from the publishers

Working Papers

PH1 (December 1965) Miss D Hudson, Yorkshire printers operating before 1865. 3 pp

PH2 (December 1965) O S Tomlinson, List of directories in York City Library, published before 1865, covering the North Riding.

PH3 (December 1965) List of directories in Middlesbrough Public Library covering the North-East prior to 1865

PH4 (August 1967) C J Hunt, A list of printed books and papers dealing with the history of the book trade in Northumberland and Durham. 7 pp

PH5 Manuscript and other miscellaneous sources of information. 3 pp

PH6 (March 1966) Notices of printing presses as required by the Unlawful Societies Act, 1799 – in the Northumberland County Record Office. 2 pp

PH7 (April 1966) List of tradesmen, artists, etc connected with the book trade, 1778–1840 – from directories in the Central Reference Library, Newcastle upon Tyne. 23 pp

PH8 (April 1966) Supplementary list of tradesmen etc, connected with the book trade, 1778–1840 – from directories in the University Library, Newcastle upon Tyne. 7 pp

PH9 Supplement to PH7. 1 p

PH10 (April 1966) D F James, Booksellers, printers, stationers etc, Westmorland to 1865. 2 pp

PH11 (May 1966) Kenneth Smith, List of printers, booksellers, bookbinders, publishers, paper manufacturers, engravers etc, operating in Cumberland to the year 1861. 19 pp

PH12 (March 1967) F Barnes, Supplement to PH11. 3 pp

PH13 B C Jones, Printers' registrations under the Seditious Societies Act, 1799 – in Carlisle City Archives. 3 pp

PH14. (November 1967) P C G Isaac, History of printing in the North – some highlights. With map showing the spread of printing in the region. 12 pp

PH15. (November 1967) F Barnes & G Wood, List of printers, booksellers, binders, papermakers etc, operating in North Lonsdale, up to 1865. 4 pp

PH16. (March 1968) List of individual research projects in progress or contemplated. 3 pp

PH17. (1971) J A Birkbeck, Newspapers of Durham and Northumberland. 4 pp

PH18. P J Wallis, The tip of the iceberg – early northern educational books. 6 pp

PH19. (January 1973) Robin Gard, Hasty notes of sources in the Northumberland Record Office of possible interest to the History of the Book Trade in the North. 4 pp

PH20. (February 1973) C R Hudleston, Excise records of papermakers. 3 pp

PH21. (February 1973) E W Wilson, Two accounts of *The Westmorland Advertiser and Kendal Chronicle.* 9 pp

PH22. (January 1974) Joan Knott, Newcastle libraries in the early nineteenth century. 5 pp

PH23. (May 1974) C J Hunt, Editing a dictionary of the North-eastern book trade. 11 pp

PH24. (March 1975) James Moran, Stationers' companies of the British Isles. 6 pp

PH25. (January 1976) M A V Gill, The Beilby and Bewick workshop. 13 pp

PH26. (March 1976) C A Chester, History of Ford paper mill – the introduction of esparto grass for papermaking. 23 pp

PH27. (March 1977) P J Storey, Some Sunderland newspapers and their proprietors. And supplement (August 1977). 13 pp

PH28. (August 1977) C J Hunt & P C G Isaac, The regulation of the book trade in Newcastle upon Tyne at the beginning of the nineteenth century. 18 pp

PH29. (1976) M J Preston, M G Smith & P S Smith, An interim checklist of chapbooks containing traditional play texts. 52 pp

PH30. (September 1977) A D Burnett Northern book trade catalogue project – report on progress at Durham. 4 pp

PH31. (September 1977) John Thackray A note on the Bell colliery collection in the Institute of Geological Sciences. 2 pp

PH32. (May 1979) J W Smith, Printing in Sunderland – some notes. 3 pp

PH33. (December 1979) W M Watson, Heralding the Mackays. 17 pp

PH34. (September 1980) Seminar on provincial printing and the book trade. [Held at Leeds University, 18 April 1980] 16 pp

PH35. (May 1982) Margaret Thompson, Some aspects of printing in Wallsend. 16 pp

PH36. (February 1983) Michael Preston, *The Newcastle Journal* 1832-1950. 27 pp

PH37. List of publications

PH38. (October 1983) Charles Parish, The Literary and Philosophical Society of Newcastle upon Tyne - the building of a library, 1793-1903. 12 pp

PH39. (December 1983) Report of the Seminar on the provincial book trade. [Held at the University of Loughborough, 12 July 1983] 30 pp

PH40. (April 1984) Charles Parish, The Literary and Philosophical Society of Newcastle upon Tyne - the development of the library. 7 pp

PH41. (February 1985) Sally Bird, The Davison Collection in the Northumberland Record Office - a treasure house of printed local history. Illustrated. 26 pp

PH42. (August 1985) Third Seminar on the British book trade - Report. [Held at the Bodleian Library, Oxford, 21 June 1985] 29 pp

PH43. (May 1986) Judith M Black, Development of the *Shields Daily Gazette*, 1864-1984. 12 pp

PH44. (July 1986) Fourth Seminar on the British book trade - Report. [Held in the University Library, Newcastle upon Tyne, 23-24 April 1986] 20 pp

PH45. (September 1986) David Pearson, Book trade bills and vouchers from Durham Cathedral Library, 1634-1740. 24 pp

PH46. (January 1987) Peter Isaac, The provincial book trade from the end of the Printing Act to 1800. 17 pp

PH47. (July 1987) C F Maidwell, Some notes on papermaking in County Durham. 20 pp

PH48. (July 1987) Peter Isaac, Provincial printing in the eighteenth century - a note. 5 pp

PH49. (October 1987) John Day, Libraries in nineteenth-century Northumberland. Illustrated 21 pp

PH50. (January 1988) Ruth Dodds, Hexham imprints: an account of the printers, presses and publishers of that town. Illustrated 67 pp

PH51. (June 1988) John Gavin, Some notes on papermaking in Cumbria. With map 24 pp

PH52. (December 1988) C F Maidwell, Some notes on papermaking in Northumberland: with an appendix on Haughton Mill. Illustrated 14 pp

PH53. (December 1989) Peter Isaac, An inventory of books sold by a seventeenth-century Penrith grocer. 23 pp

PH54. (April 1989) C F Maidwell, Some notes on papermaking in Lancashire. 22 pp

PH55. (July 1989) John Philipson, The King's Printer in Newcastle upon Tyne in 1 639. Illustrated 9 pp

PH56. (March 1990) Michael R Bailey, Robert Stephenson & Co and the paper-drying machine in the 1820s. Illustrated 19 pp

(In preparation) Michael Sharp, Andrew Reid and the creation of a famous north-country printing house.

(In preparation) C F Maidwell, Some notes on papermaking in Yorkshire.

Miscellaneous Papers

M1. (1968) L A Leake, 'The Typographical Society of Newcastle upon Tyne'. Offprint from *Private Library*, vol 1, pp 86–99.

M2. (1968) Frances M Thomson, 'A Newcastle collection of wood blocks'. Offprint from *The Book Collector*, vol 17, pp 443–57.

M3. (1969) Frances M Thomson & John Philipson, 'Dr J C Bruce and the Reid collection of engraved wood-blocks'. Offprint from *Archaeologia Aeliana*, 4 ser, vol 47, pp 147–66.

M4. (1970) Iain Bain, 'A checklist of manuscripts of Thomas Bewick'. Reprinted from *Private Library* with addenda.

M5. (1972) Robert Wood, *The Victorian provincial printer and the stage*. Newcastle Imprint Club.

M6. (1973) June W Thompson & Grace Hickling, 'A bibliography of the literature of the Farne Islands, Northumberland'. *Transactions of the Natural History Society of Northumberland, Durham and Newcastle upon Tyne*, vol 42, pp 1–64.

M7. (1975) A I Doyle, 'Hugh Hutchinson, bookbinder of Durham, c 1662 or 1665–95'. Offprint from *The Book Collector*, vol 24, pp 25–32.

M8. (1975) James Moran, *Stationers' Companies of the British Isles*. Newcastle Imprint Club.

M9. (1976) F J G Robinson & P J Wallis, 'Newcastle book subscription lists'. PHIBB 110.

M10. (1977) P J Wallis, 'The North-east book trade to 1860 – imprints and subscriptions'. PHIBB 153.

M11. (1977) C J Hunt & P C G Isaac, 'The regulation of the booktrade in Newcastle upon Tyne at the beginning of the nineteenth century'. Offprint from *Archaeologia Aeliana*, 5 ser, vol 5, pp 163–78.

M12. (1980) Susan Doncaster, *Some notes on Bewick's trade blocks*. Newcastle Imprint Club.

M13. (1981) Susan Jeffery, *The Thomlinson Library*. Newcastle upon Tyne City Library.

M14. (1986) P C G Isaac, 'Fourstones paper mill – the documents speak'. Offprint from G T Mandl, *Three Hundred Years in Paper*.

M15. (1983) John Day, *A short-title catalogue of pre-1700 books in the Newcastle Central Library*, Newcastle City Libraries.

M16. (1984) John Day, 'A short-title catalogue of early printed books in the library of the Society of Antiquaries of Newcastle upon Tyne'. Offprint from *Archaeologia Aeliana*, 5 ser, vol 11, pp 265–88.

(In press) Papers by John Philipson and Peter Isaac on the paper produced at Haughton Mill for counterfeiting French *assignats* in the 1790s. From *Archaeologia Aeliana*

Books of Reprinted Papers

Bewick and After - Wood-engraving in the Northeast, edited by Peter Isaac (Wylam: Allenholme Press for the History of the Book Trade in the North, 1990), pp xii, 144.

Index

[Numbers in *italics* refer to the illustrations]